MAXIMUM PC Guide to

EXTREME PC MODS

PAUL CAPELLO AND JON PHILLIPS

800 East 96th Street
Indianapolis, Indiana 46240

The Maximum PC Guide to Extreme PC Mods

International Standard Book Number: 0-7897-3192-4

Library of Congress Catalog Card Number: 2004107058

Printed in the United States of America

First Printing: December 2004

07   06   05   04   4   3   2   1

Trademarks

All terms mentioned in this book that are known to be trademarks or service marks have been appropriately capitalized. Que Publishing cannot attest to the accuracy of this information. Use of a term in this book should not be regarded as affecting the validity of any trademark or service mark.

Warning and Disclaimer

Every effort has been made to make this book as complete and as accurate as possible, but no warranty or fitness is implied. The information provided is on an "as is" basis. The authors and the publisher shall have neither liability nor responsibility to any person or entity with respect to any loss or damages arising from the information contained in this book.

Bulk Sales

Que Publishing offers excellent discounts on this book when ordered in quantity for bulk purchases or special sales. For more information, please contact

U.S. Corporate and Government Sales

1-800-382-3419

corpsales@pearsontechgroup.com

For sales outside the United States, please contact

International Sales

international@pearsoned.com

Que Publishing

Publisher
Paul Boger

Associate Publisher
Greg Wiegand

Executive Editor
Rick Kughen

Development Editor
Rick Kughen

Managing Editor
Charlotte Clapp

Project Editor
Dan Knott

Production Editor
Megan Wade

Indexer
Ken Johnson

Publishing Coordinator
Sharry Lee Gregory

Interior Designer
Anne Jones

Cover Designer
Anne Jones

Cover Photos
Paul Capello

Interior Photos
Paul Capello, et al.

Page Layout
Stacey Richwine-DeRome

Maximum PC   *MAXIMUM PC*

Publisher
Chris Coelho

Editor-in-Chief
George Jones

Editors
Gordon Mah Ung
Will Smith
Logan Decker
Josh Norem

Cover Designer
Natalie Jeday

Future Network USA

Editorial Director
Jon Phillips

Contents at a Glance

Table of Contents

Case-Modding: Equal Parts Science, Art, Craft, and Design

Humans appreciate and reward good craftsmanship. This is a truth I hold to be self-evident.

We appreciate physical objects that don't just merely serve a utilitarian function, but also demonstrate the best of human imagination and industriousness. That's why we hold home electronics designed by Bang & Olufsen in higher regard than home electronics designed by RadioShack. That's why we hold cars designed by Ferrari in higher regard than cars designed by Kia. That's why we hold structures designed by Frank Lloyd Wright in higher regard than structures designed by Starrco (a manufacturer of "preengineered modular office systems and portable buildings").

Have you ever seen an orrery? An *orrery* is one of those impossibly intricate 3D solar system models that illustrates the movement of our heavenly neighbors. Check out the orrery pictured on this page. It's a brilliant synthesis of science, art, craft, and design.

On a conscious level, I marvel at the orrery's aesthetics and engineering. To think that such a cool-looking—and archaic—device can model planetary paths with real-world accuracy! (The first orrery was invented around 1700, or so indicates a quick survey of orrery-related websites.) But on a deeper level, I'm awed that a human being—a member of my animal tribe—actually took the time to conceive and build the first orrery. From where I stand, the orrery is the perfect material illustration of mankind's urge to create, well, badass, neat-to-look-at, intricately engineered stuff.

Call it biological narcissism, call it whatever you want, but I'm convinced that an appreciation for human creativity is encoded into our primal DNA. We relish in the knowledge that man was not put on this earth to simply eat, breathe, procreate, and die, but also to create exciting, nifty, highly involved things just for the sheer pleasure of creation. The fruits of all this labor? The orrery. The multitooled pocket knife. The whiskey decanter cast in the shape of Elvis Presley, circa 1969.

Excuse me if all the above sounds like gobbledygook. Excuse the lofty lecturing. It's just that when I began working on the outline for this book, I couldn't help but begin thinking about what case-modding means to me and why the PC modding craze is such an important development for computer geeks, craftspeople, and, yes, mankind in general.

As editor-in-chief of *Maximum PC* magazine from 1999 to 2003, I had the pleasure of witnessing the case-modding explosion first-hand. Ever since our magazine launched in 1996, readers have been sending us photos of their home-built rigs. By the time I instituted our Rig of the Month section in the June 2001 issue, I was receiving photos of actual computer craft.

The home-built PC of the 1990s had a backyard paint job and a crudely cut-out side window. But by 2001, readers were sending us JPEGs of totally themed-out u[um]ber-rigs, replete with amazing paint jobs, elaborate dremel work, and insanely nuanced ornamentation. In effect, PC modders had discovered one-upsmanship. As the case-modding community grew larger and larger, rudimentary mods were no longer "good enough." The bar had been raised, and the new-millennium case-mod was suddenly all about personal expression, precision craft technique, and a desire to take modding where it had never gone before.

It goes without saying that craftspeople steeped in other artistic and scientific disciplines have helped make the case-modding phenomenon what it is today. Folks schooled in mechanical engineering have surely used their unique knowledge while designing extreme cooling mods. Folks with a background in industrial design have surely used their experience to create some of the more elaborate scratch-built enclosures we see today. And those mods that resemble eighteenth-century colonial furniture? I think some degree of specialized woodworking talent is required to make these cases, without a doubt.

In sum total, twenty-first-century case-modders are leading the charge when it comes to the creative merger of science, art, craft, and design. As you flip through the pages of this book, you'll see exactly what I'm talking about. What we have here might be the best collection of modding craft ever assembled. Many photos were pulled from the pages of *Maximum PC*, and many were supplied by Paul Capello, a master modder himself. To call Paul my "coauthor" doesn't do the man justice. He is, in fact, the sole instructional force behind this book, and his ability to build mind-blowingly spectacular PC mods is equaled only by his ability to explain his techniques to modding beginners like myself.

I hope this book inspires newbies to follow wherever their imaginations might take them. Explore your creativity; merge science with design. Create the first orrery mod, even. I can't wait to see it.

Jon Phillips, editorial director, *Maximum PC*

About the Authors

Paul Capello, a.k.a. Crimson Sky, has been creating custom computer case mods, fusing his passion for art, technology, and industrial design into his unique creations since 2000. His 23+ years of experience as a master model builder, carpenter, and special effects artist are reflected in works such as Metropolis, Alien Case Mod, The Matrix: Rebirth 8.0, and his most recent Doom 3: Project Mars City. The online modding forums are his launching pads for new ideas, where he can be found sharing his works-in-progress, lending a helping hand, and learning from the many creative people who make up the case modding community. Paul's work continues to be featured in books, on television, and in magazines all over the world, and in more than eight languages. Paul was born in Brooklyn, New York, where he still lives with his lovely soulmate, Jean.

Jon Phillips has 10 years of experience covering PCs and related technology and is currently the editorial director of *Maximum PC*, *MacAddict*, *Mobile PC*, and *EZ Tech Guides*. He helps each magazine refine its monthly content, design, and newsstand packaging. Jon studied journalism and graphic design in the late 1980s and became the editor of *Harpoon*, a Bay Area-based humor magazine, in 1991. In 1994, Jon moved straight into tech, becoming the editor-in-chief of *Blaster*, a digital technology magazine for teenagers, and in 1995 he joined Future Network USA's nascent Internet magazine, *The Net*, as its managing editor. Jon has since held a number of other editorial positions at Future Network USA and was editor-in-chief of *Maximum PC* from 1999 to 2003, during which time he helped set new benchmarks for newsstand sales and appeared on the *NextStep* television show in a regular weekly segment. Jon is an avid sports car enthusiast and aspires to some day pull off a perfect four-wheel drift.

About Maximum PC

Maximum PC is the market-leading magazine for hardcore PC tech enthusiasts. With wit, attitude, and uncompromising honesty, the monthly publication guides its readers through the rapidly expanding world of PC hardware hacking—PC building, PC upgrading, PC troubleshooting, PC gaming, and all the other rewarding pursuits one can do on a computer. In the Maximum PC Hardware Lab, it's all about getting the most performance possible, and having fun doing it along the way.

Since its inception in 1996 (when the publication was known as *boot* magazine), *Maximum PC* has earned a reputation for providing the highest-quality news, reviews, features, analysis, and opinion. Readers rely on the magazine to be authoritative, accurate, and scrupulously objective. "Maximum PC, Minimum BS" is the credo that our editors stand by every day.

Dedication

Paul:

To my late father, Luciano Capello, who taught me that all good things come to those who wait. In my heart, there's a sunny dock on the bay, where we still sit. And the fish are always biting.

Jon:

To Paul DeBolt, my community college journalism instructor, who was instrumental in helping me become the magazine editor I am today. Writing, reporting, opining, designing, and overall publication management: Paul inspired me to think carefully and passionately about every piece of the journalism puzzle.

Acknowledgments

Paul:

Computer case modding continues to be one of the most rewarding artistic experiences I've ever had. It has awakened my passion for creative thinking and has given me the courage to work with my hands and make it real.

I'm extremely grateful to have had the privilege of writing this book and sharing my creativity on a scale I never would have imagined. This book would not have been possible without the guidance and wisdom of the following people: Jean Marie Ogrinz, for her understanding, support, and that bottomless cup of good coffee. I'm especially grateful to Rick Kughen and Jon Phillips, who both gave me the courage to write from the very first chapter, and for their patience and enthusiasm.

Special thanks go out to all my friends, and to those modders who inspire our own creativity by so generously sharing their knowledge: Johan "Mashie" Grundstrom, William J. Lappe, Joshua "Yoshi" DeHerrera, Bill Owen, Chris "CJ" Baltar, Rich "DickNervous" Neves, Skyler "Sky" Salmasi, Keith "Hobbes" Nolen, Jeff "Dgephri" Kaiser, Lee "Bellerophon" Hancock, Christopher "Bonzanego" Norrell, Alex Wiley, James "Corg8D" Anderson, Eddie "ScopeDog" Saavedra, Peter "G-gnome" Dickison, Russ Caslis, Christophe "Piloux" Janbon, Joshua "ZapWizard" Driggs, Daniel "Dan_Dude" Jonke, Joshua Wright, Chris "KiSA" Adams, Mike "Leezard" Hermon, Terry "Scarab" Stern, Robert Harvey, and JP "PJx5x" Albergo. If I've forgotten anyone, my apologies. Send me an instant message and feel free to bawl me out.

Thanks to the owners and the hard-working people behind the online community forums and PC enthusiast websites that give us a place to share our work and visions: John "GruntmaN" Krump of Gruntville.com, Kyle Bennett of [H]ardocp.com, and Sascha Pallenberg of EpiaCenter.com.

Finally, I'm indebted to the following industry professionals for their generous support of this book and many of my past projects: Michael Smith of ATI; Joe James of Corsair Memory; Yury Reznikov of Intel; Kevin Huang of MSI Computer Corporation; Dan Stephens of Danger Den; Michal Lisiecki, Richard Brown, Fionna Gatt, and Tim Handley of Via Technologies; Henry Jakl and the entire Matrix Orbital team; Jeff Kemp of Earth LCD; Chris Francy of Xoxide.com; Clare Liu of Vantec Thermal Technologies; Christine Goutaland of Antec; Tony Ou of SilverStone Technology; Foredom Power Tools; Cristina Lee of SnapStream Media; Taner Demirci of AlphaCool; and Angus Morrison of Hoojum Cases.

Jon:

Thanks go to every *Maximum PC* reader who ever submitted a rig to one of our modding contests. It is you—the Paul Capellos of the world—who've helped establish *Maximum PC* as the go-to print magazine for hardware-hacking coverage. The magazine is indebted to your support and passion.

Speaking of Paul Capello, he deserves special props for partnering with *Maximum PC* on this immense publishing undertaking. Very, very, very few people on this planet can master not only hands-on hardware craft, but also writing and instruction. So kudos and thanks to Paul for authoring this definitive how-to guide. Case-modding is a perfect mélange of digital technology and fine art, and Paul has not only perfected the craft, but also can explain it better than anyone.

I also want to thank *Maximum PC* managing editor Katherine Stevenson and art director Natalie Jeday for all the hard work they've put into developing and editing the magazine's Rig of the Month section. This book wouldn't be stuffed to the brim with so much cool material if not for their efforts! Thanks also go to editor-in-chief George Jones and the rest of the *Maximum PC* editorial and art crew for supporting and nurturing the magazine's case-modding coverage over the years. Every staff editor, designer, and photographer is an important contributor to this book.

Final thanks go to Que Executive Editor Rick Kughen. Understanding, patient, supportive, and fun, Rick has been a champion of this project from day one. All of *Maximum PC* is grateful for his role in this kick-ass how-to guide. Thanks, Rick! Thanks, Que! Thanks to all case-modders, worldwide!

We Want to Hear from You!

As the reader of this book, *you* are our most important critic and commentator. We value your opinion and want to know what we're doing right, what we could do better, what areas you'd like to see us publish in, and any other words of wisdom you're willing to pass our way.

As an executive editor for Que Publishing, I welcome your comments. You can email or write me directly to let me know what you did or didn't like about this book—as well as what we can do to make our books better.

Please note that I cannot help you with technical problems related to the topic of this book. We do have a User Services group, however, where I will forward specific technical questions related to the book.

When you write, please be sure to include this book's title and authors as well as your name, email address, and phone number. I will carefully review your comments and share them with the authors and editors who worked on the book.

Email: feedback@quepublishing.com

Mail: Rick Kughen
Executive Editor
Que Publishing
800 East 96th Street
Indianapolis, IN 46240 USA

For more information about this book or another Que Publishing title, visit our website at www.quepublishing.com. Type the ISBN (excluding hyphens) or the title of a book in the Search field to find the page you're seeking.

Introduction

You're holding in your hands a book about the *art of computer case modding*. A bold statement calling it an art perhaps, but I will always stand by it. Like a sculptor with a block of stone or a painter before a canvas, a case modder can look deep into the metal and plastic of the ordinary desktop computer and summon its true nature. The very word *modding*, (short for *modify*) means to change and transform personal computers into works of individual expression. Or, more simply put: to make different.

In workshops, in garages, in dorm rooms, and on kitchen tables all over the world, case modders are busy customizing their stock computers. They are the hot rodders among PC enthusiasts, cutting, reshaping, painting, and tweaking their machines for stunning visual impact and ultra-high performance. Some of these are not only extreme computer makeovers, but one-of-a-kind hand-built marvels of craftsmanship and cutting-edge design. They're having fun designing, building, and showing off their own home theater PCs, car computers, and tricked-out gaming rigs.

You might be asking, "Why even bother to change the appearance of my computer when it works perfectly fine the way it is?" That's because case modding is about the expression of individuality, and about redefining what makes a computer truly personal.

Who Is This Book Written for?

This book is for anyone who loves computers and believes beige is boring, and I hope that's a good many of you. It's for PC gamers and hobbyists interested in making their computers and peripherals look better and run faster than they ever have before. Inside you'll read and learn about the techniques and tools that will make your PC stand out in a crowd or blend discretely into just about any environment.

It will teach the beginner how to jumpstart his adventures into PC case modding; the more experienced case modders will find advanced scratch-building methods to help make their own projects a cut above the rest. It's for people who want to roll up their sleeves; grab a few tools and materials; and discover their potential to create unique, customized computers they can, beyond a doubt, call their own!

 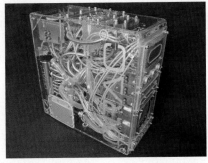 

How This Book Is Organized

Inside you'll find hands-on, step-by-step instructions on how to create custom computer case mods. You'll also find stunning works from some of the most well-known and respected case modders in the world.

Chapter 1, "Prepwork: Laying the Perfect Foundation"

In this chapter, we introduce you to the wild world of PC modding, showing you the tools and safety equipment you'll need to turn your ordinary average case from boring to badass. We also show you how to conceptualize your design using cardboard models and graphics programs. If you're a beginner, you'll definitely want to start here. Even if you're experienced in the ways of case modding, you're almost sure to learn a trick or two here, so be sure to give this chapter a read.

Chapter 2, "Choosing a Modworthy Case"

Here, we show you how to choose a modworthy case that's best for your project. Whether your vision is to overhaul a mid-tower case or create a minicase for your entertainment center, we show you how to choose the right case for the job. Of course, the truly intrepid among you might be saying, "Cases? We don't need no stinkin' cases." In that case, you'll want to be sure to check out Chapter 10, where we show you how to build your own case from scratch.

Chapter 3, "Making a Case Window"

This is where we get jiggy wid it. Literally. We show you how an ordinary sabre saw, some imagination, and a steady hand can turn an otherwise boring case panel into a veritable work of art. Sure, you can buy cases with precut windows, but where's the fun in that? Cutting a case window is a lot easier than you think—and the results can be stunning.

Chapter 4, "Painting Cases"

In this chapter, you'll discover the secrets to painting your case like a professional and achieving that show-car finish. We also introduce you to both spray painting—yes, we said spray painting—and airbrushing, with tips, FAQs, and techniques that can kickstart a new and rewarding hobby. We also show you how the pros paint cases, just like cars. While other modding books punt on the topic of painting, we dig *deep* into painting your custom rig. We show you PC painting techniques never before published in any book!

Chapter 5, "Fans, Fans, and More Fans"

In this chapter, we give you the ins and outs of case fans and what's available to help keep your PC running cool, and looking very cool. Also, we cover a variety of bay-mounted devices here, including fan-speed controllers, LCD screens, and more.

Chapter 6, "Let There Be Lighting"

In Chapter 6, you become the lighting designer, illuminating your PC inside and out with cold cathode fluorescent lamps, LEDs, and lighted fans. We show you tricks for turning your ordinary, dark case into something that will make the young girls cry.

Chapter 7, "Laying Cables"

Here, we help you make your case window worth looking into by showing you how to manage the cables and wires inside your PC for good looks and increased airflow. We show you how to install your own braided cable sleeves, split-loom sleeves, and heat-shrink tubing.

Chapter 8, "Building the Ultimate Off-the-Shelf Mod"

Who says your case mod has to be done from scratch? Although more serious modders eschew off-the-shelf mod components, we believe they're an excellent way to dip your toes into deep waters of case modding. In this chapter, we show you how to choose the best off-the-shelf enclosure and dress it up with custom lighting, cable dressings, and fan controllers. We also show you how to add a little bling-bling to your off-the-rack rig by adding colored case thumbscrews, fan-speed controllers, and other gizmos designed to crank up your mod's pimp factor.

Chapter 9, "Building the Ultimate Found-Object Mod"

Here, we take your modding adventures to a whole new level. You learn how you can transform random objects into extraordinary, fully functional computers for stealth and portability. Who says your PC has to be in a traditional case—or even look like a PC, for that matter? We show you how a little creativity, a lot of planning, and—most likely—a lot of swearing can result in something truly original.

Chapter 10, "Building the Ultimate Scratch-Built Mod"

In this chapter, we show you that you don't even need a computer case or any kind of existing receptacle to house your PC. In fact, if you're willing to use a little imagination, some nifty power tools, and materials you can find at your neighborhood hardware store, you can build your own, one-of-a-kind case from scratch.

Chapter 11, "Exotic Cooling"

No, we're not talking about exotic women fanning you with ostrich feathers and feeding you grapes. We're talking about state-of-the-art water-cooling systems designed to keep your rig both stylish and frosty cool. We first show you how to modify your enclosure to house a water-cooling unit; then we show you how to make all the connections. Also, we show you how to install after-market CPU and bay coolers, as well as how to quiet a noisy PC.

Chapter 12, "CPU Overclocking"

In this chapter, we show you how to squeeze every last drop of performance from your PC by overclocking the CPU and videocard. Be warned, however, that even though overclocking your PC can improve your bench scores and make you more deadly at LAN parties, incorrectly overclocking your PC can quickly turn your CPU into a lovely charcoal briquette.

Chapter 13, "Tweaking Your BIOS Settings"

Here, we show you how to harness the power of your PC's BIOS to eek out more power and perform-ance from your CPU, memory and some components. Most motherboard manuals are exceptionally poor when it comes to showing you how to manhandle your BIOS, but armed with this chapter, we'll show how to get it done.

Chapter 14, "Case-Modding Resources"

Wondering where we get all these cool ideas and toys? Never fear. This chapter points you to some of the best online retailers and modding communities in existence. If you're serious about modding, this is your little black book.

Chapter 15, "Showing It All Off"

Now that your rig is done and you're as proud as a new mother, you'll likely want to show it off to other modders around the world and possibly enter it in PC modding contests. In this chapter, we show you tricks for photographing and presenting your mod to the world.

Chapter One

Prep Work: Laying the Perfect Foundation

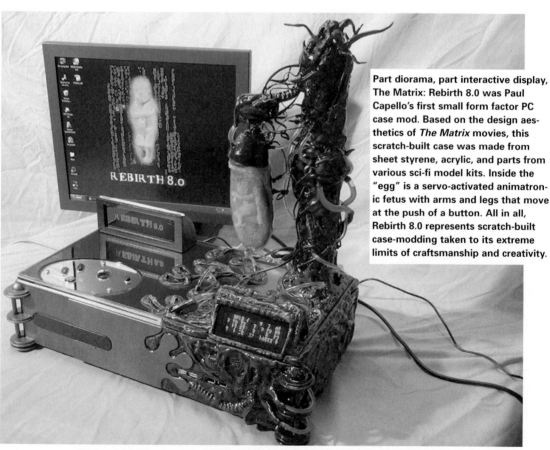

Part diorama, part interactive display, The Matrix: Rebirth 8.0 was Paul Capello's first small form factor PC case mod. Based on the design aesthetics of *The Matrix* movies, this scratch-built case was made from sheet styrene, acrylic, and parts from various sci-fi model kits. Inside the "egg" is a servo-activated animatronic fetus with arms and legs that move at the push of a button. All in all, Rebirth 8.0 represents scratch-built case-modding taken to its extreme limits of craftsmanship and creativity.

Every kick-ass modding project starts with a good idea— and good tools and safety practices can't hurt either!

It's about 3:30 in the afternoon as I push the heavy chair across the dining room floor and into the small kitchen. I'm nine years old and it's the Golden Hour—I'm alone in the apartment after school, just before my mother comes home from work at about 4:30. The television blares from the living room, and while Scooby and Shaggy skillfully craft mile-high sandwiches in a haunted mansion, I plot my own gastronomical mischief with a two-slice Proctor Silex model P20214 chrome toaster.

Kneeling on the chair, I gaze at the shiny metal box, my reflection distorted and bulging on the Fun House mirror surface as I consider what to *cook* in the toaster. I have a basic understanding of how the toaster works; with its electrical-powered heating elements and spring-loaded bread tray mechanism, the device's engineering is self-evident. A minute or two later (and with a resounding *zoinks!*) I have an idea that's so simple, so straightforward, that it just has to work. After all, what *are* grilled cheese sandwiches but two slices of toasted bread with melted cheese inside, right?

Well, yes and no, I remember thinking as I sat near the window eating a bowl of Cap'n Crunch, a box fan exhausting the last of the light gray smoke from our small apartment. While my single-slot sandwich *did* toast perfectly and the cheese *did* melt, the latter did so all over the bottom of the glowing hot toaster, just as Sir Isaac would have testified to, had he been in my R&D lab. At nine years old, my interpretation of Newton's Law had nothing to do with universal gravitation, but rather the universally accepted theory that eating too many of his fruit-chewy fig cookies would give you a bad tummy ache.

My toaster experiments ended with Project Proctor, but like any curious kid, I moved on to tinkering with other unsuspecting household devices—the very definition of softcore hardware hacking. And I'm sure that many of you have been there as well, armed with a bent-tipped butter knife or some other primitive tool from the "junk drawer," taking things apart and poking around inside. We believed that opening up that old radio would reveal the magical source of the music and voices within (alas, sadly, there were no tiny people inside), all this experimenting adding another item to our growing mental list of "Things That Are Known."

Unleashing Your Inner Case Modder

Chances are, if you're reading this book, you're already a computer case modder or perhaps interested in starting your first case-modding project. I'll tell you right now that you don't have to be an artist, engineer, or computer whiz to get involved in PC hardware hacking—you simply have to be a *time traveler*. Becoming a case modder is all about remembering the days of wide-eyed curiosity, child-like determination, and experimentation with the world around you. There's no need to overpack because all you're bringing on the trip are some readily available materials, basic hand and power tools, and of course your imagination.

I receive a lot of email from beginning modders searching for a project theme, and I always give them the same answer: The most interesting case mods are the ones that draw inspiration from your life experiences and visual stimuli you enjoy most. Ideas for hacking projects can stem from your occupation, a favorite film, a significant life event, and anything from the profound to the outright absurd.

If you spend some time browsing the Internet, you'll find amazing case mods coming out of workshops, garages, dining rooms, and dorm rooms from every corner of the globe. Customizing computers has become a worldwide phenomenon, with people from Alaska to Australia flexing their modding muscles by hacking, chopping, tweaking, and morphing their rigs to express their lifestyles and passions. PCs have become the new household appliance. We depend on them so heavily for career, education, and entertainment that it's simply an evolutionary given that we would one day begin molding and shaping them into works of art—vehicles for truly *personal* computing.

Case modding is our expression of, and response to, the inevitability of technological advancement. We are taming the hi-tech beast to help preserve, in some small way, our own fragile humanity.

If you were to research the history of case modding on Internet message boards, you would most likely come across heated arguments and colorful language relevant to the topic. There are those who argue that case modding was first pioneered by hardcore over-clockers, the "more bang for the buck" crowd who strived to push stock CPUs beyond their warrantied clock speed thresholds. On the opposing side, we have the red-in-the-face fist shakers who proclaim the first true case mods were more aesthetic—perhaps custom-paint finishes on previously vanilla cases.

Notwithstanding the difference of opinion, for this book let's just sit on the fence and agree that, at present, case modding is about both creativity *and* performance.

Time to Get Organized

Now, before we go any further, let's break down the structure of this book. In this chapter, we'll focus on the fundamentals: idea-generation, tools, and tool safety—all the things you need to consider before actually tinkering with raw case-modding materials. Immediately thereafter, in Chapter 2, "Choosing a Modworthy Case," we'll get into picking the best off-the-shelf enclosures for "simple" modding projects. Then, in Chapters 3–7, we'll get into step-by-step, how-to examples for doing case-modding basics. We're talking about simple hacking projects such as cutting case windows, painting your rig at home, adding trick fans, installing dazzling interior lights, installing custom cables, and modding your PC's front panel. All this rudimentary case-modding culminates in Chapter 8, "Ultimate Off-the-Shelf Mod," with a single, comprehensive case-modding project in which I show you how all these individual elements can be integrated into a single unit. I call it the "Ultimate Off-the-Shelf Mod" because all the parts and materials I use can be purchased from retail outlets.

In Chapters 9 and 10, we progress to "extreme" PC hardware hacking—how to break the rules by exploring mods that don't involve traditional enclosures. You'll discover how to put computers into toys, furniture, and other found objects, as well as how to fabricate your own enclosure from raw materials, piece-by-ever-loving-piece.

We then attack more performance-oriented hardware-hacking in Chapters 11, 12, and 13: installing exotic cooling, overclocking your CPU frequency, and tweaking your BIOS settings. Finally, we close the book out with some basic resource information that should be of interest to all modding enthusiasts, newbie and hardcore alike. This includes mod-oriented trouble-shooting advice, a guide to online component retailers, and a list of modding events and contests.

Why in the World Would Anyone Fenestrate a Computer Case?

If you've ever been to a custom hot rod meet or auto show, you've seen people gathered around the open hood of a tricked-out ride, with tilted heads and facial expressions not unlike those of primitive humans around an alien obelisk—a mixture of amazement, curiosity, and bewilderment. In the world of case-modding, the acrylic window is the analogue to the popped-open hood. Installing a custom window in your computer case not only reveals the secret inner workings of your PC and any interior craftsmanship you might have done, but also adds another level of dimension and character to an otherwise sealed box. It's a great feature to begin with when planning your first project.

Window-cutting was one of the first do-it-yourself modding trends, and it continues to be very popular, especially now that case manufacturers are including windows in off-the-shelf models. As you'll discover in Chapter 3, "Making a Case Window," it's easy to create your own custom case windows, not to mention all the interior flair that justify windows in the first place.

Indeed, with windows opening up our rigs for all the world to see, we need to install interior lighting to illuminate dark corners and reveal subtle details. Custom lighting found its way into case modding early in our hobby's history. Computer power supply units are models of *electrical redundancy*—that is, they carry enough juice to power both necessary computer components *and* quite a few added extras. So, with more neon pulsing through their rigs than what you'll find over the streets of Tokyo, modders are firing up their enclosures with 12-volt sticks of red, green, and blue—*and it looks really sweet*.

Painting with light is probably the easiest of all modifications. A tremendous retail selection of easily installed lighting products is available for every nook and cranny of your case, both inside and out. Dramatic lighting can significantly enhance the beauty of a simple case mod, adding sparkle to a custom-etched window. But, of course, custom lighting isn't the only visual flourish that lends pop to a case interior....

Did Someone Order a Nice Cold Coke?

You're looking through the window of a custom case mod at a computer technology convention. Your brow furrows and you wonder what those plastic hoses are for, and then you realize there's some sort of tasty-looking liquid flowing through them. Well, before you embarrass yourself and ask the marketing rep at the booth for "a large with no ice," I'll tell you right now that you're not staring at a fountain-drink machine, but rather at a water-cooled computer system. And it looks quite spectacular behind that case window, doesn't it?

In the never-ending quest for performance—CPU speed, video card speed, and hard drive speed—hardcore PC enthusiasts pay a heavy price. Oh sure, all these components cost a lot, but they also generate a lot of heat—heat that needs to be dissipated come hell or high-water. An overheated component can only run for so long before causing a system crash, so some type of cooler must whisk its heat away. In traditional PCs, simple fans and heatsinks can keep components cool, but they also typically cause quite a racket.

Enter much more exotic cooling methods, which borrow their cooling strategies from technology used in the automobile, refrigeration, and medical industries.

Water-cooling, the most common of all exotic cooling strategies, is fast becoming a familiar scheme for keeping temperatures down and PCs quiet. Even more radical are the vapor-phase systems that can chill CPUs to sub-zero temperatures using the same technology found in air conditioning and refrigeration units. Electronics and water don't mix, you say? Well, you're right: It's safe to say that we never want our PC components touching H_2O. That said, exotic cooling strategies are growing more popular (and easier to implement) thanks to the availability of plug-and-play kits. And they all look quite bad-ass when viewed through a case window.

Redefining the Meaning of "Fanboy"

If you're not quite ready to take the water-cooling plunge, there are alternative approaches to keeping things cool, quiet, and spectacular-looking. Indeed, a lot of money and research is going into traditional CPU and case fans that offer adjustable speed levels. When set at their low-speed settings, the fans run noticeably quieter but can't cool a system generating excessive heat. When set at their higher-speed settings, noise increases but so does cooling headroom.

So, how do you control the fan speeds? Aha! Even the basic issue of fan-control offers the hardware hacker some modding opportunities. Some of the newfangled fans come complete with inline potentiometers for adjusting speed (and thereby lowering noise levels). There are also built-in thermal regulators on motherboards that ratchet down fans as well. But if you want to control fan speed yourself while simultaneously making a visual statement, you can install a snazzy front-panel *fan bus* that comes with an array of user-adjustable fan-speed control knobs. Some of the cooler front-panel options even include programmable LCD displays that provide read-outs on critical system temperatures. You might also be interested to know that the very material you choose for your case can play an important role with regard to system cooling, performance, and noise.

If you're a first-time case-modder, we recommend that you work with a prebuilt case for your first project. This is the best way to become familiar with every component in a computer system and the manner in which hardware is properly installed. Plus, the companies that engineer and sell prebuilt cases typically spend a lot of effort in making sure their thermals are correct. All this factory testing ensures that your first-time mod will have an efficient airflow design from one end of the case interior to the other—a critical consideration for component cooling.

Once you have a few notches in your modding belt, you might want to carry your skills to the next level by designing a scratch-built custom case from the ground up. Building cases piece-by-piece, panel-by-panel gives you not only absolute control of design and function, but also a certain satisfaction that your project is completely handmade and one-of-kind. Scratch-built cases can be made from wood, plastic, metals, and even more exotic materials such as carbon fiber and polyester resin.

Many scratch-built rigs are made by those who bring their unique life experiences to case modding, such as woodworkers, metal smiths, sculptors, and other artisans. Although you don't have to be a skilled craftsman to get into scratch-building, you do need to be familiar with many tools and materials and have a good understanding of their properties, benefits, and limitations. For the how-to section of this book, I created a scratch-built case from polystyrene plastic, aluminum, and other materials to create a truly unique PC.

Beginning Your Project in Earnest

Let's face it—all hobbies have their share of pleasures and disappointments, and hardware hacking is absolutely no exception. So, to avoid the most common pitfalls, there's no better preventive medicine than beginning with a well-thought-out plan.

Most likely, your first case mod will be an experiment in using new techniques, new materials, and new tools. You'll have to absorb a lot of information during your efforts, and you'll make a fair share of mistakes (we all do). So, take it slow, follow your heart, have fun, and *just get it finished*. Even if your project doesn't turn out exactly how you would have liked it to, the experience you'll gain will be well worth it.

That said, a good strategy not only prevents your project from becoming a footrest, but also helps to conserve two very important commodities: time and money.

Creating a truly fantastic mod can easily be done without a fat wallet or breaking the bank. Some of the best mods I've seen had far more inspiration put into them than cash. As with any hobby, spending can get out of

What Makes a Case Modworthy?

When shopping for parts to use in your modding project, keep in mind that a good review should examine every aspect of a modworthy product, including

- Included parts and accessories
- The product's overall fit, finish, and availability
- A description of the materials used
- Ease-of-use and integration
- Basic installation instructions
- Clear, easy-to-see photographs
- MSRP (manufacturer's suggested retail price) and street price
- Benchmarking results, if applicable

control, and case modders are frequently lured by the siren call of bleeding-edge hardware and shiny chrome trim. For this very reason, you should plan a realistic budget for yourself and try your best to work within it.

Unlike purchasing a complete computer system that comes with a blanket warranty for the entire unit, acquiring PC and modding components á la carte is a tricky business. Although your local computer shop might have some modding supplies, it probably won't have everything you need, and thus online shopping becomes your only option for purchasing hard-to-find parts at decent prices. Purchasing products sight unseen is one of several shortcomings of Internet shopping, but with a few helpful tips you can safely buy the mod parts you need.

Picking the Right Parts

Type the name of any modding product in your favorite search engine and the first result will most likely point to a review website. Good hardware review sites are your first line of defense against purchasing products that haven't made the grade with fellow case modders.

On these sites (some of which are listed in Chapter 14, "Case-Modding Resources"), you can also find information there about fair-market pricing and which retailers are reputable and which are deadbeats. A well-written, in-depth review of a hardware component is almost as good as having the product in your hand, and it can save you a lot of shopping time, not to mention headaches.

> *MAKE NO LITTLE PLANS; THEY HAVE NO MAGIC TO STIR MEN'S BLOOD AND PROBABLY WILL THEMSELVES NOT BE REALIZED. MAKE BIG PLANS; AIM HIGH IN HOPE AND WORK, REMEMBERING THAT A NOBLE, LOGICAL DIAGRAM ONCE RECORDED WILL NOT DIE.*
> —DANIEL BURNHAM, ARCHITECT (1846–1912)

With so many online reviews available, I usually limit my consumer research to just three (and no more than five) critiques. Typically speaking, if the world's reviewers have reached consensus, that consensus opinion can be trusted. Online community forums are another great resource for feedback and for posting your own opinions on a particular product.

It also goes without saying that you should visit the website of the manufacturer that made the product you're considering. In most instances, these are the best places for accurate information on how best the product might fit into your mod project. You can search the site for images, manuals, and technical data that can be difficult to find elsewhere. If the information on the site is vague or nonexistent, don't hesitate to write or call the company with specific questions, especially if it's a new product offering. Although some companies offer their products for sale directly, they might also have a Where to Buy section with a list of authorized retailers that sell the products at street prices.

Creative Visualization

Planning the aesthetics and theme of your case is every bit as crucial as finding the right parts at the right price. Two of the most essential items in my own arsenal of modding tools are a trusty sketchpad and an assortment of pinky-sized number 2 pencils. While I'm no Leonardo da Vinci, I always begin composing simple sketches and line drawings before I begin whacking any actual case-modding materials. Whether you're figuring out the lines for a case window or sketching the basic shape of a scratch-built enclosure, putting concepts on paper is the first step in the path of realization.

Personally, I have a rather freeform approach to case modding, and this allows my initial designs to take on a life of their own and eventually tell me what they want to be. For this reason, I recommend that beginners not worry about planning every single detail of a project, or they'll wind up becoming overwhelmed by distracting minutia. Now, of course, if you are already an accomplished artist or modeler, and you're comfortable designing in the digital realm, software applications like SketchUp and the more advanced 3ds max are alternatives to pencil and paper.

Here are few tips to consider when purchasing from online modding supply retailers—you'll want to protect yourself from shysters:

What to look for

- Positive and consistent customer ratings from reliable consumer watchdog websites. (Some online retail sites host their own sections for customers to post opinions on products and services; just be aware that these opinions might not be completely reliable.)

- Policies on returns and exchanges. Companies often charge anywhere from 5% to as much as 15% for restocking fees; even though this might seem like a questionable practice, it's perfectly legal.

- Detailed descriptions of products with good photographs.

- Safe and secure ordering forms.

What to avoid

- Sites that have little or no company contact information. If you have to return a product for refund or replacement, you'll want to deal with a company that keeps open the lines of communication.

- Retailers and auction sites that sell products through a third party. Investigate the policies of both companies before purchasing.

- Bait-and-switch schemes. Unscrupulous salespeople can push "similar" products on you when preferred items are out of stock.

- Sites that set limits on the amount of products you can buy. If you need six widgets for a project, and the site will only sell you five, you'll have to go shopping for one more elsewhere. And that would be a pain.

And once you actually have the product in hand:

- Inspect all your packages when they arrive. Even slightly dented packaging could be an indicator of physical damage inside.

- Make sure all packages are factory sealed. Sloppy packaging could be an indication that a product was returned and then resold to you.

- If you've purchased a full-retail version of hardware, make sure the packaging it arrives in is from the manufacturer. Many companies repackage OEM goods in plain white boxes and sell them at reduced prices, and often without the full suite of accessories.

Planning: Paper Models

In addition to sketching out your designs, another good practice that can help you visualize your project in 3D is to create a full-scale mock-up of key components. Imagine having all your components, accurate in size and shape, right at your fingertips before making a single purchase and voiding warranties. Not only is this easy to do and extremely accurate, but it can also help you avoid costly case modding mistakes with both scratch-built mods and those made from stock cases. If you consider most computer components, they can be very easily broken down into their basic geometric shapes. With decent images and the manufacturer's specs handy, you can create your scale models and use them over and over.

When planning for a water-cooled system, one of the most difficult parts might be finding room for the pump. Let's take a look at building a simple model of the popular Eheim 1250 pump.

Here's what you'll need:

- Razor blade or craft blade
- Foam board, cardboard, or printer paper
- Hot glue gun
- Straight edge
- Ruler or tape measure
- Accurate specs and measurements of components, many of which can be found on the manufacturers' websites.

Below, I show you how to build a simple cardboard model.

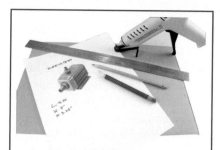

Use cardboard, a razor blade, a glue gun, ruler, and a pencil to create your own scale models. Putting the time in here will save both time and money later when you're bringing your creation to life.

1

The Eheim 1250 pump is simply a rectangle with beveled (chamfered) edges, one inlet barb, and one outlet. Based on the width, height, and length from the manufacturer, I estimated the size of each side and its corresponding bevel. I then made a pattern on a sheet of scrap cardboard with a pencil and straight edge.

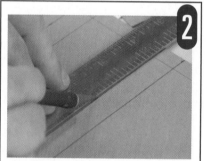

2

By lightly scoring the cardboard along the pencil lines with an X-acto blade, you create clean crisp edges that can then be folded to create a rectangle.

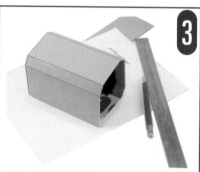

3

Carefully fold the cardboard into the desired shape. Recheck your measurements and make sure everything is right before moving to the next step.

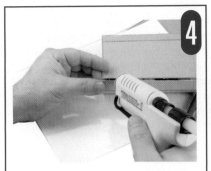

Run a bead of hot glue along the edge and then hold it in place while it cools to close the rectangle.

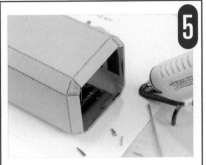

I decided to add a bit of accurate detail by snipping the front edges and creating a beveled face.

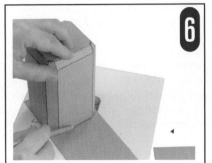

Here I traced out both ends of the model and cut out the patterns.

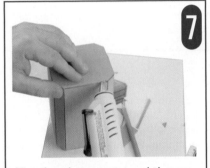

Use the glue gun to seal the rectangle. I find it's a lot easier to hold the pieces in place and weld it by running a thin bead of hot glue along the edges.

Cut strips of paper and roll them up with a pencil to create the two pump barbs.

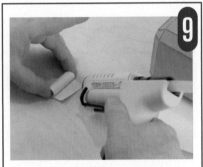

It takes very little glue to hold paper in place, so use it sparingly by squeezing the trigger gently.

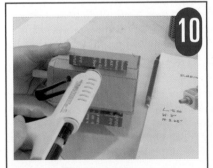

After gluing the barbs on, I decided to add the mounting plates to give me a better idea of where this pump might fit inside a case.

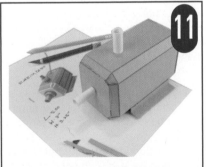

The completed paper model.

Use the model to find a mounting spot for the actual pump.

Never Run with Scissors

It's past midnight and you're not quite sure where the heck you are, or how you got here. Your vision is blurred, and your head is heavy and nodding, like an anvil balanced on a drinking straw. Voices sound echoey and far away; you hear your name called but you can hardly move. Zombies in bloody, torn clothing amble past you, dragging their heavy feet. You slowly lift your arm and try to brush something off your shoulder, and in a moment of dumbfounded terror, you realize it's the floor.

Welcome to the Emergency Room.

I certainly hope that you never have to visit the ER while case modding, but it's a frighteningly real possibility. You should be so concerned with accidents, in fact, that the following advice becomes writ and scripture for you. If it sounds like I'm getting a little preachy, I make absolutely no apologies. During the 20 years I worked as a carpenter, I never received more than a few minor cuts and bruises on the job—and I attribute this not to good luck but to due diligence. Of course, I have had my share of close calls and heart-stopping moments, but every single one of them was caused by carelessness or inexperience, not bad fortune.

Anyone who works in any building trade needs to depend on three things to keep out of harm's way: experience, common sense, and respect for tools and safety practices.

As for experience, hey, you're a *beginning* modder. You'll be constantly gathering information, filtering it, and using what you need to become better. Just accept the fact that you might not know, for example, the correct way to cut through aluminum with a Dremel tool and that you should consult the advice of others (or this book!) before making the first incision. Same goes for other building techniques that involve sharp blades, extreme temperatures, or volatile chemicals.

As for common sense, most would argue that we're either born with it or without it. That said, I can advise you to be *deliberate* with every case-modding step you take. Actually *think* about what you're about to cut, shear, fuse, or connect before you actually do it. Think about ramifications—and what's reversible and what isn't.

Finally, we come to the most important part of the puzzle: tool knowledge and basic workplace practices. I outline a basic overview in the following paragraphs, and I close the chapter with close-up looks at every important tool in the case modder's arsenal.

Eye, Hand, and Lung Protection

Protective Eyewear: You've probably heard the phrase before: "Hey, watch it! You can poke an eye out with that thing." And it's certainly a possibility during case modding. Protective eyewear should be a top-level piece of safety equipment, especially when you consider that eye injuries are the most common and preventable of all workplace accidents.

Common prescription eyewear (unless safety-rated) should not be used as an alternative to proper protection. Good safety glasses are inexpensive and easy to find, and many will fit over existing eyewear. You should wear your eye-protection when cutting, grinding, sanding, polishing, and using any type of powered machinery. Before I even begin working, I make sure my safety glasses are around my neck (I use a shoestring) and ready to use.

Safety glasses will inevitably get scratched up, so replace them immediately or use a plastic polish such as Novus to buff out the scratches. Never attempt to clean your safety glasses with solvents. Using badly scratched or damaged eyewear is equivalent to using nothing at all and can result in injuries caused by vision impairment. Protective eyewear should be OSHA-certified.

Gloves: Leather work gloves are your first line of defense against hand injuries from sharp metal, splinters, cutting tools, and hand fatigue. Proper gloves should be form-fitting and comfortable to wear, and they should allow you to feel your tools and materials as you work. Those big, cheap, loose-fitting gloves might be good for digging holes with shovels, but they have no place in the mod shop were you do delicate work.

Gloves should *not* be worn when using machinery such as lathes, drill presses, and table saws because blades can catch a glove and pull you in. Also, you should use latex rubber or silicon examination-type gloves (ouch!) when working with acrylic paints and other noncorrosive materials. (Keep in mind that some people are allergic to latex and can have adverse skin reactions.) Chemical-resistant gloves must be worn when using resins, epoxy adhesives, acid, and other harmful chemicals.

Respirator and Dust Mask: NIOSH/MSHA-approved respirators should be used when painting, sanding, and using hazardous materials such as resins and auto body fillers. Certain plastics like the kind used for computer case bezels can seem harmless, but when you start sanding and cutting them, they can give off harmful dust and vapors. Good-quality respirators have replaceable cartridges, each designed to protect against different kinds of chemical exposures. Always read the labels and find out which type of respiratory protection is recommended.

Respirators work in a two-stage process: The first layer filters out larger particles (such as paint particles), and the second-stage organic filter protects your from vapors and fine mists. Respirators are *not* a replacement for a properly vented work area because harmful vapors can build up and cause serious injury and death. Please note that nuisance or dust masks offer *no* protection from harmful vapors and should not be used when painting. Dust masks should be used only when harmful materials and vapors are not present.

Respirator: $42

Using hazardous chemicals without risking brain damage and or death: Priceless

Ear Protection: The loud noises that result from metal cutting and grinding can quickly damage your hearing, so ear protection is imperative. (If you've ever cut a window in the side panel of a case with a jigsaw, you know exactly what I mean.) Go to your local drug store and buy whichever earplugs offer the best noise-reduction rating. When cutting metal with high-speed tools, the material surface basically becomes a nice big speaker, vibrating and projecting tooth-rattling, brain-numbing decibels right into your inner ear—enough noise to cause permanent damage. Can you hear me? Gooood.

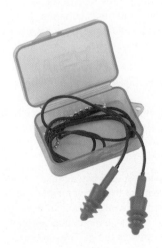

Clothing: Finally, a word about clothing: It's a basic workshop practice to not wear loose, baggy clothing when using power tools and machinery. Clothes can snag and catch on spinning blades, resulting in loss of control of your tool and serious injury. When cutting or grinding plastic, wood, or metal, hot dust and particles are directed toward you, so long-sleeved, close-fitting shirts are recommended to prevent burns and injury. Long hair should be tied back and tucked away from spinning blades, soldering irons, and other hazards. We all want to be comfortable and relaxed when we work, but going barefoot is a great way to get splinters and amputate a toe when you drop a 15-pound aluminum PC case on it. No more roast beef for that piggy!

Planning Your Workspace for Efficiency and Safety

Let's face it, not all of us have the luxury of home improvement TV–style workshops decked out with expensive tools and sprawling space. Most of us make use of garages, bedrooms, and kitchens for our modding pursuits. Even the smallest of spaces, however, can be made safe, comfortable, and efficient. The following guidelines apply to workshops of every size and shape and in every room of your house.

The Work Table
A sturdy work surface is a must in any work area. Tables can easily be made from plywood and simple 2' × 4' framing or found at garage sales for a few bucks. An old solid-core door fitted with steel legs can also make a great table. Care should be taken with folding tables, though, because they can sometimes collapse. These tables should be made of strong metal and have locking leg mechanisms.

A good worktable will offer the proper height whether you're sitting or standing. If the table is too low, you'll have to hunch over and won't be able to pull a chair under it. If it's too high, your hands won't be at the proper level.

If you're using a kitchen table or desk, you can protect the surface with a piece of 1/4'' thick hardboard. Always have a safe place on your table to rest hot tools such as soldering irons and heat guns (a piece of scrap metal or a cookie sheet works perfectly). Your worktable can clutter up pretty quickly, so take a break once in a while to organize your space for safety and peace of mind.

Lighting If you're straining or hunching over to see your work, you probably need better lighting conditions. Inexpensive work lights can be found at home improvement and hardware

Universal Checklist: Common To-Do Points for All Case-Modding Projects

1 **Brainstorm the basic concept of your project.** Is it an homage to Iron Maiden? A replica of a Sherman Tank? A Habitrail PC? Start thinking about your theme, color palette, and overall aesthetics. At this point, you should also determine the overall function of your computer (for example, whether it's a full-tower workstation or a mini PC for living room deployment) because this will influence your design as well.

2 **Sketch out your ideas on paper, or use your favorite drawing program.** This is the stage when you begin giving definition to paint schemes, window designs, fan and lighting placement, and all the other little details that make a case mod undeniably yours. At this stage, you should also determine the physical compatibility of all your components: Take stock of the sizes, shapes, and angles of all your intended parts, and use length notation to spec out how your hardware will live in perfect harmony.

3 **Plan your budget.** Figure out how much money you can comfortably spend, and then begin plugging in numbers for computer parts, case-modding materials, and tools. Obviously, this stage requires a lot of price-checking online, and you might have to redesign your sketches if budget restrictions demand so. When you have a clear idea of all the ingredients you need to buy, make a comprehensive list and tally it thrice.

4 **Acquire all your ingredients.** I use the word *acquire* because you might be able to borrow tools from friends. But, in general, in this stage you'll be buying everything you need from some type of retailer: tools, safety equipment, traditional computer parts, and case-modding parts and materials. Remember to follow the consumer-protection advice provided in this chapter.

5 **Inspect your purchases.** Make sure the part you ordered is the part you actually received. Make sure nothing is damaged, either externally or internally. If you bought some type of kit (for example, maybe a water-cooling kit), make sure that all its individual pieces are present and accounted for.

6 **Prepare your workspace.** You'll need as much room as you can get, so clean off that kitchen table and warn your family that they won't be able to use it for a few days (or maybe weeks). Even better, set up a proper workbench or table in the garage—some place you can spread out in. You'll be making a mess, so the more space you have at your disposal, the better organized your tools and materials will be.

stores. Daylight or color-corrected bulbs and fixtures are a must for accurately mixing and applying paints, and they cause less eyestrain. Start your workspace off with a good amount of indirect lighting, and then combine it with table lamps to see fine details.

Storage   I've been obsessed with plastic storage containers ever since I started case modding. Sagging cardboard boxes have been replaced with an army of inexpensive storage boxes that keep all my parts and tools neatly organized and readily available. Clear plastic containers are great for at-a-glance identification, and containers with trays and compartments are great for holding small hardware items. I have a separate toolbox or container for each of the following:

- Small hand tools
- Power tools
- Electrical supplies
- Cables and wires
- Finishing supplies
- Fans and grills
- Nuts and bolts
- Case hardware
- Miscellaneous

Sketch Your Creation Before You Grab the Power Tools

These case-mod concepts were modeled in SketchUp, an easy-to-use 3D modeling program. The nice thing about SketchUp is that you can find dozens of user-drawn components online—parts such as case fans, pumps, radiators, and entire cases. Simply import them into your document and integrate them into your custom concept.

3D modeling and sketching software can create extremely detailed case-mod designs. This concept drawing of a video editing workstation took only a few hours to complete using SketchUp.

Even simple designs like this full-tower case can help you plan and visualize your mod project. This sketch was used to help decide on the placement of water cooling components.

Safety Checklist: How to Create a Killer Mod Without Getting Killed in the Process!

1 **Get a home fire extinguisher.** Always have one on hand, fully charged and ready to use. Check its safety ratings, and buy one that's capable of putting out as many types of fires as possible.

2 **Consider ventilation.** Never work in windowless rooms or areas that have little or no air circulation. Do not use aerosol paints or other hazardous materials indoors without proper ventilation.

3 **Watch the weather report.** Don't work outdoors in bad weather or when poor lighting might keep you from using tools safely. Cold hands and extremities can prevent you from operating tools safely as well.

4 **Pay attention to what's underfoot.** Protect carpets and floors from debris and flammable liquids. Keep garage floors clean and free from oil and loose wires, and never work with electrical tools in damp areas.

5 **Don't tempt electrical fate.** Make sure you have enough available outlets to handle the power requirements of tools and other electrical equipment. Don't overload circuits, and be certain that extension cords and surge suppressors are properly grounded. Always repair tools with loose or frayed wires before using them.

6 **Provide ample lighting.** Good lighting prevents eyestrain and fatigue, shows colors properly, and allows you to work safely and accurately with tools.

7 **Wear workshop attire.** This means wearing eye, hand, and ear protection and avoiding baggy clothing that can get stuck on tools or materials. If you have long hair, get it under control as well.

8 **Keep a first aid kit.** It should include bandages, burn salve, antibacterial cream or spray, and eye wash solution.

9 **Working alone.** For safety, you should always let family members know what you're up to. If you're in a garage or shop, have a reliable phone handy in case of emergency.

Stocking Your Tool Chest

We hereby inventory the case-modder's most indispensable paraphernalia

If you're the typical case modder, picking out tools is as fun as picking out modding materials and computer parts. Indeed, as you peruse the next few pages, you'll probably feel like a kid in a candy store.

We'll start our inventory with a look at the most popular and indispensable of all modding tools—the rotary hand tools, which can be used for cutting windows, shaping plastic, etching, and grinding.

Dremel Tool

With dozens of head attachments, the legendary Dremel is a small, lightweight, and versatile rotary tool for cutting, carving, sanding, polishing, and drilling—and much, much more. The Dremel company motto is "Tools for the Imagination," and it's a motto

that's well-deserved. Dremels can be either AC-powered or cordless, and because they offer variable

speeds between 5,000rpm and 35,000rpm, they're perfect for working with a variety of materials. However, they are noisy; they tend to run hot; and, because they vibrate, you might get hand fatigue after prolonged use. They're also not suitable for cutting really heavy-duty materials. www.dremel.com

Foredom Flexible Shaft Power Tool

The Foredom flexible shaft tool has been a workhorse for hobbyists, sculptors, and jewelers for many years. With strong, quiet, 1/8-horsepower motors offering butter-smooth performance, these are the BMWs of the rotary tool world. And

because the flexible shaft and hand piece are separate from the motor, users don't suffer heat and vibration fatigue. The motor assembly is available in hang-up and bench-style models, and you can vary your rotational speeds via either a foot or tabletop dial controller. The tool is compatible with a wide variety of attachments, and it has enough high-torque power to really do some seri-

ous business. Its only real negative is its high price. www.foredom.com

Jigsaws

When your rotary tool just can't handle a task, the jigsaw is your best bet for fast, smooth cutting through metal, wood, and plastic. Jigsaws employ stroke-action blades that can be used for both straight cuts and intricate scroll

patterns. Strong and powerful, yet easy to handle, jigsaws are

indispensable for window and fan hole cut-outs in steel, aluminum, and acrylic—you just have to choose the right blade. Unfortunately, really good jigsaws can be prohibitively expensive, and these aren't the best tools if you're trying to do work in tight spaces.

Hand Drills

Cordless and AC-powered hand drills are perfect for making small, precise holes in metal, plastic, and wood and are a must for clean, finished fan openings. Hand drills can also accommodate sanding, grinding, and buffing accessories. Good drills can last a lifetime and help out in all types of home improvement projects, but they can be expensive and sometimes they're too large for working in tight spaces.

Drill Presses

When you need to make truly accurate holes of the most extreme order, a stationary drill press is your answer—it prevents both your material and drill bit from moving off-target, and it accepts all the same bits and accessories of its handheld counterparts. Drill presses can also accommodate sanding, grinding, and buffing accessories.

Drill Bits

Standard twist bits, hole-cutting bits, and spade-type bits can be used in many types of tools.

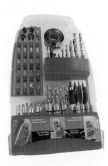

Power and Hand Sanders

Removing the paint or powder coat finish from an entire PC case can be an arm-numbing experience if you're working by hand and a complete mess if you're working with chemicals. That's why every hardware hacker needs a power sander, so he can get the job done lickety-split and move on to fun stuff like painting and finishing. Palm-type sanders, utilizing standard-size sheets of grit paper, are the most

economical. Random orbit sanders use adhesive-backed or hook-and-loop replacement discs. Variable speed models can be used with buffing and polishing accessories, and detail sanders can get into all sorts of nooks, crannies, and corners.

The alternatives to the AC-powered power sanders are the faithful and inexpensive sanding blocks. Blocks are great for very fine wet sanding and finishing on flat surfaces. They also come in handy when you're modding on a desert island.

Airbrush

I have to admit that I was intimidated by airbrushes before I decided to purchase one. But after only a few hours of tinkering, I discovered how easy they are to use and operate. Of course, mastering the art of airbrushing can take a lifetime, but these tools do provide the very finest paint finishes for simple applications. Airbrushes can spray acrylic, enamel, and lacquer paints for very precise line art as well as entire cases.

Nibbler Tool

This inexpensive tool is handy for cuts in sheet metal up to 18-gauge. It can also be used on plastic, soft copper, and aluminum up to 1/16. Operation is simple: You just drill a 7/16'' hole in your material (or start from an edge), insert the cutting head, squeeze, and begin to "nibble" the material to your desired shape. It's an easy tool to use, and it cuts through a variety of gauges and materials, but many people find it to be too time-consuming and the basic operation causes significant hand fatigue.

Files

Files are used for cleaning and deburring cuts in metal, wood, and plastic, and they last for years—assuming they're not abused or misused. Large, flat files are best for cleaning edges and fast material removal. Riffler files come in many shapes and sizes and can get into very small places for detail finishing. When filing soft materials like plastic or wood, files eventually become clogged and should be cleaned with a steel wire file cleaning brush.

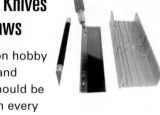

Hobby Knives and Saws

Precision hobby knives and saws should be found in every modder's tool kit. There's no better set of tools for extremely fine cutting, carving, and scribing of plastic parts, non-ferrous metals, and other materials. For accurate 90° and 45° cuts in tubing and small stock pieces, a miter box can be used together with a hobby saw. Replacement blades for hobby knives are easy to find and don't cost much.

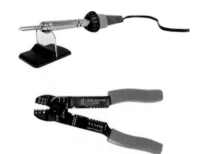

Squares, Straight Edges, and Measuring Devices

"Measure twice and cut once." You've heard it before, and these tools will help you get it right the first time. Combination squares help make repetitive marks a breeze. Straight edges are a must when scribing, marking, and cutting. Compasses, of course, are must-haves when marking holes for fans, switches, and cut-outs.

Soldering Iron and Wire Strippers

Inexpensive and easy to use, these two tools often work as a team. Soldering irons are needed when making custom switches and wiring lights, fans, LEDs, and other electrical parts of your case mod project. Models of 15–30 watts are good for electronics, whereas higher-wattage irons are suitable for joining metal parts. Wire strippers remove the sheathing from every gauge wire found in your PC—and once your wires have been stripped, the soldering can begin!

Pliers, Snips, and Multi Tools

All toolbox classics, these instruments help you hold, clamp, cut, bend, and shape metal, wire, and plastic. Chances are, you already have some type of pliers hidden in some junk drawer, but I recommend you invest in various sizes for every task you might encounter. Needle-nose pliers are especially helpful during case modding.

Extraction Tools

When braiding and wrapping the cables attached to power supplies and other items in a case, these tools make removing Molex headers and ATX power connectors a breeze. Extraction tools are simple in design but can be ridiculously expensive. In a later chapter, I show you how to make some of these tools from items around the house. They're very helpful, but they need not be professionally made.

Hot Glue Gun

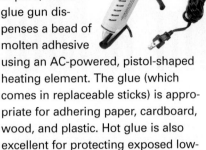

Like the name implies, a hot glue gun dispenses a bead of molten adhesive using an AC-powered, pistol-shaped heating element. The glue (which comes in replaceable sticks) is appropriate for adhering paper, cardboard, wood, and plastic. Hot glue is also excellent for protecting exposed low-voltage wires and other connections. Hot glue should not be used where a strong bond or structural strength is required. Also, they're not great for use on metal, glass, and painted finishes.

Heat Gun/ Paint Stripper

The heat gun is an excellent multiuse piece of equipment to have in your modder's toolbox. A good variable temperature model can strip paint, can form and shape plastic parts, and is perfect for setting heat-shrink tubing. It's good safety practice to have a piece of scrap metal or an old cookie sheet handy to set the tool on during and after use.

Allen Wrenches

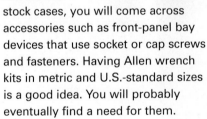

Although Phillips-head screws are standard in stock cases, you will come across accessories such as front-panel bay devices that use socket or cap screws and fasteners. Having Allen wrench kits in metric and U.S.-standard sizes is a good idea. You will probably eventually find a need for them.

Tweezers

Great for retrieving small screws from tight spaces, tweezers are also good for removing jumpers from motherboards, optical drives, and hard disk drives.

Screwdrivers

Phillips-head screws are the standard fasteners inside stock cases, so it's a good idea to have several, different-size Phillips-head screwdrivers on hand, including the tiny jeweler's type. Everything from motherboards to optical drives use Phillips-head screws, but it's also important to have flat heads available for lifting and prying.

Bench Vise

Bench vises are excellent for safely securing pieces when cutting, drilling, and filing. Bench vises can be found in many sizes, from small hobby-type vises to the large ones that bolt permanently to a worktable. They are used to hold heavy materials. I prefer vises that clamp onto the worktable edge so I can reposition them easily while working.

Clamps

A good set of various-size clamps is indispensable when cutting metal side panels—by locking down your material, you prevent it from vibrating and jumping. Quick-type bar clamps are my favorite when drilling or filing, and their soft rubber protectors don't mar finished surfaces. Spring clamps are handy for holding small pieces securely while glue dries.

Chapter Two

Choosing a Modworthy Case

Feast your eyes on what a good craftsman can do with an Enermax 5190-EL case. Chris Moore's Iron Chef project includes a custom Plexiglas faceplate, a custom front-panel fan controller, a custom-installed 14.5" LCD peaking out of one side panel, and a custom-cut window on the other side panel. Peek through the window and you'll find custom water-cooling.

A prefab enclosure might be the perfect blank canvas for hardware-hacking exploits.

You're ready to try your hand at modding, and you have a sweet idea for a killer project. Perhaps it's a sleek, low-profile home theater PC for your living room. Or maybe it's a monster gaming box for toting to LAN parties.

So, do you build the whole mod from scratch, fabricating the enclosure with your own bare hands? Well, unless you're an accomplished craftsperson, you might be better off basing your first modding project on a prefab case. Indeed, there has never been a larger selection of stock, prefab cases, with models running the gamut from practical and utilitarian cases to garish theme cases that almost qualify as "premodded."

With countless retail cases to choose from, selecting the right one for your modding project is a key decision because whatever you choose will directly influence the outcome of your rig. For this very reason, you should see every retail case as a blank canvas—the very fabric and foundation on which your ideas will be applied. The case-choosing game is all about exposing a stock enclosure's full potential and turning it into a work of art that is unique in appearance and distinctively your own.

Design and aesthetics aside, you also need to consider basic PC-building issues when choosing your case. After all, when you get right down to it, the computer is still just an electronic tool, an amalgamation of digital circuitry and moving parts. So you must consider the ultimate function of your computer, its components, and the environment it will live in.

These considerations will directly influence your choice of case materials, the size (or *form factor*) of your PC, and your ability to do future hardware upgrades on your mod. For example, if your rig will be sitting on a physical desktop in your home office, you might consider modding a small form factor (SFF) case for its small footprint and quiet, elegant presence. On the flip side, if you're planning on building a gaming PC, it might be better to choose a larger case with easy access to internal components because you might want to swap videocards every other week and do what hardware hackers do best: fixing what isn't broken.

In my opinion, the single-most attractive rationale for choosing a stock enclosure is self-evident: The basic internal design and engineering have already been done for you. The standards that case and hardware manufacturers follow enable most of your hardware components to bolt, slide, snap, and otherwise click right into place. Just as importantly, case manufacturers typically pay strict attention to the thermal properties of the cases they design. In other words, if you use a prefab case, you probably won't run into terrible over-heating dilemmas—assuming you're not overclocking and that you're running a sufficient number of fans for the parts you've chosen.

All types of computer parts retailers carry stock cases, and nothing beats seeing cases in person, opening them up, and checking them out before you purchase. Brick-and-mortar retailers probably won't be able to match the huge case selection of the online retailers, but if you decide to buy off the Internet, make sure you hit the PC hardware review sites before buying anything. Read every available review of the case you intend to buy. This will help you avoid the duds and aid in narrowing down your choices.

The creator of this June 2003 Rig of the Month winner said, "I believe there is more to case modding than just purchasing the items. I wanted this case to include mods that took work on my part, from cutting and painting to custom fabrication of brackets and components."

Barry "Cold Dog" Collins built his Copper Top mod from a prefab case. He included tons of fine details, including a handmade front bezel—proof positive that even the most inconspicuous-looking case can become art.

It Pays to Be Materialistic

The material on which your case is based will factor into most of your modding decisions. Some materials are better for painting. Some materials are better for cutting. And some materials simply look better when left in their raw, unmodded states. When you begin shopping for prefab cases, you'll mostly find enclosures made from steel, aluminum, acrylic, and plastic, and some cases will be based on combinations of all four. Once you get a feel for the properties of all these materials, you'll know which one is best for you particular hacking plans. Here's the basic 411 on case materials:

- **Plastic**—Back in the day of "plain beige boxes," most PC cases were made of plastic— boring, thin, brittle plastic. Today, even in this modern age of metal cases, the front bezels (or frames) of many enclosures are still made from injection-molded plastic, which is then dyed or painted to match the rest of the case. Yes, you *will* find metal bezels in high-end models, but not as often as

you'd think. In fact, I caution you to be aware of the trickery involved with "chrome bezels." Even though they typically look like metal, they are most likely plastic parts that have been sprayed with a special conductive paint and then coated using a chroming process.

Drive bay covers made from plastic can be easily cut, drilled, and painted, which is good news if you intend to add custom bay devices (such as fan busses) to the front of your modded case.

- **Acrylic**—If a case window just isn't a big enough to show off the mysterious inner workings of your rig, an acrylic case is the bare-all, naked-truth solution you've been looking for. Acrylic is a transparent, man-made fiber famous for its ability to retain molded shapes, as well as its resistance to heat, aging, and electricity. It also takes dyes very easily. This is why you'll find acrylic cases in so many colors, including ultra-violet, which glows brilliantly under proper lighting.

If you choose an acrylic case, you'll need to maintain a clean and tidy interior because your rig's innards will be on permanent public display. In fact, if the interior of your rig doesn't boast its own clever design aesthetic, you might want to avoid acrylic altogether because what you end up with might just look like a storage box full of random computer parts.

Acrylic cases are available in the form of both build-it-yourself kits and factory preassembled units, although the latter usually costs

a lot more. Modding an acrylic case requires a good degree of patience and careful planning because you need to avoid cracks and scratches to parts that might be impossible (or, at the least, very expensive) to replace.

As you can surmise, acrylic is the most fragile material you can use in case modding, and it doesn't hold up well to constant travel and relocation.

- **Steel**—Synonymous with durability, steel is a metal alloy based on iron, small amounts of carbon, and small amounts of other metals. Steel is the most common and inexpensive metal used for cases, and steel cases can be found in dozens of designs and just about all form factors. Steel is the strongest and most durable case material you can get, but it's also the heaviest, so consider this if you plan on creating a portable rig.

Salar Madadi fashioned this grim design— appropriately dubbed Grim Bandelero— from a prefab case, adding a custom-cut window and a wicked skull to the front bezel. Salar won *Maximum PC*'s coveted Rig of the Month award in January 2002.

Steel is a very forgiving metal that can be welded, bent, reshaped, and even repaired if necessary. For cutting elaborate window shapes in side panels, steel is typically a good choice. See Chapter 3, "Making a Case Window," for more details on cutting windows.

- **Aluminum**—This metal is the most common metal found in the earth's crust and is actually an element (atomic number 13). It has great thermal properties (in that it can quickly dissipate heat), and it is often used to form strong, light, corrosive-resistant alloys. Aluminum cases can be quite pricey, but they're very popular with modders and gamers because they're light, they look good when left "unfinished," and they can shed heat better than steel enclosures.

Aluminum is a great metal to work with because it can be easily filed, sanded, cut, painted, and polished. That said, aluminum cases are not all created equal, and some are downright flimsy and useless for serious hardware hacking. When shopping for an aluminum case, check online reviews for overall build quality and read the fine print to find out the thickness of the aluminum used.

Keep in mind that, once bent or damaged, aluminum is easy to repair but replacement panels can be expensive.

What to Look for in a Modworthy Case

Raw materials aside, plenty of other factors affect a prefab case's suitability for modding. So, at this point, let's get into the nitty-gritty of physical case design—what to look for in a new case and what should be avoided at all costs:

- **Unkind cuts**—Case-modding shouldn't be like working on an Alaskan fishing vessel: Tetanus shots and late-night visits to the emergency room should never be part of the plan. Nonetheless, metal cases can pose dangers to your flesh. So, when buying a metal case, be on the lookout for die-cut tabs, poorly installed rivets, and mounting clips that have sharp edges. These edges can not only cause injuries to your hands and fingers, but can also lead to pinched wires and electrical shorts. So, if you're not into hair-raising adventures or sacrificial bloodletting, make sure that any metal edges in your case have been rolled or somehow blunted for safety.

- **Difficult entry**—Even in the roomiest of enclosures, installing hardware and modifying parts can be a knuckle-busting, tool-throwing nightmare if you're working within the confines of a poorly designed case. Some interior parts of a case can be very hard to reach or blocked off entirely by some ill-conceived "design feature."

It's for these very reasons that smart manufactures are now selling cases with removable parts— removable motherboard trays, hard drive racks, floppy bays, and so on. Detachable motherboard trays really come in handy when installing CPU heatsinks because it's simply much easier to install the heatsinks when you're not working within the confines of a metal box. Water-cooling components can also be a bitch to install, so it's always nice to work outside your case when mounting these heavy components.

Knurled thumbscrews are another welcome addition. These fasteners replace the tiny Phillips screws used for exterior panels and PCI slot covers, allowing you to batten down your hatches, as it were, without ever having to touch a screwdriver.

Mark Purney's force-inducted PC uses an honest-to-goodness automotive turbocharger to help cool down his internal components. Mark's fast rig was runner-up in *Maximum PC's* 2003 Coolest PC Case Modding Contest.

Bottom line: Removable mobo trays and drive cages are preferred. Ditto thumbscrews. And you should always check the removable side panels of a case to see whether they have any handles or locking mechanisms that might interfere with your design ideas.

- **Airflow friendliness**—When shopping for a prefab case, take into consideration the number and placement of fan mounting points. Most cases include the very basics: one or two 80mm or 120mm fan ports on the front and the equivalent number on the back. But some prefab designs go over the edge with options for as many as eight or more fans. It can be tempting to create a screaming vortex of wind inside the air plenum (the empty space inside an enclosure), but air, like water, prefers the path of least resistance for efficient heat exchange. The upshot is that if you install a greater number of intake fans than exhaust fans, you'll simply be blowing warm air around the interior of your case and noise levels will increase needlessly.

Also remember that cases that come with precut fan holes on the top and side panels can limit your design options. Sure, they can be covered up if you don't use them, but a better option is to find the same case model *without* the holes.

Some hard drive bays come with fan-mounting frames as well. Placing fans in these frames is perfect for cooling off several drives at once—a must-have feature for video-authoring stations running numerous

high-speed storage drives. However, I do have a note of caution on hard drive fans: Depending on the case design, installing these fans can increase the depth of your hard drive bay, forcing your drives to hang over your motherboard. This, in turn, makes the installation of RAM, IDE cables, and other components that much more difficult.

Finally, with higher-end cases, your fan ports might come with removable and washable fan filters, which are perfect for keeping the inside of your rig looking pretty and those pesky dust bunnies at bay.

- **Designer cases: love 'em or leave 'em**—It was only a matter of time before retail manufacturers caught up to the case-modding phenomenon and began designing "premodded" enclosures. We're talking off-the-shelf, retail cases complete with windows, blow holes, LCD displays, rainbows of blinking lights, and more. From alien themes to insect themes, case manufacturers have decorated their offerings with countless design flourishes, hoping to appeal to PC enthusiasts who lack the skill and patience to mod their own cases.

Although you can certainly work your designs around factory-installed mods, and even modify the manufacturer's livery if necessary, you'd probably do better to start with a clean slate. After all, you're reading a case-*modding* book, not a book about buying premodded parts.

One final note about premodded cases: It's becoming more

and more difficult to find cases *without* preinstalled windows, and because of this, modding and design options are becoming more of a challenge. Unlike DIY window kits that come with precut acrylic sheets and special rubber gasket material, cases with factory-installed windows often use small, plastic buttons to secure the window to the side panel. To lower weights (and thus production costs), these windows are usually made from flimsy, 1/8'' acrylic—not ideal. I highly recommend that you avoid cases with factory-installed windows; they're only worth buying if you want to concentrate your modding efforts on other parts of the case. Personally, I'd rather have full artistic control of window size, placement, and materials.

Case Design Personalities

Before we talk about specific case form factors, it's important to first discuss the various prefab case styles that have emerged. Serious modders will want to start with a blank canvas and create their own look, but beginning modders might want to start with a case that's already tricked out to some degree.

Years ago, when aesthetically minded PC enthusiasts like ourselves would sit around talking about the future of our favorite technology/hobby, we'd wonder aloud why more people weren't into computers. "It's the cases," we'd always argue. "Mainstream consumers don't like ugly, beige boxes. When they can purchase PCs that aren't in beige boxes, everyone will own PCs."

Ironically, we were right about the last part of the argument, but our causality was inverted. Motivated by affordable prices and easier-to-use operating systems, the mainstream masses flocked to the PC in the late 1990s. Cases, for the most part, remained homely looking and plainly designed, although a few companies innovated by using black or even gray colors. This stood in stark contrast to the innovative design philosophy of the iMac, which was embraced by and responsible for energizing Apple Computers.

But as millions of people bought millions of PCs, a funny thing happened: Some of these users got hooked on the concept of building, upgrading, and tinkering with computers. Enter case design. If you're going to custom-build your own PC, you're probably going to look past the boring beige (or black) box when you go to Frye's and reach for something a little cooler-looking.

As more and more people began to upgrade their PCs, the demand for more colorful designs increased. This need was filled by companies such as Cooler Master, Antech, SilverStone, and scores of others. Consumers began to snatch up these companies' early designs, and the PC case boom was on.

Years later, the growing build-it-yourself trend shows no sign of abating. In fact, it's escalating. Over the last 12 months, we reviewed close to 50 different cases; no 2 were alike. During the same period of time, we probably heard about approximately 10 times that number.

What's interesting is that, as a wide variety of people from every possible age, racial, geographic, and socioeconomic background have begun to build their own PCs, their widely ranging aesthetic desires have resulted in a preponderance of different designs. At *Maximum PC* we're in favor of both of these trends. Because we're enamored with PCs, the more people and types of people who get into them, the better, from our perspective.

Over the last 12 months, we've begun to notice an interesting phenomenon that is a result of this diversity: Cases are beginning to fall into several categories. Here's a quick breakdown—if you're in the market for an off-the-shelf PC case, you should probably think long and hard about what type of look you consider most appealing. We've broken the various styles down into seven categories:

- **The Classic**—This is your standard plastic-and-steel PC box. Plain-jane in color, design, and functionality, this type of case lacks doors and uses standard screws for its drive-bay slots and other apertures.
- **The Neo-classic**—This variant of the Classic also tends to emphasize function over form, but the Neo-Classic embraces a more jazzed-up version of the traditional Classic design. Elegant, sleek, and simple, the Neo-Classic embraces brushed aluminum (or other solid, non-garish colors) cases with doors that cover the optical drive bezels. SilverStone's Nimiz is a great example of such a case.
- **The Bling**—This is the low-rider of PC case design. Featuring cycling lights, colored tubes and wire coils, and transparent case windows, the Bling takes the notion of a PC and "streets it up."
- **The First Person**—This design aesthetic can be best described as PC-as-animated-creature. Want a PC that looks like a Transformer? You're in this category.
- **The Neon**—This PC design tends to embrace transparent case walls; after all, if you're going to light up the inside of your PC like the Fourth of July, you probably want to make sure the light show can be seen from all angles.
- **The Demonic First Person**—Inspired by games such as *Quake* and *Doom 3*, this PC also embraces the PC-as-animated-creature notion but adds a more evil touch.
- **The Media Center**—If you want to build your computer for the living room—a growing trend—you probably want it to look more like a stereo component than a PC. You also probably want it to be small. We'll explore the small form factor rig in detail later in this chapter.

Case Form Factors: Up Close and Personal

We hear the term *form factor* bandied about quite often. What does it mean? Does it refer to a case's size? Its shape? What?

The answer is all of the above, plus a whole lot more. A case's form factor does indeed refer to the enclosure's basic size and shape, but it also describes what type of motherboards

Bearing the look and feel of an SGI workstation, the SilverStone Nimiz is a great prefab candidate if you're looking for a true desktop-style box rather than a tower design. And don't let the horizontal white striping scare you: This all-aluminum enclosure can be easily resurfaced and its uninterrupted, flat expanses provide plenty of space for design flourishes. Just be aware that desktop-style enclosures can present cooling issues and don't offer oodles of interior room.

the case supports; which kind of power supplies it runs; how internal airflow is handled; and the number, size, and type of components that can be stuffed inside. The following descriptions of the five main form factors should help you get started in choosing the right case. But rest assured, form factor science runs deep. For more information, check out www.formfactors.org.

Desktop-style Cases

Desktop cases—once relegated to office and school PCs—have recently found their way into the modding world for use in home theater personal computers (HTPCs). You can find steel, aluminum, and plastic versions of these low-profile cases in a variety of colors to match your existing home theater components.

Desktop cases can easily slip into wall-unit shelving, and some can be placed vertically on bookshelves or small tables.

Space is tight inside desktop-style cases, so careful planning is a must when selecting hardware, cooling components, and add-in devices. In garden-variety desktop cases, you'll find at least one exposed 5 1/4'' drive bay for an optical drive or front-panel device and extra 5 1/4'' bays in larger models. Some desktop cases require proprietary power supply units that are low-profile and fit within the specs for the desktop chassis, so consider your power requirements during project preparation. (In most cases, these proprietary PSUs come preinstalled.) As always, be sure to verify that the desktop-style enclosure you want to use supports the motherboard form factor you have in mind.

SilverStone Nimiz

SilverStone is a high-end case manufacturer with the goal of building the absolute best cases in the industry, price be damned. A prime example of this philosophy is the company's warship-sounding Nimiz—an expensive case absolutely loaded with features.

The all-aluminum Nimiz is certainly pleasing to the eye. In a market dominated by bling, we're happy to see such elegance. The front bezel sports a dual-door design that uses tiny embedded magnets to keep the doors shut. The top door swings out to reveal six 5 1/4'' drive bays. The lower door provides convenient access to the front fan filter and sports a push release cover for the bay of I/O ports. FireWire, dual USB 2.0, mic, and headphone jacks are all present and accounted for. Despite the case's overall sturdy construction, we admit to feeling slightly disappointed with the flimsy nature of the two case doors. Both rattled around on their hinges, and the weak magnets used to keep them closed consistently failed. When tipped to the front or side,

the doors come loose and swing open, which makes transporting the Nimiz a nuisance. Even though full-tower cases like the Nimiz aren't designed to be transported, we'd still like to see more powerful magnets for the front doors.

SilverStone bucks the current side-window trend by going with a solid side panel and maintains a clean, classy look as a result. The side panel is attached via three thumbscrews, allowing it to be easily removed along with the motherboard tray. Complementing the six 5 1/4'' bays are six internal 3 1/2'' bays, which is more than sufficient. Located on the case's rump is a power supply slot that accepts either a redundant power supply or a standard ATX unit. Interior cooling is achieved with 80mm fans mounted on the front and top; two optional rear 80mm fans bring the total up to four.

With its utmost accessibility, room for growth, and superb cooling system, the Nimiz is a power user's dream come true.

And, of course, it's a wonderfully blank canvas for all you would-be modders out there.

Chenbro PC6166 Gaming Bomb

We know what you're thinking: The Gaming Bomb pictured here looks cheap. This was our first impression, too. However, looks can be deceiving. Upon closer investigation, we found the Gaming Bomb to be surprisingly, er, bomb-like.

This mid-tower case's front bezel comes in four colors (blue, green, silver, and orange) and is easily removed via two plastic tabs on the case's interior. Although the rest of the case is made of metal, the bezel itself is made of plastic and includes a perforated lower half with a soft filter on its interior—perfect for sifting the air that enters the case from the front. Holes are drilled for 80mm or 92mm fans, but no fan is included. A well-stocked front I/O port is included as well, with two audio jacks, two USB 2.0 ports, and a FireWire port. Overall, the front of the case is well-designed and packed with useful features.

The case's side panel includes a standard locking mechanism, and the door is released by shifting a single plastic tab upward. Operating the door is effortless, and we dig the subtle-yet-cool design. If you're into the currently popular clear look, the Gaming Bomb optionally comes configured with a transparent acrylic door.

The case's internals surprised and delighted us. The seven internal bays (four 5 1/4'', three 3 1/2'') are mounted with included plastic rails. Extra rails are kept secure in a holder on the floor of the case, and a cable caddy helps you keep your front I/O wires tidy. The Gaming Bomb uses an innovative screwless design for holding add-in cards in place; although it works fairly well, the plastic parts it uses feel flimsy. The case's rear includes mounting holes for a 92mm or 120mm fan, but again, no fan is included.

The Chenbro doesn't come with a power supply, but it costs just $45, for crying out loud! Considering its rock-bottom price, this low-cost case totally exceeds our expectations. It's not just a fantastic case for the money, but a fantastic case overall.

The Gaming Bomb possesses features you'd find in cases costing more than twice as much. It's a decent case for beginning modders who want to earn their first modding stripes by adding custom lighting, groovy fans, and bay-mounted controls.

The Antec P-160 Performance One Series case is not only a pretty good-looking unit, but is also well-made and a pleasure to work on. With features like a removable motherboard tray, quick-release hard disk drive rails, stealthy optical drive covers, and a digital temperature display, it's hard to beat for the price.

Mid-Tower Cases

These cases are by far the most common and come in hundreds of designs, flavors, and configurations, ranging from 16'' tall to as much as 20'' in height. For building a gaming rig, aluminum and steel mid-towers are probably your best choices, at least in respect to cooling and friendliness to future upgrades.

The interiors of mid-towers offer a nice amount of work room, but space can become quickly cramped in the smaller models, depending on the amount of hardware you've installed inside. As for drive bays, most mid-towers should feature four exposed 5 1/4'' bays and two exposed 3 1/2'' bays, giving you plenty of room for installing control and display devices. Mid-towers are suitable for turning into LAN party rigs, especially if you integrate case handles. The larger mid-towers also offer enough interior room for many water-cooling setups.

Full-Tower Cases

Full-tower and server cases are the titans of the case world—so big, in fact, that you might be tempted to climb right in! Their heights range from 20'' to a whopping 30'', and some server cases are almost as wide as they are tall. Does anyone remember the

Witness the epitome of blank-canvas case design. The SilverStone Nimiz will cost you a pretty penny ($285 at press time), but its all-aluminum construction is sturdy, cooling-efficient, and absolutely ripe with hardware hacking possibilities. Good God, it's like giving Christo access to the Bonneville Salt Flats and saying, "Here's your canvas. Have at it, Tiger!" We at _Maximum PC_ say in our review of the case, "The classy exterior provides a welcome reprieve from a [prefab] market dominated by side windows, neon tubes, and laser lights."

photographs of the *Maximum PC* editors riding their server cases like bucking broncos? Hmmm, maybe these somewhat embarrassing "stress test" images never made publication, but it is a fact that some server cases are so sturdily built, a 250-pound PC geek can sit on one without risking damage.

Full-tower cases will always offer the largest battery of exposed drive bays; typically from four to six exposed 5 1/4" bays and two or more 3 1/2" bays. With plenty of room for modding and water-cooling every single possible device you can imagine, these behemoths make a great choice if big and bold are the statements you're aiming for. Full towers are the least portable of all case types, but many come with casters, making back panel access easier and enabling wheeling (well, more like *driving*) it around the room, should you need to.

Maximum PC has always endorsed Cooler Master cases as near-perfect examples of blank-canvas prefab case design. The Wavemaster model you see here is made of an aluminum alloy that's not only easy to cut (ideal for window jobs), but also appropriate for painting. All surfaces, save for the wavy front bezel, are flat and unadorned, making the Wavemaster ideal for modders who need a lot of room to express themselves. You might recognize this case as the one *Maximum PC* used for its Dream Machine 2003 project.

Micro-ATX Cases

Micro-ATX cases are typically slightly smaller in footprint than mid-tower cases and can often be positioned either horizontally or vertically. You'll find them in a variety of styles, including tower-shaped, low-profile, and cubical. Some of these cases can accept standard ATX components, but most are too small and require Micro-ATX form factor motherboards, power supplies, and special PCI riser cards. Thus, the name of the case form factor: Micro-ATX. The spec was created to facilitate a bold new generation of smaller PCs.

A limited number of Micro-ATX motherboards is available on the market, and finding the right one requires a fair bit of research. Like desktop cases, the Micro-ATX form factor is ideal for HTPCs, automotive entertainment centers ("car-puters"), and small home office spaces. Materials range from plastic and steel to all-aluminum. Be aware that Micro-ATX power supplies are not capable of running an excess of

power-hungry hardware. Also be on the lookout for Micro-ATX cases that include PSUs and motherboards built right in.

It's probably safe to say that the majority of small form factor case-modding projects have been based on Shuttle's fine enclosures, such as this XPC SB51G. This case's aluminum chassis helps wick away heat and provides a neutral canvas on which to cut, drill, and paint. Note that the air venting is extremely simple in design, allowing for more integration opportunities by the wily hardware hacker.

Small Form Factor Cases and Cubes

Chances are you've heard the term *Shuttle Cube* in reference to small form factor (SFF) cases; that's because the Shuttle company pioneered the market with its sleek, powerful, and sexy cube designs. Shuttle sells its cases as "bare bones" systems, which means the case, a proprietary motherboard, and the power supply unit are all included in the retail packaging.

The unique design of the SSF case and components lets you use fast processors and full-sized AGP videocards—two must-have components for any serious gaming PC. Small cube cases are portable and thus ideal for taking to and from the office or to LAN party events. You might think the tiny sizes of these cases make them poor modding candidates, but I've seen some fantastic airbrushing artwork, front panel devices, and even water-cooling systems added to SFF cubes.

The Cubit[3] case from Hoojum Design, a small company in the U.K., is a beautiful example of the Mini-ITX breed of hand-made small form factor enclosures. Seemingly carved from 2.5kg of solid aluminum, the Larkpsur blue matte finish shown here is just one of several yummy finishes available. The Cubit[3] also offers its own Quickslot system for easy hardware installation and upgrades. The Earth-friendly folks at Hoojum will even recycle your old Cubit[3] when it's time for replacement (www.hoojum.com).

Mini-ITX Cases

These tiny cases are made specifically for the thin-client Mini-ITX motherboards developed by VIA Technologies. Every Mini-ITX includes a VIA chipset.

If you're into small form factor boxes and want an awesome, premodded SFF case, it's hard to go wrong with the Hornet Pro 64. If you're biased toward high-end videocards with the GeForce moniker (you probably already know the two don't mix well these days), the Hornet Pro is a welcome surprise. Few SFF boxes can accommodate these cards' two-slot design. And no SFF machines we know of have the cojones to match the merciless power requirements of NVIDIA's new GeForce 6800 Ultra.

But somehow, Monarch not only has managed to stuff a GeForce 6800 Ultra into its Hornet Pro 64, but has also integrated a bunch of other high-end components.

The GeForce 6800 Ultra is paired with AMD's new Athlon 64 3700+ in a VIA K8T800-based motherboard. This equates to a smooth 2.4GHz of computing that's damn-near as fast as an FX-53 CPU in most tests. A pair of Corsair Micro DDR400 Pro modules light up to indicate memory access activity, while a pair of RAID 0 Western Digital Raptor 74GB 10K drives handle storage. Also new to the mix is Plextor's PX712A, a recent upgrade to our favorite multiformat burner: the Plextor PX-708A. Rounding out the hardware configuration is a Sound Blaster Audigy 2 ZS card.

The case itself sports a Ferrari red custom paint job that looks fabulous. None of this matters to gamers, though, so much as cold, hard performance results. This is a category where the Hornet Pro 64 doesn't disappoint. In our *Jedi Academy* OpenGL test, the Hornet Pro 64 gave us a Lab record 115fps. In *Halo*, the Hornet Pro coughed up an

The Hornet Pro packs a fistful of power, with 10K RAID and NVIDIA's latest and greatest GeForce 6800 videocard.

amazing 78fps, more than double our zero-point reference system. Even though it's not part of our official suite, we also ran *3DMark 2003* and recorded a shockingly fast 12,034. In *3DMark 2001 SE*, it threw down a 24,747. Needless to say, the NVIDIA GeForce 6800 videocard is one bad mutha.

In application testing, the Hornet performed well, but the 200MHz speed advantage of its Athlon 64 3700+ was nullified by the dual-channel capabilities of our zero-point Athlon 64 FX-51. With that said, Monarch's little red box posted 12% faster scores in our *MusicMatch* test, which measures a PC's ability to encode MP3s. Our software tests consistently demonstrate the power of Intel's architecture with regard to software performance—the Hornet ran behind our P4EE-equipped system—but the Pentium 4 is considerably more expensive. In our mind, these savings justify Monarch's decision to go with an Athlon-based CPU.

Some boards are designed to run with passive cooling (that is, no fans), and the Mini-ITX spec calls for a maximum mobo size of 170 × 170mm and a PSU of less than 100 watts. Like most of the diminutive form factor mobos (including Flex-ATX and Micro-ATX), Mini-ITX mobos include plenty of integrated hardware features, such as onboard USB, LAN, sound, and video support. Thus, the fact that Mini-ITX mobos feature only one PCI slot might not be so discouraging.

Only a handful of Mini-ITX cases are available, but these wee enclosures are perfect if you're looking to cook up an HTPC, a music jukebox server, or a carputer. Most of these cases are made from aluminum.

Yeah, you guessed it: The case itself acts as a giant heatsink, dissipating heat generated from the hardware inside. For more info on the Mini-ITX spec, visit http://www.mini-itx.com.

BTX Form Factor

In addition to ATX, Micro-ATX, and Mini-ITX, there's a new player in town—BTX.

Here's a tough question for you: Look at your PC and contemplate which component, besides the mouse and keyboard, would remain useful after eight years. The CPU? Hardly. RAM? No way. Videocard? Impossible.

There's actually only one part that could still be kicking around after nearly 10 years: the ATX case, a standard for case and mobo design that has become increasingly outdated due to the increasing amounts of heat modern PC components generate. That's about to change. This year, we'll see the first systems using the new BTX form factor.

This doesn't mean the ATX case standard will be replaced overnight; it will take a few years for BTX to take over. Why make a new form factor for desktop cases when the current approach seems to work fine? Because the Advanced Technology eXtended (ATX) form factor was designed for 1996 PC technology. To give you an idea of how ancient the design is, ATX was originally supposed to suck air in through the power supply and blow it over the CPU to keep it cool—an idea that has long since fallen by the wayside. In contrast, BTX is designed to meet the thermal requirements of tomorrow's CPUs and videocards.

The immediate difference you'll see on a tower case is the reverse-mounting of the motherboard. In most BTX towers, you'll have to pop open the right side instead of the left to access the interior. BTX also makes a major change with the CPU placement. In ATX cases, the CPU is positioned just under the power supply. In the BTX design, the processor will reside in the middle-front of the case—an area the ATX case typically reserves for hard drives. This way, a fan can suck cool air from outside the case and blow it directly over the CPU first. This is a big shift; in an ATX case, cool air is usually pulled in from the front and is heated by other components before even reaching the CPU. Airflow in a BTX case will be routed in from the front; come over the CPU; and then come over the chipset, RAM, and voltage regulators for improved flow patterns.

BTX will also call for a new power supply with a 24-pin connector. The BTX spec will be released later this year, but it will take several years for it to completely supplant ATX. So don't sweat it if you just bought a $200 aluminum ATX case.

Other Future Case Design Changes

BTX is definitely the big change coming, but because it will take a few years to become firmly established, we still anticipate seeing further development in the following categories:

- **More small form factor boxes (SFF)**— More will be released as more and more PC enthusiasts migrate toward building PCs for nontraditional reasons, such as media centers, portable digital jukeboxes, and LAN party boxes.

- **Stereo component-looking cases**—It appears that the PC is destined to migrate into the living room. With this in mind, we'll see more and more cases designed to look like traditional stereo components.

- **More radical cooling schemes**—In our June 2004 issue, we detailed a company named Nanocoolers that is working on an even more extreme cooling system than water. By using liquid metal and an electromagnetic pump, this company claims it will eventually revolutionize PC cooling by making it smaller, easier to install, and less risky. Time will tell, but it's clear that, even with the BTX shift due, cooling will remain a high priority.

All these changes mean good things for the modders of the world.

Choosing the Best Material for Your Modded-Case-to-Be

When choosing a prefab retail case as the foundation for a modding project, you're essentially looking at four main materials: plastic, acrylic, steel, and aluminum. Each medium has its own strengths and weaknesses, so be sure you pick the right one for whatever project you have in mind.

Plastic

Based on organic and synthetic compounds, plastic is a highly malleable manmade material that can be easily molded and extruded into different shapes.

Pluses: Lightweight. Easy to cut, drill, and paint.

Minuses: Can often look cheap. Not very sturdy under heavy weight. Tends to be brittle. Repairs can be expensive, if not impossible.

Acrylic

A transparent, manmade fiber, acrylic easily holds color and resists aging very well.

Pluses: Lightweight. Allows your entire case to be transparent. Even colored acrylic retains its see-through qualities.

Minuses: Easily cracked and scratched. Requires a careful touch when cutting and drilling. Repairs can be expensive, if not impossible.

Steel

Steel is a metal alloy based on iron and small amounts of carbon and other metals.

Pluses: Extremely strong, durable, and inexpensive. Can be easily welded, bent, reshaped, and repaired. A great medium for case windows.

Minuses: The heaviest of all case materials. Large steel enclosures are not easy to transport. Cutting and drilling requires some serious elbow grease and/or power tools.

Aluminum

An abundant metallic element found in the earth's crust, aluminum also serves as the base for many strong alloys.

Pluses: Lightweight and resistant to corrosion. Looks great raw. Dissipates component heat very well. Often an appropriate material for cutting windows.

Minuses: Expensive. Although thick slabs of aluminum are relatively strong, flimsy aluminum panels do not hold up well to cutting and other types of hardware hacking.

The Gospel of the Case According to Maximum PC

Looking for a prefab case to start your mod off right? See our reviews to help you pick a killer case.

Like leg warmers, Cabbage Patch dolls, and poignant soft saxophone solos, the beige PC box is dead and has been for years. In its place: a thousand different PC case enclosures. Some are big; some are small. Some are light; some are heavy. Some are flashy; some are classy. Some are chrome; some are colorful. And some are downright ugly. But none of them are beige.

With such a wide variety of cases available for modders, it's tempting to grab the first cheap or attractive case you see. We deem this a bad idea. We've found that we hold onto our cases longer than our drives, cards, CPUs, and even motherboards, which means choosing the right case is a crucial decision. And if you're pouring your cash and sweat into a modded PC, chances are you'll be bunking with the case you choose for a long, long time.

The tricky thing about buying a PC case is that everyone has specific PC-building needs. With this in mind, it's important you consider the type of computer you're building before you buy the chassis. Even with the right mentality, however, case hunting can feel pretty overwhelming. We requested, tested, and reviewed the best cases on the market today to make things easy for you. All you have to do is decide which case is right for you, and you're set. And, on the off-chance none of these enclosures floats your boat, we've also included a detailed reviewer's guide that readily illustrates what we look for when we evaluate cases.

Our emphasis is on real-world system building, so we do just that—build a system within each case. We add the mobo, the optical drive, a hard drive, a video-card, and a soundcard; then we fire it up to see how it performs in its running state. Next, we break it down, noting how easy it was to install all the parts, how cramped or uncramped we were for space, and the time commitment involved in the assembly.

1 **Case construction**—Cases are built from a variety of materials, the most common being steel and aluminum. Steel is sturdy and inexpensive, but aluminum is way lighter and provides much better cooling properties. Some cases are even made out of acrylic and are completely transparent so as to show off your case's innards and lighting effects. We prefer aluminum when given a choice.

2 **Case fans**—Case fans help air circulate inside your case, keeping your parts nice and cool. Most cases include several fans, or at least places to mount them. The bigger the fans and the greater the number, the cooler (and louder) your computer will be. If you plan on running several hard drives and a high-end videocard, the case's cooling setup should be a primary consideration. We prefer a minimum of two 120mm fans—one in front to draw air into the case and one above the AGP slot to blow hot air out. See Chapter 5, "Fans, Fans, and More Fans," for more on case fans.

3 **Motherboard tray**—All cases have a flat surface on which you attach the motherboard. Because it can get rather cramped inside a mid-size tower, some high-end cases let you remove the motherboard tray so you can install the motherboard and cards with greater ease. We look for a slide-out tray because it lets you assemble almost the entire PC outside the confines of the case and then slide everything back into the case in one fell swoop.

4 **Power supply unit (PSU)**—Power supply units provide your computer's juice. PSUs range in output from 250 watts to over 500 watts of power. Because each component in your PC draws a bit of power from the PSU, a high-output power supply enables you to use more components in your PC than a lower-output supply. We recommend a minimum of 350W for a standard gaming system, and 450W or more for a fully loaded rig.

5 **Case window**—Case windows have replaced the opaque case doors of yore and enable you to show off your PC's interior. They're typically made of acrylic. Some of the best cases don't include windows, but if you have a jigsaw and a pair of safety glasses, you can change all that lickety-split. See Chapter 3, "Making a Case Window," for more on cutting your own case window.

6 **Front bezel**—This is a case's detachable faceplate. Bezels vary from bland, shapeless plastic contraptions to smooth and curvy chrome jobbies and everything in between. The bezel doesn't have any features per say, but it's often a case's most distinguishing trait. Some bezels include a door that hides the 5 1/4" bays for a clean look.

7 **Front I/O port**—USB, FireWire, and audio jacks used to be found on the rear of the PC, but it's a pain in the butt to crawl back there just to plug in a USB key. Thus, the front I/O port was born. It is always found somewhere on a PC's bezel and lets you plug in new devices with relative ease. We need at least two USB and one FireWire port up front but don't really care if audio jacks are included or not.

8 **5 1/4" bays**—These bays are primarily used for optical drives such as CD and DVD writers. Their most popular secondary use is housing sundry case accessories such as fan controllers, LCD displays, and even cup holders and cigarette lighters. Most ATX cases have four of these bays, which is more than enough because most people use only one or two optical drives. We demand at least two of these bays in a case.

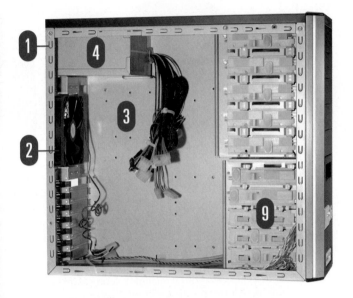

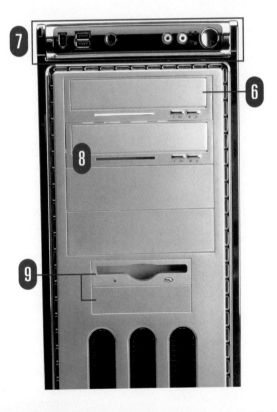

9 **3 1/2" bays**—These smaller drive bays are generally reserved for hard drives, floppy drives, and media readers. If you have more than one hard drive, the number of these bays is a critical consideration when shopping for a case. We require a minimum of four with a separate fan in front of the drive cage to keep our hard drives chilly.

Chenbro Xpider II

With its web-patterned front bezel and strangely angular side window, a casual observer might think the Xpider 2 is Chenbro's attempt to cash in on *Spider-Man II*'s popularity. Be that as it may, this budget enclosure is an excellent mid-size tower that offers plenty of bang for not much buck.

The Xpider II feels solid, with a strong frame under its colorful plastic exterior. The case is easy to work inside thanks to handy features like drive rails and a removable hard drive cage. Unfortunately, it has a plastic locking system for the card slots, which we found awkward and flimsy and made us doubt our PCI cards would remain secure.

The front bezel maintains the spider motif with a web pattern and large metallic arachnid adorning the face. Well-stocked I/O ports hide just under the spider behind a small plastic door.

The case's steel and plastic construction makes it a bit heavier than an aluminum enclosure, but it's rare to find a fancy aluminum case at this price point. In fact, the only real drawback to the Xpider II's budget price is that no fans are included, nor is a PSU.

Pros: It's a great case for the money.

Cons: An awkward card-lock mechanism and gaudy looks.

Xoxide X-Blade Extreme

This mid-size tower is a budget system, but you'd hardly know that by looking at it. The front bezel looks vaguely like a mutated Alienware case, thanks to its glowing eye grills on the sides. It's not the most subtle design, but we dig the shiny logos and clean-looking custom-cut side window, which lies completely flush with the side and has a chrome fan built in to its center.

Puzzlingly, while the X-Blade uses conventional screws for its side panels, motherboard, and PCI cards, drive installation is completely tool-less. The drive bays use rails that snap easily onto drives, and the hard drive cage can be removed with the twist of a thumbscrew. Tool-less designs give us warm fuzzies.

On the downside, the case is made from heavy, plain steel instead of lighter, more aesthetically pleasing aluminum. Also, the front I/O port conspicuously lacks a FireWire port; oddly, we found a small FireWire-shaped hole in the case where this port would normally reside.

With two included 80mm fans and room for two more, the X-Blade offers decent cooling capabilities. We weren't too disappointed about the lack of an included power supply given the low $70 price tag.

Pros: Looks nice and includes tool-less drive features and a stylish window/fan.

Cons: Non-aluminum construction makes it slightly heavier and uglier than need be.

Antec Super LANBOY

Antec's Super LANBOY is a revamped version of the hugely popular LANBOY case, and it adds several new features to the already ultra-light package. This new version holds even more hard drives than the older case and adds a filtered 120mm fan to the lower portion of the front bezel. Both are welcome additions. Two other cool new features are a completely tool-less interior and a handy little tool/screws/memory-card drawer that pops out of the front bezel. And, like its predecessor, the Super LANBOY includes a carrying case. Not bad for a sub-$100 price tag.

Also like the original LANBOY, Super LANBOY's greatest flaw is that it's so darn light we find ourselves doubtful it can withstand even the mildest abuse. The case sides and motherboard tray wobble and bend if too much pressure is applied, which made us a bit nervous when installing parts. Even though we didn't experience any problems building our test system in this case, we felt like we were building a PC on a bed of egg shells. The basic configuration we reviewed doesn't include a power supply, but Antec does offer a few variations that do.

Pros: Super-light, lots of neat features, and a clean internal design.

Cons: It feels flimsy and lacks a front FireWire port.

Kingwin KT-424

This mid-size tower looks unassuming and generic, but behind its nondescript front bezel is an extremely well-built case. The KT-424 is made of aluminum but has a solid, sturdy feel to it and features the kind of niceties we favor, such as tool-less construction and a slide-out motherboard tray.

The case is a cinch to work with, mainly because of the aforementioned mobo tray and push-lock drive bays. Even the PCI slots are tool-less, so swapping parts in and out of this case is relatively painless. Unfortunately, the front I/O panel is awkwardly placed in the lower-right corner of the bezel, tucked behind a tiny window. The I/O panel also lacks audio jacks, but it does include two USB 2.0 ports and a FireWire port.

Cooling is provided by two fans up front and one in the rear, and the front fans also include a filter over them to keep the dust and dander at bay. The case does not include a power supply.

We appreciate this case's classy, understated exterior, but its simplicity makes it seem almost retro. Although it certainly doesn't go the extra mile in any one category, it covers all the bases with aplomb.

Pros: Great features, classic look, and tool-less design.

Cons: Has an uninspired design and no audio jacks.

Cooler Master Cavalier 1

The Cavalier looks like the little sister of Cooler Master's extremely popular Wave Master case, with a similar but less curvy front bezel. Smaller than the Wave Master both in length and height, this case is decidedly more retro, with a subdued paint job and an old-school analog dial on its face that measures sound output. Why sound output? We don't know—a temperature or fan speed monitor would have been much more useful.

Once we got past the inexplicable sound meter, we were impressed with Cooler Master's characteristic sturdy construction and appealing design. The case itself is great to work with; its tool-less features make component installation a snap. You'll seldom have to pick up your screwdriver because both drives and device (PCI) cards are secured by surprisingly sturdy tool-less locking systems.

Sound gauge aside, the Cavalier 1 is a very solid, tasteful case, with all the features we've come to expect from Cooler Master.

Pros: Pretty looks and great locking systems.

Cons: Um, what's with the sound gauge?

ClearPC Secret Agent Briefcase

The Secret Agent Briefcase takes the concept of a clear case one step further by fashioning an ATX case out of a briefcase-shaped enclosure for easy transport as well as inspection by drooling onlookers. Although it's a novel design that's fairly well-built, the case is not suited for use as a full-time ATX case, but rather for periodic LAN gaming or show purposes because of its lack of electrical grounding.

The case fits any standard ATX motherboard and can accommodate two optical drives as well as two hard drives. Cooling is provided via a 120mm fan mount over the PCI slots as well as four 40mm fan mounts (two pairs of two), which allow the case to maintain its slim profile. All in all, we found the included cooling to be adequate.

Our main complaint with this case is that we experienced difficulty securing the optical drives because of slightly misaligned screw holes. And because the case is clear, there's nowhere to really hide cables, so our case looked like a portable snake pit when assembled; however, we could have made it look better using braided or split-loom cabling as we discuss in Chapter 7, "Laying Cables." Finally, one of the door hinges repeatedly came loose during our testing process.

The Special Agent is certainly one of the more intriguing clear cases we've tested, but we wouldn't recommend it as a standard desktop case because of its fragility and lack of grounding.

Pros: A slim design, novel approach, and sturdy build.

Cons: A lot of assembly is required, it has imprecise screw holes, and it's heavy when full.

Cooler Master CMStacker

The CMStacker is a big, beautiful full-tower case with so much interior room you could almost sublet the extra space to house other people's PC components. Like most Cooler Master enclosures, the CMStacker comes loaded with almost every feature and doodad known to man, making it worth the extra dough you'll cough up to own it.

The CMStacker sports an all-aluminum construction, which makes it surprisingly lightweight given its size. It's also extremely rigid and, like the company's Jazz 5 enclosure, features a ventilated exterior on all sides except the bottom for improved airflow.

Hardcore PC builders will appreciate the fact that this case supports up to eight case fans, can accept ATX *and* BTX motherboards, and is also dual-PSU ready. Be warned, though—the BTX conversion is time-consuming and difficult.

The spacious interior makes system building a walk in the park. It includes seven 5 1/4'' bays in stock trim and up to eleven with some minor modifications. With bays running the entire height of the case, you can use as many optical drives, fan controllers, and cup holders as you want. The front I/O port is equally impressive, sporting a whopping six USB 2.0 ports, on top of the standard FireWire and audio ports. The CMStacker is even available with a case window, but it does not include a PSU.

Pros: A spacious interior and front USB 2.0 ports aplenty.

Cons: BTX conversion is a pain in the ass.

Antec Performance One P160

The P160 is the big brother of the Super LANBOY and features a much sturdier build and some additional features that *almost* justify its high price tag.

At the top of its shiny plastic front bezel is a slick I/O port that pivots upward 45° and comes with a digital temperature gauge as well as the standard USB 2.0, FireWire, and audio ports. The case's cooling system concerns us, with just a single 120mm case fan and a mount for only one other fan in front of the hard drive cage.

We found the P160 easy to work with; it has a fair amount of room for a mid-tower enclosure. It has a lift-out motherboard tray that makes installation a bit easier, but we found ourselves wishing for a slide-out tray, which is even easier to use. Unfortunately, the tray holds only the motherboard, so PCI cards have to be removed before lifting the tray from the case.

With its clean design and solid construction, this is a decent midrange case, but we're puzzled by why it costs so much. Antec jokingly says the case is made from recycled fighter planes, but aside from its snazzy front bezel, not much sets the P160 apart from its competition. However, for the intrepid among you, we turned this average case into a work of art in Chapter 8, "Building the Ultimate Off-the-Shelf Mod."

Pros: The tilting I/O port is handy and the onboard temperature display is a nice touch.

Cons: Exorbitant price; the lift-out motherboard tray is not as handy as a slide-out one.

Thermaltake Xaser V Damier

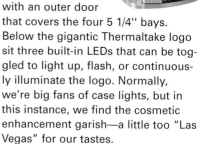

Pronounced *zaser*, this all-aluminum mid-tower features a lavish two-part front panel with an outer door that covers the four 5 1/4'' bays. Below the gigantic Thermaltake logo sit three built-in LEDs that can be toggled to light up, flash, or continuously illuminate the logo. Normally, we're big fans of case lights, but in this instance, we find the cosmetic enhancement garish—a little too "Las Vegas" for our tastes.

The Xaser's design emphasizes user control. The top bay of the front panel holds the Hardcano, which lets you control the case's impressive six-fan array. An I/O port at the top of the case puts FireWire, dual USB 2.0, and dual audio jacks at your fingertips.

The side door of the case sports a large X-shaped window that would reveal more of the Xaser's interior if the view weren't obstructed by a swing-out fan holder for the PCI slots. The spacious interior features a screw-less design, with plastic tabs holding the PCI cards and drive rails for the three 3 1/2'' bays in place. Sadly, there's no motherboard tray.

Overall, the Xaser offers a feast of features and ample cooling. And though the acid-flashback lighting effects will certainly appeal to some builders, we geezers think it's a bit over the top.

Pros: Well-made, plenty of cooling, and easy access.

Cons: The Thermaltake logo is plastered all over the case, and overdone lighting.

SilverStone Temjin SST-TJ05

SilverStone's newest tower is a drop-dead beautiful behemoth that is fully loaded and highly reminiscent of Cooler Master's famed Wave Master case. This makes sense because we've heard that both cases were designed by the same person. The Temjin J05 combines many of the Wave Master's features—including a subtly curved front bezel—and the clean, neat design of SilverStone's Nimiz case (which received a 9 verdict and a Kick Ass award and is home to 2004's *Maximum PC* Dream Machine). The front panel even has a small LCD screen that displays time, motherboard temperature, and other features.

The Temjin J05's interior is just as brilliant as its exterior. Maneuvering through the incredibly spacious case is a simple matter of turning thumbscrews and sliding plastic levers—no tools needed here. Every drive bay uses a rail that is stored neatly on the case's floor. PCI cards are secured using a set of plastic locks that, while not the sturdiest we've seen, work quite well. The only time you'll need a screwdriver is when installing the motherboard.

The downfall to all this ATX real estate is that this baby weighs a ton, so don't plan on taking it to any LAN parties. Its full-size stature and weight limit the case to stay-at-home duty, but we can't think of too many better cases for the job.

Pros: Beautiful, sturdy, clever design, and has tons of great features.

Cons: Aluminum would have been better than a steel frame.

Windy Jazz Take 5

This case is imported from Japan and boasts a super-lightweight design thanks to its aluminum mesh construction. The mesh material also enhances airflow by allowing cool breezes to float in from any angle. The most notable design element, however, is its unusual stepped front bezel, which is comprised of seven 5 1/4'' drive bays. Unfortunately, none of the steps have front I/O ports.

The Take 5 is well-constructed but not incredibly sturdy—the mesh walls don't feel nearly as resistant to bumps and scratches as other solid metal or aluminum case enclosures.

The case is a snap to work on and in, with a slide-out motherboard tray and two removable drive cages that hold two drives apiece. The slanted step design makes things a bit cramped near the top of the case, but it's not a major issue. Cooling options are barely adequate, though, with a 120mm fan above the AGP slot and a 60mm in the bottom of the front bezel. Several additional cooling kits are available, but considering this case already costs $400, they should be included. The outrageously high price tag can be partly attributed to the 500W PSU. A nonPSU version is available for $300.

Pros: Super-light with lots of nice features.

Cons: Way too pricey, no front I/O ports, and extra fans shouldn't cost more.

Xoxide UFO

This unusual case is part Borg, part Battlebot, and part Hellraiser all rolled into one 18'' cube. Easily the size of two mid-towers placed side-by-side, the UFO is a three-windowed beast that consumes more than 3.3 cubic feet. The model we received was fully equipped, with no less than seven cold-cathode lights and almost a dozen fans. It also includes five 5 1/4'' bays and room for nine hard drives. The sheer terror this case evokes doesn't come cheap, however: The bare-bones version of the case costs more than $300, and the fully loaded version is twice that amount.

Unfortunately, the case's coolness factor diminished as we worked with it. Instead of individual panels, the case is built out of two three-sided sections. These oversized sections are difficult to work with because the top section must be lifted out and the fan connectors unplugged. With so many fans and lights, the case's interior is a massive tangle of wires before you even install your first PC component (though we do show you how to fix that problem in Chapter 7). Worse yet, for all the case's bells and whistles, it's missing a front I/O port!

The UFO is a huge, pretty, creatively built, and certainly unique. Unfortunately, its awkward design will turn off all but the most hardcore case modders. Anyone?

Pros: It's one of the most creative prefab cases we've ever seen.

Cons: It's awkward to work with and pricey, and has a rat's nest wiring.

To Think This Was Based on a Prefab Case

James T. Anderson's Heavy Metal mod is a world-renown example of extreme hardware hacking. Indeed, the monster truck–themed PC is remarkable for its many special details, not the least of which is its final price tag. I won't spill the beans on how much this project cost, but can I testify that I have never heard of any other mod that consumed so much of its creator's money.

But for the purpose of this chapter, I'm highlighting *Maximum PC* magazine's July 2003 Rig of the Month winner because it is actually based on a prefab, retail case: the FS-1500 server chassis from Enermax. This project just goes to show that even the most spectacular feats of creativity can be based on an off-the-shelf enclosure. James says he in part chose the hefty case for its preinstalled systems that monitor temps, fans, and power. In fact, he even uses this workstation in his job as a programmer!

And this sucker is big. When standing next to it, the tip of the chrome wing reaches James's waist, thanks to the lift it gets from the 8'' × 11'' Burris racing tires. All told, the rig weighs 150 lbs.—J.P.

Originally an LCD occupied the lower-right corner of the case window, but for aesthetic reasons, James replaced it with the Heavy Metal emblem, which is made from laser-cut and polished stainless steel. The exhaust headers, inlets, processor stacks, and wing are all custom-made from 6061-T6 aluminum. The front covers, drive cages, fan caddies, mobo tray, and power supply foot are all show-chromed, and red metal-flake acrylic paint was used both inside and out.

A fully functional tachometer (operating on software that James wrote) represents the CPU load, with each 1% of load equaling 100rpm.

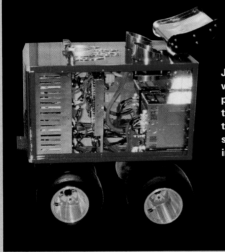

James says, "The wiring harness for pretty much everything was soldered together from scratch and covered in red Flexwrap."

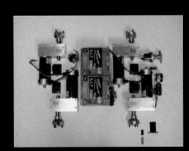

Racing-kart axles, bearings, cassettes, and hubs ensure this rig can roll.

Here's the case's front panel—opened up, in all its server-box glory.

Chapter Three

Making a Case Window

Exposing your creation's innermost secrets

Cliff Rockson's Star and Stripes Forever made us salute, earning Cliff the runner-up award for the Patriotic PC contest in our July 2003 issue.

Modding and performance-tweaking has created nothing short of a revolution in PC hardware design and manufacturing. Thanks to the pioneering spirits who hacked the first windows into the sides of their cases during the early days of the case-modding revolution, the dingy-looking case interiors of yesteryear are becoming history. Indeed, if you're going to expose your components for all the world to see, you better bring the bling with a snazzy-looking chest cavity.

Multicolored printed circuit boards (PCBs), lighted fans, and other components that add flash and flair to case interiors can now be purchased right off retail shelves. And it has never been easier to design your case mod from the inside out, what with all the color-matched videocards, motherboards, cooling devices, and cabling available. Even with a simple, square-shaped window cutout, your case mod can become a diorama, giving onlookers a glimpse of the once-concealed world of PC electronics and gadgetry.

Best of all, for the beginner, a window cutout is easy to do and can be the entire focal point of a well-executed case mod theme.

Your design possibilities are endless when it comes to windows and cutouts, and the side panels of a case are the perfect blank canvases for cutting any shapes you can dream up. That said, there are several fundamental design theories when it comes to case windows. The most basic scheme is defined by a side-panel cutout with clear acrylic mounted behind it, providing a portal-type view of interior lighting and hardware elements. This type of window is already found in garden-variety, premodified retail cases.

While I'm no fan of premods, there is hope for retail windows—you can always add a bit of your own handiwork, such as etching designs on the acrylic, appliqués, and even airbrushing with translucent paint.

Windows and similar openings aren't just limited to the side access panel of your case, either. You can add clear sections to front-mounted doors to expose front-panel devices, and you can cut custom fan grills on the top of your case as well. One of the most underutilized parts of a case is the right side panel (in most

Cliff used some of the same window-cutting techniques we describe in this chapter to give his mod a uniquely patriotic feel.

cases, the motherboard attaches to this panel). I've found that with most cases, there's enough clearance between the mobo mounting tray and the actual side panel to place a couple of CCFL lights. For example, whatever design pattern you apply to your left access panel could be repeated on your right side panel with a piece of translucent acrylic—perfect for a unified design theme.

Why Prefab Is Not Preferred

Case windows are now sold in prefabricated kits that are available from online case mod shops. These kits include a precut sheet of clear or colored acrylic in round, oval, rectangular, or square shapes, along with a length of rubber grommet (or molding) material. Installation of these kit windows is pretty straightforward: First, you cut the appropriate pattern in your side panel. Next, you cut the grommet to size with a razor knife or scissors; then you fit it inside the opening, along with the acrylic piece. You next press a provided strip of rubber into a channel on the grommet, creating a pressure fit and locking the window in place.

These kinds of kits were the first ones made commercially available, and they're still being sold today. However, in my opinion, these windows are still as uninteresting as ever. Sure, if you want an industrial-themed case mod, these kits might be what you're looking for, what with their heavy black rubber grommet and primitive-shaped windows. But because you're going to break out the tools and cut your case anyway—that's why you bought this book, right?—you might as well go a few extra steps and make a window that is much cooler and more customized.

Applying appliqués is an easy way to dress up a boring window and perhaps add a little oomph to the overall theme of your case mod. These self-adhesive vinyl stickers are mounted to the inside of a case window with a mist of water from a spray bottle and a plastic squeegee to smooth it out. A few dozen designs are available at online modding shops, such as hazard symbols, cute alien heads, and the infamous "whiz kid" pattern. Another good source for appliqués is your local automotive supply store, where you can find racing-inspired company logos, lettering, and the obligatory stacked bombshell in the martini glass. The adhesive used on vinyl stickers and lettering won't harm your acrylic window and can be easily peeled off and replaced.

To make your window more interesting and custom-looking, here's a trick you can easily do with vinyl appliqués: Once the appliqué is mounted on the back of your window, mask off the front of the glass with paper and apply a few coats of enamel spray paint to the back of the window, right over the appliqué. You'll know when you have enough coats by holding the window up to a lamp and checking for opaqueness (make sure you hold the window by its edges!). Before the enamel paint completely dries, very carefully and slowly remove the appliqué using the tip of a hobby knife to lift the edges. When the paint is dry (about 24 hours), you can remount the window to your PC, and you'll have a clean, frosted stencil pattern in the shape of your appliqué. A variation on this technique is to evenly sand the back of the acrylic with 200-grit paper before applying the appliqué, creating a frosted look beneath the appliqué.

Creating Custom Cutouts

The most interesting windows are those cut from unique, personalized patterns that have been drawn or transferred right onto the metal side panels of a case. Silhouette windows allow you to create a cutout that is customized for your particular case's size and shape, and it can perfectly complement your overall design theme. These simple "line art" cutouts become stunning and dramatic silhouettes when lit from inside with colored cold cathode tubes.

The basic procedure for creating line art windows is not unlike carving a Halloween pumpkin in that you only need to cut out the most basic of shapes. Indeed, with even a simple personalized cutout, you can count on internal lighting to fool the eye as it plays with opaque and transparent areas, creating shadings and shadows and capturing the moody essence of your cutout pattern. With this style of window, just about any shape can be prepared with an editing program like Photoshop. Simply print your line-art design and use it as a cutting pattern—perfect for landscapes, portraits, lettering, logos, and much more. The level of intricacy in your pattern is completely up to you. As you become more comfortable working with new tools and materials, there's no limit to the detail and originality you can achieve.

Now, at this point you might be feeling some trepidation. You're saying to yourself that you have no experience with the various metals and plastics that make up a case and its window, and you're worried you'll botch the job royally.

Have no fear. These things aren't as difficult to work with as you might think.

Stock cases are based on one of three main materials: steel, aluminum, or plastic. Steel cases are generally made from between 0.8mm- and 1.2mm-thick SECC sheet metal (essentially, electro-plated commercial grade) and can be cut with a jigsaw, scroll saw, or rotary tool, assuming you're using the proper bits. Most aluminum cases have similar thickness specs and can be cut with the same tools. Some higher-end aluminum cases might be made with heavier gauge material, but they too can be cut using the same methods; it just takes a little more persistence. Plastic front-bezels and doors are common on low- and mid-priced cases, and these are easily cut and shaped with rotary bits (perfect for making drive bay windows and custom grills).

When it comes to cutting windows, aluminum and steel cases both have issues that need to be addressed *before* you begin your project. While aluminum cases are generally revered for their thermal dissipation qualities, they do pose a few problems for hardware hackers: Unlike steel, aluminum isn't very forgiving when kinked or bent out of shape. Thin aluminum sections also tend to crack easily.

As for steel, it can be hammered, welded, brazed, and repaired without the use of adhesives or special equipment. To its disadvantage, however, steel is much heavier and requires more time (and power tool bits) when cutting windows and intricate patterns. Also, when cutting steel using the abrasive cut-off disks of a rotary tool, you'll be showered with a considerable amount of sparks, so wear gloves and keep flammable materials safely at a distance.

Steel cases are usually electro-plated with a protective, micro-thin coating of rust-resistant material such as zinc. So, keep in mind that your cutting will create unprotected surfaces, and any exposed material will be prone to corrosion. If you plan to paint your case after cutting a window, remember to use a rust-inhibitive base coat to protect it. If painting is not part of your project plans, spot-paint the edges of your cutout with a small sable paintbrush, using clear or colored enamel.

Aluminum is probably my favorite metal to work with because some of its qualities remind me of wood. It can be easily cut, shaped, drilled, and filed with a minimum of effort, yet it's also very strong and lightweight—two qualities we like in our case mods! Also, compared to steel enclosures, aluminum cases are better at shedding the heat generated by internal components, and they weigh much less than their metallurgic cousins. It can corrode over time, but aluminum won't rust, so it can be left unpainted with its natural finish. I recommend clear-coating aluminum, but only to protect it from stains and smudges. Finally, with the proper rubbing compounds and some elbow grease, aluminum parts and surfaces can be wet-sanded and then buffed to an eye-catching reflective mirror shine.

Yes, You Can Put an Eye Out!

Safety considerations are extremely important when grinding and cutting metal cases and case parts. Safety glasses are an *absolute must* when cutting aluminum, steel, and plastic, especially considering the high speed of the cutting bits that are used. Even the smallest particles of steel dust and splinters can cause serious eye infections as they rust very quickly. Abrasive disks spinning at high rotational speeds can

crack and shatter if unbalanced or if they get twisted or pinched. Cutting bits can even fly out of their chucks if not properly tightened. Aluminum dust isn't healthy at all, so wear gloves and a dust mask when sanding, and keep your hands and tools clean at all times.

I cannot stress this enough: Eye protection, hand protection, and dust masks are required!

By now, you should have a pretty good idea of the types of windows and cutouts you can include in your case mod project. So let's grab some tools, a mod-worthy case, and make a really cool cutout!

Boom Baby!

Now's also a good time to get into explosive dust hazards. There's a very important shop safety rule concerning the sanding, grinding, and cutting of metals that must be followed to prevent fire and serious injury. Although steel and aluminum are not combustive on their own, when fine dust (or finely ground) particles from both metals are mixed (on your shop floor or table, for instance), you've just created *thermite*, a highly explosive compound. Although this compound is difficult to ignite because high temperatures are required, it's best not to take any chances. So, always keep in mind these safety precautions to prevent a hazardous situation:

- Never collect steel and aluminum dust together in a shop vacuum.

- Do not sweep steel and aluminum dust together in a pile.

- If your sanding tools have a dust collection bag, clean them out very thoroughly before sanding each metal.

- Clean your tools (wheel grinders, sanders, and rotary tools) very carefully before switching between these metals.

Up Close: Window-Making Materials and Tools

I don't know what kinds of gear you have sitting around your case-modding shop, but I'm more than happy to show you some of the stuff I have in my case-modding shop. Like the infamous Maximum PC Lab, my shop is well-stocked with all the materials one might need for a window project. Let's investigate....

Aluminum cases—like this one made by SilverStone—are lightweight; rust-proof; and easy to cut, shape, and drill. Aluminum can also be sanded to a beautiful natural finish or polished to a mirror shine. The downside to aluminum is that it can be very brittle at thinner gauges and requires special equipment to weld and repair.

Steel cases are very strong and can be welded and repaired easily. Side panels can hold finely cut details without cracking or breaking. However, in addition to being heavy, steel is also difficult to cut with wimpy rotary hand tools. Also, hand-filing of detailed windows takes a lot of time and patience.

Acrylic sheets make the best material for case windows—and they can also be used to form the body of entire cases! Extremely durable acrylic is available in many translucent and opaque colors, from 1/8'' to 1/2'' thick. Also known as Plexiglas, acrylic is easily cut, drilled, and tapped with hand and power tools. Acrylic can be easily scratched, but these scratches can usually be removed with rubbing compounds.

Jigsaws are my tools of choice when cutting windows and other holes in steel and aluminum cases. With some practice, a variable-speed jigsaw can be used to literally "carve" designs into soft metals (such as aluminum). Always have a good selection of metal cutting blades available for jigsaw modding projects.

Rotary tools like those made by the Dremel company are great for grinding and finishing tasks on all types of materials. Fiber-reinforced cutoff disks are a must for making case windows when a jigsaw isn't available; just be prepared to spend many hours using this method. A good set of tungsten carbide bits for your rotary tool will get the job done when detailing window designs and cutting patterns.

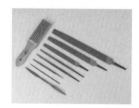

Files and rasps of various sizes should be on hand when cutting windows. They are perfect for making very flat finished edges and for cleaning hard-to-reach areas of intricate cuts in steel and aluminum.

Liquid acrylic paints can be found in many colors and are perfect for airbrushing and hand painting. A good set of small sable artist brushes should also be a part of any modder's painting kit.

Hands-On How-To: Case Windows

Stop with the yakking and on with the window hacking!

Materials Used for Our Project

- SilverStone TJ03 Aluminum Case
- 1/8'' yellow acrylic at 12'' × 14''
- Acrylic artist's paint: black, red, and yellow
- Flat black enamel model paint

Tools Used for Our Project

- Jigsaw with metal cutting blade with 24 TPI (teeth per inch)
- Dremel rotary tool
- 1/4'' sheet palm sander
- Metal files (flat and riffler)
- Small sable paintbrush
- Airbrush or aerosol spray paint in cans
- Water-based acrylic paints (red, orange, yellow, and black)

Estimated Time Commitment

- 6 hours

When I took the SilverStone TJ03 case out of its shipping box, I immediately knew that it was a prime candidate for hosting a really nice silhouette window. This streamlined, all-aluminum case sports a black powder-coat-type finish on the top and side panels and a lusciously thick front panel with two hinged doors that provide access to drive bays and an intake fan.

At more than 23'' deep, the case provides ample room on the side panel for a big, dramatic cutout, as well as a very roomy interior for lighting installation. I did find the aluminum on the side panels to be a little thin, but, as you can imagine, a thicker metal would have added considerable weight to the unit. All that said, in the case's defense, I knew the panel would be a breeze to cut and considerable detail could be had with careful planning on my part.

When planning your window or cutout design, it's good practice to break down your case by removing the side panels and giving the whole thing a visual once-over. When you do this, think ahead about lighting requirements and whether the enclosure can provide ample room to mount lights that will properly illuminate your intended cutout.

In fact, it's not a bad idea to have spare 4'' and 12'' CCFL tubes on hand—you can tape them, or temporarily mount them, to the inside of your case to ensure your plans are sound.

If you plan on mounting lights directly on the inside of the panel featuring your window or cutout, tape them on beforehand to make sure they don't interfere with the opening and closing of the panel. Also, consider the dimensions of the acrylic material you will mount behind the panel, and figure these dimensions into your lighting and design plans as well. If your side panel has an indented or mechanical-type handle mounted on it, now's the time to figure this into—or out of—your design.

The inside or back of the side panel is the place to consider when mapping out the absolute dimensions of your window. When you have these measurements, you can start sketching out your design on paper or begin entering these dimensions into your favorite image editing program.

NOTE: As with all the step-by-step articles in this book, be sure to read every step before making any design plans, purchasing any product, or hacking any piece of hardware!

Step 1: Conceiving Your Vision

Even simple designs can be transformed into amazing cutouts. The palm tree and mountains were carefully placed to create a pleasing symmetry and composition.

Whether your window is part of a larger case theme or a singular element that will define your mod, creating a design that is original and eye-catching should be your ultimate goal. For this chapter, I went through three design ideas, each inspired by the look and feel of the stock case I was using for the project.

The black powder-coat finish was the spark that ignited the idea for the dramatic silhouette cutout I finally decided on. I also wanted to utilize some of the techniques that sign painters use—such as simple airbrushing and hand painting—to create striking graphics. With its stylized, tightly spaced font, the FarCry logo provided a good challenge for my jigsaw. After measuring the side panel, I decided on a 16''×10'' cutout (perfect for printing my stencil design on two sheets of paper). I decided on a translucent, lightly frosted acrylic background that would hide wires and cables and help foster a sunset effect behind the mountains. The most striking part of the game FarCry is its lush island terrain—swaying palms and rugged mountains. By using these two elements, I was able to create a design that captures the spirit of this incredible title.

The supplies I needed for this project included an Acrylite window sheet, a few bottles of paint, and two CCFL lights. My local plastics supply store charges by the square foot for clear acrylic in many colors. I selected a transparent yellow as my window color because yellow was the lightest shade I wanted for the overall effect of the sunset. Like most acrylic projects, this one called for latex-based paint, which is easy to mix into any shade and clean up with soap and water. These paints can be applied with regular sable brushes or thinned down for use in an airbrush. For the lights, I chose 12'' cold cathodes (one red and one yellow—perfect for creating a sunset effect inside the case). I also had on hand a jar of flat black enamel paint for touching up the cut edges of the window after the design was cut out.

Step 2: Selecting Materials

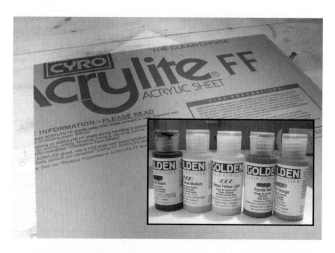

My yellow acrylic window was purchased from a plastic supply store and cut to size for $12 total. Find a shop that charges by the square foot for the best deal.

Step 3: Preparing Your Pattern

With basic image-editing skills (I used Photoshop), you can design and print the perfect pattern for your window or cutout.

Creating a silhouette is easy to do with Photoshop; the one you see here took me only a few minutes to create! For raw digital content, I started with a palm tree from a clip art gallery, a mountain screenshot from the game, and the FarCry logo from the official website.

First, I created a canvas in Photoshop that was 16"×11" and 150dpi. Using the magic eraser tool, I removed the white background from all the images. Next, for each image, I used the brightness and contrast sliders to turn them way down to zero, creating black and white silhouettes. I then dragged the images onto the 16"×11" canvas and began scaling and placing them. Next, I made a new layer with a white background and applied a black stroke to its border, making a black perimeter for the entire cutout. I didn't want the palm tree to "float" in my cutout, so I used the leaves to overlap the mountain and the square perimeter, thus creating connection points. Once I had the silhouette design to my liking, I flattened the image layers; then I dragged a vertical guide from the ruler bar and split the image into two 8" sections. Finally, I copied and pasted each half into a separate new document and then printed each one.

After I printed the two halves of the Photoshop pattern, I used a strip of clear tape to join them along a seam. Assuming you're installing a clear window to see the inside of your case, placement of the window is an important step. You'll have to consider the interior framework of the case, which areas you want to be visible, and which areas you want to conceal.

For my project, I wanted my graphic centered both horizontally and vertically on the side panel. However, depending on your design, you can cheat the placement on the panel until you nail down the sense of composition you're after. Using a tape measure, I carefully squared the pattern on the side panel from top to bottom, and left to right. After I had the pattern taped down and aligned properly, I used a piece of chalk to make tick marks on each corner in preparation for mounting.

Step 4: Deciding on Window Placement

Window placement is a critical step, so get it right the first time! Once you begin cutting, there might be no turning back to correct bad alignment or crooked patterns.

Step 5: Transferring Your Pattern

A light coat of spray adhesive is my choice for mounting the paper pattern to the side panel. When the cutting is complete, the adhesive is easily removed with a rag and some mineral spirits.

There are basically two methods for transferring a pattern to the side panel of a case. The best method for any project depends on the specific case, the complexity of the pattern, and whether you plan to paint afterward.

If you have a bare metal surface you intend to paint later, you can simply cut the paper pattern out with a hobby knife, tape it down, and then trace around the pattern with a sharp pencil. Conversely, if you plan to keep the original case finish, I suggest applying the pattern with a spray adhesive. With a medium to heavy coat of spray adhesive on the back of the paper, carefully place the pattern, using the chalk marks made earlier as positioning guidelines. Don't wait for the adhesive to completely dry because it won't stick to your panel. Once in place, rub the pattern down with a soft cloth and make sure it's completely flat and wrinkle-free. Now use the tape measure once again to make sure the pattern is properly aligned. There's no need to worry about the adhesive on the panel because, after you cut the design, you can pull up the pattern and remove the glue with a little mineral spirits.

After I mounted the pattern on the side panel (using the adhesive method), I put several strips of painter's masking tape on the exposed metal of the case. Why? Because if you're planning on keeping the factory finish of your stock case, you should protect the paint. Cutting with a jigsaw creates a lot of particles that can get trapped under the base of the tool as you cut. These stray particles can scratch the finish down to bare metal, presenting a problem that's beyond repair.

If you're using a rotary tool to cut your window, it's also a good idea to protect the surrounding area of the side panel by taping on heavy cardboard or even thin sheets of tin, which can be purchased from a plumbing supply store. At high speeds, rotary tool bits often jump and skip, causing scratches and gouges in a paint finish.

Step 6: Preparing for Surgery

When cutting windows, it's very important to protect the finish of your side panel. Even if you plan on painting afterward, metal particles can scratch and gouge the metal surface.

Step 7: Preparing Your Surgery Room

Clean work areas mean clean case mods and peace of mind. Get in the practice of keeping your work area clean, safe, and ready for every step of your project.

Cutting and grinding metal produces a big mess of fine particles that can fly everywhere, so it's a good habit to clear your work surface of debris and stray tools on a regular basis. In my shop, in fact, I keep a roll of painter's masking paper handy and roll out fresh, clean work surfaces whenever necessary. Sure, it might sound a bit obsessive-compulsive, but it can be absolutely critical if you want a professional-looking mod. Think about it: Would you buy a new car if it had even a single blemish on it?

When cutting windows, it's also important to have a flat surface on which to work. This helps prevent dimples and scratches on your side panel. Use a putty knife or scraper to clean your worktable of bumps caused by glue and splinters, and be sure there are no nail or screw heads sticking up. You can also have a clean board cut to table size at a lumber yard (use this board for finishing work only). Quarter-inch to half-inch hardboard works great. Keep a small dust broom handy to periodically sweep the table of dust and debris. Now is also a good time to grab your shop glasses, dust mask, and other safety equipment and have them ready.

I decided I needed to cut my elaborate FarCry design with a jigsaw, so I needed a way to support the side panel and still have enough clearance for the stroke (up and down travel distance) of the jigsaw blade. So, rather than cutting my pattern with the panel on the edge of the table, I made a frame using 1"×3" pine. I cut the four sides of the frame slightly larger than my cutout and joined them with 1-3/4" screws. Now I had a sturdy surface on which to support the panel while cutting. When you're cutting small sections of your pattern, you can position the frame anywhere you need to support the panel. This prevents the metal from bending or, worse, breaking off and causing big headaches.

Step 8: Everyone Needs a Little Support

By making a simple wooden frame from 1"×3" pine, you can support the side panel as you cut the pattern with a jigsaw.

Step 9: Drilling a Starting Point

Using a 3/8'' drill bit, I made holes on my side panel where I would need to insert the jigsaw blade. This next point is important: I decided to keep the black parts of my pattern and cut out the white parts. You'll need to make a similar decision when you're designing the pattern and its border, and you'll need to follow through on that decision when you begin drilling your starting holes. It's easy to forget which part of the pattern to cut out, but this issue is critical, so make sure you get it right. A hole in the wrong place can spell disaster—you might have to relocate your pattern, design a new pattern, or get a replacement side-panel or case.

Before and during cutting, I sprayed a light coat of WD-40 right on the jigsaw blade; it serves as a metal lubricant. Without some kind of oil, the metal of the side panel can bind on the blade and cause bending and other damage to the cutout.

Jigsaw blade starter holes were drilled in the areas to be cut out. Using a lubricant such as WD-40 on the blade before and during metal cutting helps prevent the blade from binding and jumping.

It's your moment of truth! Depending on your skills with a jigsaw, you can cut as close to the edges of the pattern as you feel comfortable with. Cutting close saves time and elbow grease during the finishing work phase, but it also gives you very little wiggle room to make mistakes. Cutting farther away means there will be a lot more cleanup work to do later, but at least you'll have the luxury of defining your cutout edges with your most sensitive, high-precision tools—your hands.

Cutting aluminum doesn't require tremendous jigsaw speeds, and low speeds will give you better control of the blade and tool. Let the machine do the cutting. Don't push too hard. Just gently guide the tool through the pattern and let the blade do the work. In the photo, you'll see the correct placement of your free hand and fingers. This hand should be used to keep the base of the jigsaw flat against your work. Your other hand should be used to hold and steer the tool through your pattern. When stopping your cut, back the blade up slightly to prevent the teeth from grabbing the metal as the tool slows down. Take frequent breaks to review your cut and give your hand a rest. And when you stop a cut, take the opportunity to put another coat of WD-40 on the blade to get it ready for your next series of cuts.

Step 10: Gettin' Jiggy with It!

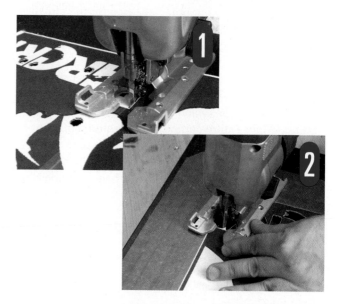

Begin cutting your pattern slowly and carefully. Cut the design as close to the pattern as you're comfortable with. Use your free hand to hold the base, or *shoe*, of the jigsaw lightly against the work. Let your other hand do all the steering and guiding.

Step 11: Advanced Maneuvers

When using a metal cutting blade, sharp turns are difficult to make in tight spaces. The trick is to ease the pattern out by making a series of cuts to free up the blade. In Figure 1, you'll see I made two cuts along the letter *Y* and then backed out the blade completely.

It would be impossible for me to make such a tight radius cut, so in Figure 2 I started a new cut and slightly curved this toward one corner of the *Y*. Now, with more room for my blade to maneuver, I made a cut to the opposite corner and the scrap fell right out, leaving me with a little point, shown in Figure 3.

A neat little trick when cutting a pattern with a jigsaw is to use a side-to-side motion at low speeds to let the blade "carve" the material, as shown in Figure 4. Aluminum is soft enough for this type of carving, and it really helps save a lot of time during hand finishing. When your cutout really starts to take shape, the panel becomes more fragile. When this happens, clamp the panel and the wood frame beneath it to your worktable. Now you can apply very little pressure on the panel by slightly lifting the jigsaw off the surface.

When the cutout was complete, I gave my worktable a good brushing to clean up all the metal shavings and dust. I then peeled off the paper pattern and gave the panel a good cleaning with a soft rag and mineral spirits to remove any traces of the spray adhesive. (Be sure you go nice and easy with the rag; otherwise, you'll catch the fabric on your cutout, possibly damaging it.)

I also used a small hammer to gently flatten out bends and dings on the cutout.

Step 12: Cleaning the Cutout

With the paper pattern peeled off, I cleaned the adhesive from the side panel with a soft rag and some mineral spirits. Kinks and bends can be flattened out by gently tapping with a small hammer.

Step 13: Finishing Touches

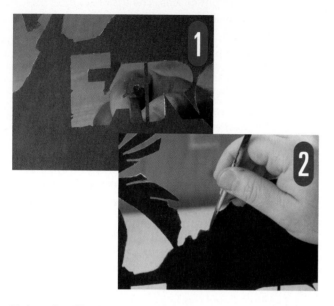

After cleaning the cutout, I pulled out my small files to clean the edges and perfect the rough cuts made by the jigsaw. This is the most time-consuming part of the project, and the one phase that will determine how nice your window or pattern ultimately turns out. Use the files with circular, side-to-side, and up-and-down motions to gently clean the cutout and remove any sharp edges. After filing, I was left with bright silver aluminum on the edges, so I used a flat small brush and some flat black enamel paint to hide the bright edges. When this was dry, it was time to get that yellow acrylic painted and mounted behind the cutout.

Various-size riffler files are indispensable for cleaning intricate metal cutouts. A small, flat paintbrush and some black paint put the finishing touches on the edge of the metal.

Quick note: When you get to this stage with your own project, put on your dust mask!

For this particular cutout design, I didn't want the interior of the case to be completely visible. So, I put some clean paper down on my worktable; then, with a palm sander and 300-grit paper, I frosted one side of the yellow acrylic (Figure 1). I sanded the plastic lengthwise because this was the direction of my sunset horizon. Now my window would let interior light shine through, but wires and framework would be hidden from view. I cleaned the dust from the window with a damp paper towel and water.

The next step was to trace the logo onto the frosted side of the yellow acrylic in preparation for painting. Using a tape measure, I calculated exactly where the yellow acrylic would be mounted on the back of the cutout side panel; then I transferred these lines to the front. I temporarily mounted the acrylic on the front of the panel with some tape and flipped it over flat on the worktable. With a sharp pencil, I then traced the logo (Figure 2).

Step 14: Painting and Mounting the Acrylic

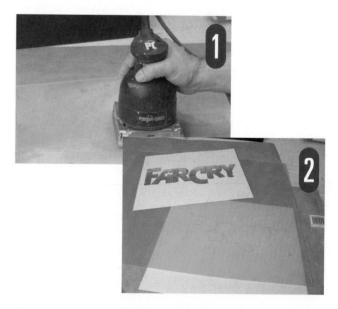

Use a palm sander and 300-grit paper to frost one side of the yellow acrylic. Trace the logo onto the acrylic.

Step 15: da Vinci Time

Flip the acrylic so it's shiny side up, and use foil to create a palette for mixing your paints. Use a damp sponge to lightly apply paint to the acrylic.

After the logo was traced out, I flipped the yellow acrylic over to the shiny finished side (Figure 3). Then, using the logo printout as a color reference, I began mixing the paints on my fancy foil palette (Figure 4). I broke a rough piece off of an ordinary kitchen sponge, dampened it with some water, and began stippling the paint lightly onto the acrylic (Figure 5). Notice that I applied my paint in a block that covers much more than the FarCry logo strokes. No worries! You need to remember that all this "overage paint" will be covered up by the case's side panel. Refer to the final beauty shot in this chapter if you don't believe me!

I wanted enough paint on the acrylic to create the texture from the logo, but not so much paint as to block the light from coming through. So, after a few minutes, I thinned out the paint with a few drops of water to prevent it from becoming opaque. If I wasn't happy with the paint job, I could have easily washed it off with some soap and water and started again. I created a sort of stippled fade, starting with dark reddish orange on the bottom of the logo and blending to more yellow at the top of the text. When I was satisfied with the look, I gave it a few minutes to dry.

For the "sunset horizon" effect, I broke out my airbrush for a quick paint job. I mixed up a nice dark orange right in the airbrush reservoir using red and yellow paint. I also mixed a few drops of water into the color to thin it out, and to provide me with a nice, even mist of paint. Starting from the top of the window, I created a fade on the front side of the yellow acrylic that extended about a third of the way down. (This was another very light coat of paint.) After this paint was dry, I sealed the front of the window with two coats of clear acrylic enamel from a spray can. This type of sealer coat helps prevent the paint underneath from easily scratching off. Because I sanded the back of the yellow acrylic, I didn't seal that side with a clear coat (doing so would have basically "unfrosted" it).

Step 16: It's Airbrush Time

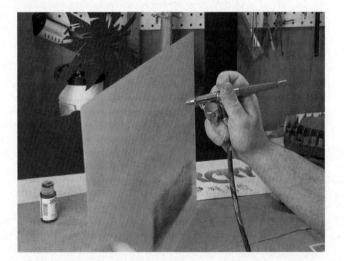

An airbrush came in handy for creating a subtle sunset effect on the reverse side of the window. Aerosol spray paint can also be used with great results.

Step 17: Mounting the Window

Mounting an intricate window design like this one should be done slowly and carefully. Double stick tape, epoxy, and silicon adhesive will do the trick, and it's a good idea to experiment with scrap pieces from your project just to be sure.

When it comes to mounting windows, you have several options. Some modders like to use strips of double-sided foam tape. Another method is to bond your two pieces together with a thin bead of clear silicon caulking, placing a heavy book on the assembly so that the caulking dries under pressure. Just be aware that if you're not neat and careful during this phase, the silicon can squeeze out onto the front of your window, causing a mess. An alternative to silicon is 5-minute epoxy mixed up and carefully applied to the acrylic with a small disposable foam brush. It's a good idea to experiment by using scrap pieces of metal and acrylic from your project because every surface has its own adhesive properties.

For my project, I used a super-strong and thin double-stick tape, first applying it to the case panel. When the panel was done, I placed the acrylic in the desired position and applied some pressure to it with my hands and a soft rag. Sadly, the "super-strong" double-stick tape wasn't so strong after all, so I decided to put a few beads of super glue on the edges of the acrylic, and this finally did the trick.

Cutting text and logos can be tricky. Having used a jigsaw for this project, I managed to break off only one small triangular piece of the *F* in the logo (Figure 1), and I did this by accidentally fumbling the panel and dropping it on the table. Mixing up some epoxy and gluing the piece directly on the window itself easily repaired this.

Addressing the "holes" for the letters *R*s was another small task. With my rotary tool and some scrap aluminum left over from the cutout, I shaped the appropriate parts with a sanding drum at a medium speed (Figure 2). Once I was satisfied with the shape and size, these small pieces were then edge painted in black and glued on the window with 5-minute epoxy. To finish up the look of the logo, I did a bit of brush painting to create the cracks and chips on the letters.

Step 18: Repairing Mistakes

You can repair mistakes, such as the botched *F* in the logo, which are hard to avoid when making intricate cuts. Fortunately, a little epoxy saved the day. I used a sanding drum to shape pieces of scrap aluminum to complete the two *R*s in *FarCry*.

Step 19: Cleaning Up and Finishing

I used my work lamp to test the effect of the painted sunset. I really like the way it turned out. Careful placement of the cold cathode lights creates the same effect inside the case. The stippled-paint effect worked out pretty nicely. The finishing touches of the painted cracks and crevices really brought the logo to life. Sometimes it's the little things that make all the difference.

You would think that a powder-coat finish is good at hiding smudges, but I was wrong. As it turns out, the powder-coat was great at lifting the aluminum dust from my fingertips (even after washing my hands!), so I had to carefully clean the panel with a damp cloth. I rigged up a power supply (more on this in Chapter 6, "Let There Be Lighting") with two white cold-cathode lights and placed them inside the empty case. When I put the panel on and fired up the lights, I was *very* happy with the results.

What's nice about painting the acrylic is that even with the lights off, the window still looks cool. When I turned the shop lights down to LAN party levels, the entire design was even more dramatic. With this type of window, experimenting with various colored lights is a good idea. Perhaps a couple of red and yellow lights would make a pleasing sunset glow. I might even try making reflective baffles to direct the light onto the acrylic window instead of illuminating the entire inside of the case.

Looking back on the cutting process, I came up with an idea that would help prevent breaking the aluminum next time around: If I had temporarily laminated a piece of 3/16" hardboard on the back of the panel using spray mount, it might have helped support the metal as I was cutting. I'm going to keep this in mind next time I cut an intricate window. You should always come away from even the smallest project with new ideas on how to improve your general craft skills. This kind of thought and experimentation is the key to growing as a case modder and craftsperson.

Step 20: Admiring Your Work

Here's our beauty shot—the finished project in all its glory!

A Study in Sublime Window Dressing

Sure, the *Maximum PC* editors have seen crazier paint schemes. And, yes, we've seen nuttier cooling contraptions. And, of course, we've seen rigs based on wilder themes. But during our Rig of the Month judging deliberations, we sometimes grow tired of all the visual excess—all the fluttering flags and cartwheeling clowns of the case-modding scene. So, during December 2001 judging, we all wanted some relief, a touch of subtlety, if you will. And in rushed a breath of fresh Air.

We ultimately chose Dev Jugdeo's Air Machine rig for its sublime integration of form, symbolism, and function. And as you can quite plainly see with your own eyes, the mod is a stellar example of window-cutting. No, it's not a "traditional" case window covered with acrylic, but it was executed with the same type of craft and artistry described in this chapter. We dig the way his glyph plays off of the symmetry of his case fans and how his metal fan cages work so well with the silver enamel paint on his case.—J.P.

Dev Jugdeo Describes His Work in His Own Words . . .

"The symbol is the Chinese symbol for air. The first thing I did was pencil templates of the fans and the symbol itself on the inside of the case. After all the measurements were done—positioning the fans at the same level as the CPU, for example—it was time to start cutting.

"I chose to use a Dremel MultiPro Kit. Everyone said this wouldn't cut the case properly, but I wanted to see for myself. I purchased reinforced metal cutting blades—make sure you buy a lot because you'll go through a lot. The Dremel went through the case like a hot knife through butter! The key to cutting the case so precisely is patience. Cut in short blasts. Don't just cut continuously because that causes the blade to heat up faster, which will make it break more easily.

"After everything was cut out, I used the sanding tool that came in the Dremel kit and went around the edges to the point where you could run your finger across the edges without feeling any sharp edges."

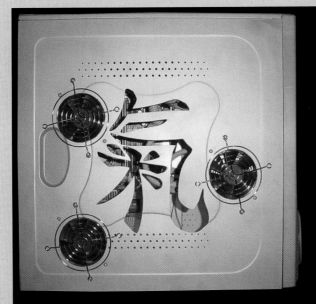

"As you can see from the images, the fans and symbol are very close together, which doesn't give me much room to work with a Plexiglas cover. People have suggested that the [open symbol] will affect the cooling, but because of the high number of fans in the case, I don't see any problems at all. My temps range from 15° to 19° C at idle, to 34°–35° C max at full load."

"On my CPU, I have a 60mm Delta fan that spins at 7000rpm—nice and loud! I also have three 40mm drive bay fans, one 80mm case fan in the front blowing air inside, and three 80mm fans on the side. All totaled, I have nine fans— three bay, one front, three side, one rear, and one on my power supply."

"Inside, I have a Pentium III 733MHz. I'm using the Asus CUV4X jumperfree motherboard. The CPU is overclocked to 854MHz, with the PC133 memory running at 155MHz. When benchmarking, I run my system at 881MHz with the memory at 160MHz. My videocard is an AOpen GTS Pro PA256 Deluxe II 32MB. Its stock rating is 200/400, but I have overclocked it to 235/435. I'll push it more when I get better cooling!"

Chapter Four

Painting Cases

Transform your case from basic to badass.

To create a corrosive look, Piloux started with a flat gray paint layer, added a rust-colored layer, and finished with orange highlights. You'll have to play *Half-Life 2* to understand the motivation for the jagged, craggy surface creeping up the side of the glass—or you can just read more about this Rig of the Month winner in the November 2004 issue of *Maximum PC*.

We so fell in love with this PC that we pictured this bad boy on our July 2004 cover. We started with Cooler Master's sublime Wavemaster enclosure, stuffed it with top-end hardware, and asked the pros at Smooth Creations to "make it look fast." The results? This Hugger orange rig, reminiscent of the 1967 Camaro, damn near made us cry. Breathtaking.

For 2004's Dream Machine case, we wanted a paint job in sync with our PC's forward-thinking, future-proof nature. Words like *abstract*, *sleek*, and *post-modern* dominated our thoughts. With this and Art Director Natalie Jeday's early drafts in mind, we enlisted the aid of the custom-painting PC wizards at Smooth Creations. And the rest, as they say, is history. See the September 2004 issue of *Maximum PC* for more about this affordable (who are we kidding?) rig.

Here we have another stellar example of the work of Smooth Creations, a professional case-painting studio whose technical prowess is rooted in automotive painting. The rig was created specifically for *PC Gamer* (one of *Maximum PC's* sister magazines) for a contest giveaway. Original, high-resolution *Half-Life 2* artwork —supplied directly by Valve—was turned into a decal, which was then applied directly to the case. Next, Smooth Creations used careful airbrushing to eliminate decal seams and add artistic accents to the tableau.

The Hypersonic SonicBoom is quite fetching (it reminds us of an angry bumble bee) and proof positive that if you aren't of a mind to paint your own case—or shell out the bucks to have a pro do it—you can purchase a decent painted case off the shelf. Although the paint job isn't Falcon Northwest caliber, it's vibrant, professional-looking, and durable. On the inside, Hypersonic attached foam to the case's side door and sundry other empty spots in an attempt to dampen any noise the aluminum chassis might emit.

Taking a 1968 candy apple red Mustang convertible or a 1967 Camaro done up in delicious hugger orange for inspiration, case modders take these classic colors off the street and put them right on their desktop rigs. Although not nearly as exhilarating as a neighborhood cruise in a muscle car, a slippery smooth paint finish can transform a PC case from basic to *badass*.

For the most part, stock cases are available in only a few color choices and with paint finishes that leave a lot to be desired. A good majority of these are your basic blues, metallic grays, silvers, the dreaded beige, and of course—the timeless favorite—black. These paint finishes tend to be satin, metal flake, or powder (lightly textured) and far from what can be called "show quality." The better manufacturers, such as Cheiftec, Lian Li, Cooler Master, and Silverstone, are more interested in durability than looks, although their paint finishes are of much higher quality than your garden variety cases. I have an old-school Chieftec Dragon case in the shop, and although it's a stock finish, it is one of the best-looking (and durable) factory paints I've seen. On the other hand, the dirt-cheap cases that litter the shelves of some retailer warehouses have entirely laughable paint finishes that flake off if you look at them wrong.

When you must have a hot-rod-quality paint finish, there are two roads you can take: handing your case over to a professional or rolling up your sleeves and taking the challenge on yourself. A growing number of cross-over craftspeople have brought their skill and experience with automotive and motorcycle paint finishing to the world of case modding. As a result, you can ship your case to them and, for a fee, have it shipped back to you with a high-quality custom-paint finish, airbrushed graphics, logos, or any design you can imagine. These skilled artists have the experience and the equipment to create the most stunning paint finish your case will ever have, and with that comes a hefty price tag. It's not uncommon to find prices from a few hundred dollars to more than a thousand, depending on the design and complexity of the project.

This Smooth Creations custom paint job was created for Falcon Northwest and is found on its Mach V Icon Exotix gaming rig. Dubbed "Red Death," this custom paint job depicts a Khmer Rouge motif—a pile of skulls painted along the oceanside. At $7,300 for the rig, including the paint job, it's more than a little salty, but we guarantee you'll get noticed at your next LAN party.

See "How the Pros Paint Cases" later in this chapter for an insider's look at how professional painters can transform a garden-variety enclosure into a veritable work of art.

If you don't have the bucks to spend on a custom paint job or a "friend in the business" with the free time and equipment to help with your project, you can get a very respectable finish on your case (and keyboard, monitor, mouse, and so forth) with about $25, some elbow grease, and the patience of a saint. More than a few modders on the scene are masters of the spray can paint finish, and there's no reason you can't achieve the same expert results with lots of practice, some common sense, and a helpful guide to point you in the right direction. I have no doubt that after you do the first paint job right, you'll be addicted and will strive to make the next one even better. Secrets to great paint finishes are locked away in those hardware store rattle cans, and if you're unfamiliar with the techniques in this chapter, you're in for a surprise.

For those of you skilled with an airbrush, a PC case can be an interesting canvas. Cases with windowless, unadorned side panels provide good surfaces on which to work your airbrushing magic. I've always envied the airbrush artists with their mastery of light, shadow, color, and composition. When you study the work of airbrushing professionals and see how they capture incredible detail and subtlety in their work, you can easily become intimidated. Have no fear, though, because airbrushing is all about method and technique, and these skills can be learned just like anything else. If you don't own an airbrush, serious case modding is a good excuse to invest in a starter kit and begin exploring all the artistic possibilities.

In this chapter, we show you how to get stunning results using spray paint, as well as an airbrush. In the end, however, you'll find the techniques we show here just scratch the surface of what you can achieve with a little practice, some patience, and paints you can purchase at your neighborhood hardware or paint store.

Project Silicon Rising is a commissioned piece, created by Paul Capello for Intel Corporation. This work of art not only showcases a beautifully done airbrushed metallic paint job, but also show's Paul's talent with clay molding and casting.

Before You Get Started— Safety Precautions

You're probably saying to yourself, "Here he goes again, talking about case modding safety." Well, as we say in Brooklyn, "Yeah, you got a problem wit dat?" I'll put it simply: *The same safety precautions workers at the factory take when getting the paint into the can should be followed by the consumer who lets it out of the can.*

Here are the basic safety items you shouldn't start without. Don't say we didn't warn you. Note that these safety items should be worn when using spray paints or an airbrush. Don't even *think* about painting without them.

This should go without saying, but before you go and ruin your favorite Moby shirt or low-rider jeans, make sure you wear clothes and shoes you don't care about. If you're painting outdoors—and we wholeheartedly recommend it—mild breezes can cause paint overspray to wash back over your clothing. You might also want to consider wearing a hat, lest you end up with a blue metal flake 'do.

Safety Glasses

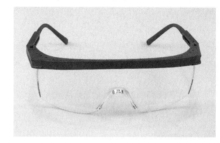

Common prescription eyewear (unless safety-rated) should not be used as an alternative to proper protection. Good safety glasses are inexpensive and easy to find, and many fit over existing eyewear. You should be wearing your eye protection when painting, cutting, grinding, sanding, polishing, and using any type of powered machinery. Safety glasses inevitably get scratched, so replace them immediately or use a plastic polish such as Novus to buff out the scratches. Never attempt to clean your safety glasses with solvents. Using badly scratched or damaged eyewear is equivalent to using nothing at all, and it can result in serious injuries. Protective eyewear should be Occupational Safety and Health Administration (OSHA)-certified.

Respirator

Spray enamels, lacquers, oils, and alkyds are manufactured from extremely poisonous materials that must be used in areas with adequate ventilation while wearing a properly fitted National Institute for Occupational Safety and Health (NIOSH)-approved paint respirator. Read the warning label on the can. Seriously. Read it, and follow the instructions.

Gloves

You should use latex rubber or silicon examination-type gloves when working with acrylic paints and other noncorrosive materials. Keep in mind that some people are allergic to latex and can have adverse skin reactions. Chemical-resistant gloves must be worn when using resins, epoxy adhesives, acid, and other harmful chemicals.

Tools and Materials for Our Spray-Painting Project

- Spray paints (primer, color, and clear topcoat)
- Rubber sanding block
- Wet/dry sandpaper (2,000-, 1,500-, 1,000-, 600-, 500-, and 400-grit)
- Automotive rubbing compound
- Automotive polishing glaze
- Denatured alcohol
- Painter's masking tape
- Clean, lint-free cotton terry cloths

- Spray bottle with fresh water
- Plastic bowl containing water and a few drops of dishwashing soap
- NIOSH-approved paint respirator
- OSHA-approved protective eyewear
- Gloves
- Pretrashed clothing
- Random orbital sander and abrasive disc (optional)

Your local hardware or paint store should have everything you need to paint your case. If you can't find a particular brand or color, try visiting the Krylon, Plasti-Kote, and Dupli-Color websites. See Chapter 15, "Showing It All Off," for contact information.

A liquid rubbing compound and polishing glaze are used to create a "wet look" mirror finish. These are what make people go "oooh" when they look at your finished creation.

You'll spend a lot of personal time getting to know your sanding block, so be sure you get a good one with a comfortable grip. Also, make sure you have a wide selection of A-weight sandpaper, ranging from 600- to 2000-grit.

Use denatured alcohol on bare metal because it evaporates quickly and removes any oils left over from the original manufacturing.

About the Materials We Use

Paints

The best aerosol paints for getting a good finish on your case are enamels and lacquers. Both of these paints are formulated for the best possible adhesion on metal, wood, plastic, and previously finished surfaces. Enamels are the most common and come in a wide range of colors. Generally, they are more easily wet-sanded, are durable, and shine up pretty well. The downside to enamels can be the drying time—up to twice as long as lacquer-based paint. Lacquers give you the best aerosol can shine you can get and have good durability; for the beginner, this is an excellent choice. Brands such as Plasti-Kote and Dupli-Color are popular and come in many automotive-flavored and matched colors. When selecting a brand, you should also purchase the suggested primer and clear topcoat to ensure the best compatibility and save the time of having to do a test piece. Lacquer applied over some enamels becomes an effective paint stripper and can basically ruin your day. Your best bet is to read the labels carefully.

The first and most crucial coat of paint is the primer. Whichever brand you choose, make sure it is *wet-sandable* (or even *dry-sandable* for that matter) by carefully reading the label; if it's not stated right on the front of the can, then generally it is not wet-sandable. *Wet-sanding with an incompatible primer results in peeling, lifting, cursing, redness of the face, and sometimes throwing.* My personal favorites are Krylon wet-sandable black and ruddy brown primer; for light-colored paints, I use their gray or white primer.

For painting parts such as bezels, CD-ROM faceplates, and other plastic parts of your case, you can use the same materials and methods we discuss later. There are also specialty products you might like to experiment with, such as the Plasti-Kote automotive vinyl dyes and Krylon Fusion brand paint. The vinyl dyes from Plasti-Kote are sold in aerosol cans and are applied much the same way as your basic spray paints. The consistency is more akin to a plastic "stain." Krylon Fusion paints are said to bond to plastic on a molecular level, creating a durable and scratch-resistant finish on hard-to-paint plastic surfaces. I've used this paint with great results on my Boblbee found-object case mod (see Chapter 9, "Building the Ultimate Found-Object Mod"). The drawback of plastic paints and dyes is the limited colors available, but if they happen to fit your color scheme, give them a try.

Wet/Dry Sandpaper and Sanding Block

A block of rubber and a few sheets of wet and dry sandpaper are your most important tools for creating a show-car-quality finish on your PC case. You can find these at hardware and automotive supply stores just about everywhere. A favorite in the automotive restoration business is 3M and its Imperial brand of silicon carbide papers. Good-quality sandpapers have fast cutting properties and a tendency to last a bit longer before clogging up with paint residue and requiring replacement. Wet and dry sandpapers for paint finishing also have a weight specification: *A* is a light paper, and *B* is slightly heavier. For this project, we used A-weight papers from 600-grit to 2,000-grit.

Rubbing Compound and Polishing Glaze

After your painted case parts are made as smooth as they possibly can be with 2,000-grit paper, a liquid rubbing compound and polishing glaze are used to create a wet-look mirror finish. Rubbing compound is a liquid that contains fine abrasives and removes the fine scratches, swirl marks, and imperfections left behind by the 2,000-grit sandpaper. Your best bet is to get the type that can be used by hand because some are formulated for use only with high-speed buffing machines. Hand glaze is another liquid that is applied after the rubbing compound and contains no abrasives, but rather special polishing agents that create the final shine. For these final steps, be sure to have plenty of clean, lint-free cotton cloths on hand, so you should get yourself one of those "big bags-'o-rags" at the hardware store. For the paint jobs in this chapter, I used 3M Perfect-It 2 fine-cut rubbing compound and 3M's Imperial Hand Glaze.

Denatured Alcohol

After you've stripped any factory paint from your case and sanded it silky smooth, you should clean up the case with denatured alcohol before you begin painting. Remember, hand, eye, and lung protection is a must.

Step 1: Preparing Your Case for Painting

When I set out to gather the materials for this project, my goal for the PC case was to purchase the cheapest, most hideous case I could find. If I could then make it just a little bit better with a few coats of paint, the project would be a success. My neighborhood haunt on 8th Avenue in Brooklyn is a small PC shop called CompuStar, and it's there I found the perfect subject for this chapter. This sad, nameless steel case was stacked underneath three others, and for $25 I brought this unwanted puppy home from the pound. I removed the right side panel and the plastic front bezel with the weird "alien eyes" shaped intake vents. The power and reset buttons, along with the USB/speaker ports, were also removed and stored in a plastic baggie for safekeeping.

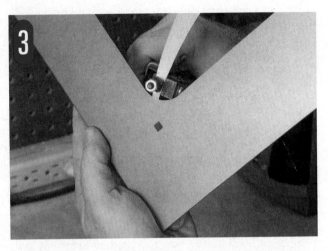

I removed the plastic window and took the hand nibblers to the offending side panel. With my rotary tool and sanding drum attachment, I cleaned the cut edges and sanded them smooth with some 300-grit paper. See Chapter 3, "Making a Case Window," to learn more about cutting case panels.

I was most frightened by the Nike swoosh-type metal design on the window panel, and without hesitation I grabbed my tools.

Make sure your own case is at a point where you're ready for paint. For the amount of work you put into a primo paint finish, you should avoid making structural or design changes afterwards.

Step 2: To Strip or Not to Strip

If you have a decent quality case, chances are the factory paint finish doesn't have to be removed down to the bare metal. Manufacturers use special etching chemicals prior to painting that help with adhesion and durability. If your paint finish is fairly sound, proceed to step 5 and begin wet-sanding. Apparently, the creators of my scruffy little case didn't bother with this etching process, and after testing with sandpaper on a small area, the finish was easily removed to the metal. When cases are manufactured, the sheets of metal are put through a series of bending and breaking machinery, folding and stamping the material to create the parts. This leaves the tops and side panels with edges that are slightly curled, and it can pose a problem when you sand the coats of paint. Your nice, flat-sanding block will find all these high spots and remove the paint down to the primer or, worse, the bare metal. Of particular concern are those pesky indented handles that are stamped into some side panels, so be sure you get those areas nice and flat. The key to putting a good paint finish on your case is getting all the parts sanded as flat and true as can be. Like a good-quality mirror, the flatter the glass is, the better the reflective qualities.

It's important when using an orbital sander to apply very little pressure on the tool because this can distort the rubber pad that holds the abrasive and create an uneven surface.

I decided to use my Bosch random orbital sander fitted with a 400-grit disc to the case; this tremendously helped flatten all the high spots on the panels.

By just guiding the tool along the surface and allowing the weight of the machine to do the work, you can get nicely ground case panels like this as a result.

Step 3: Cleaning and Masking

Now is a good time to prepare your work area, preferably in a sunny spot outdoors away from people, plants, and other fragile living things. If you're painting outdoors, do it on days that are low in humidity. Water vapor in the air significantly slows down drying time and can even cause the paint to haze as moisture is trapped between the coats of paint. If you have no choice, get your parts into a warm, dry place between coats of paint. Aerosol spray paint is best applied when temperatures are between 50° and 85° Fahrenheit and when winds are low, so keep this in mind when selecting your work area. For the work surface, a pair of sawhorses with a plywood top is perfect. Protect your work area from overspray with newspaper; just remember to tape the paper down to avoid a gust of wind (or the spray can propellant) from blowing it onto your painted parts.

Be sure to clean your case with denatured alcohol and mask off the areas you don't want painted.

We probably don't need to tell you this, but make sure you're not standing downwind when applying your paint!

Painter's masking paper is your best bet for protecting your case from overspray, drips, and the little accidents that are bound to happen with painting. Using newspaper to protect your case is acceptable only if you apply the sheets in several layers because it can tend to be porous and allow the paint to bleed through.

Having sanded all my panels, it was time for a little cleanup. I like to use denatured alcohol on bare metal because it evaporates quickly and removes any oils left over from the original manufacturing. Removing the oils is important if you decide to paint the interior of your case, even though this is often left unfinished. Painting the interior, however, does give your rig a nice, finished (dare we say it?), automotive look.

Using a low-tack painter's masking tape like the blue tape shown here is recommended because it will be left on for a few days while the paint dries between coats. Carefully cut away excess masking tape with a pen knife, being careful not to mar the surface of your case.

Step 4: Priming

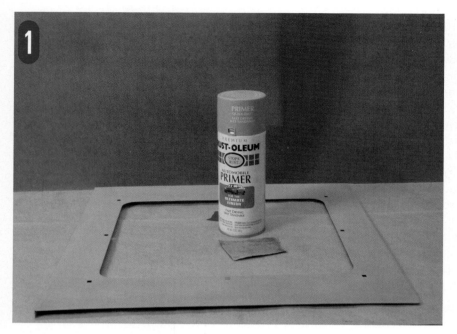

1

It's time to get that rattle can shaking and get down to business. Use a clean rag or tack cloth to remove any debris or particles on your work. After shaking the can of spray primer for a minute or so, give a 3-second blast of paint onto a piece of scrap paper to charge the can and clear out any dried particles. Start spraying the paint for a moment off of the panel and then across it in a sweeping motion about 10" away from the surface, ending each course of paint off of the panel. You should start painting at the bottom of the panel and work toward the top, holding the can at a slight angle to the work so the spray pattern is evenly distributed and slightly overlapping each course. Don't stop in the middle of your work and change directions. Stopping or changing painting directions can cause the paint to pool up and create heavy spots. Your first coat will only be a light dusting of paint, and after about 8–12 minutes, you can apply another. The primer coat doesn't have to be perfect, so it's a good opportunity to practice your sweeping motions for the color coats.

2

From three to four coats of primer should be enough to cover the surface; after that, let your piece dry for about an hour in a warm, dry area or a nice sunny spot where it won't be disturbed. At the beginning of the chapter, I mentioned needing the patience of a saint, remember? This is where you begin to be put to the test. We all hate waiting; we like to get results ASAP. Unfortunately, with paint finishing, these results do not come quickly. Let the paint dry properly and thoroughly—don't poke at it, pick debris from it, or otherwise look at it funny. Leave it be, and go do something else.

Step 5: Wet-Sanding the Primer Coat

When your primer coat is dry, it's on to the wet-sanding to get that paint flat and silky smooth. Prepare your work area for a messy job by covering your work surface with a canvas or plastic drop cloth. Have plenty of paper towels on hand for cleanup as you work. I keep a spray bottle filled with fresh water handy so I can clean up the "mud" wet-sanding leaves behind and inspect my progress. Put a few drops of dishwashing liquid in a bowl or container and fill it with warm water. The soap helps the paper glide over the work by reducing the surface tension of the water. Load your sanding block with 400- or 500-grit paper and let it sit in the soapy water for about a minute until the paper is soaked and properly conditioned.

Begin sanding the panel in an up and down direction and with light pressure until you've reached the opposite side. Now turn your panel clockwise so the left side becomes the top; begin sanding again, this time crossing over the grain of the previous pass.

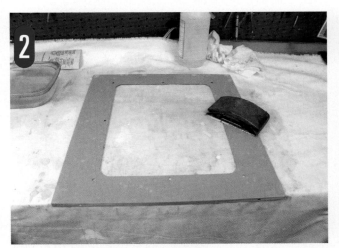

Going in a diagonal direction also helps to get an evenly sanded surface. A circular motion is not recommended for wet sanding because this can cause the corners and edges of your sanding block to dig into the paint and cause problems. Dip your sanding block in the water several times to rinse off the paint after each pass. If you find the sanding block sticking to the surface, you might have too much water on the panel, which can create a suction effect. In this case, remove some of the water from the surface with a paper towel. After a few passes with the 500-grit to get the heavy particles from the surface, load your sanding block with either 600-grit or 1,000-grit and higher depending on your progress. For trouble spots like the side panel handles, you should avoid using the sanding block and get these tight areas by hand, using a small piece of sandpaper.

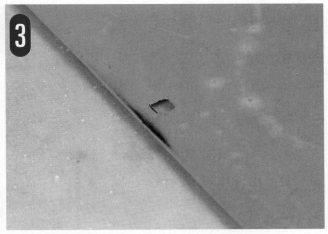

If you sand down to the previous layer of paint or even the bare metal, don't get discouraged; it's your panel's way of saying, "I have a high spot that needs sanding!" As you can see here, that's exactly what happened to me. If this happens, you just have to sand down that high spot and then give it a few more coats of primer after a good fresh water cleanup of the panel. Your final wet-sanding should leave your panel with a buttery soft satin finish that is even and free from heavy scratches.

Step 6: Applying the Color Coats (and, You Guessed It, More Wet-Sanding)

Just like you did when you applied the primer, shake the can of paint for a minute or so and give a 3-second blast of paint onto a piece of scrap paper to charge the can and clear out any dried particles. Start spraying the paint for a moment off of the panel and then across it in a sweeping motion about 10" away from the surface, ending each course of paint off of the panel. You should start painting at the bottom of the panel and work toward the top, holding the can at a slight angle to the work so the spray pattern is evenly distributed and slightly overlapping each course. Don't stop in the middle of your work and change directions because this can cause the paint to pool up and create heavy spots.

One drawback of painting with aerosol cans is the dreaded "orange peel" effect, which is bound to happen. Spray cans do not have the finest of mist patterns, and this causes the paint to create a dimpled surface texture, resembling the skin of an orange.

Color coats should be applied a little more heavily than the primer, creating a nice wet-looking surface after a few passes. Color paint takes longer to dry between coats than primer, so give each one about 15 minutes drying time. After from four to six coats of color, let your work dry overnight or, better yet, a full 48 hours before beginning the wet-sanding. This gives the paint time to harden up and helps prevent the paint from getting soft during sanding.

The object of your next course of wet-sanding is to sand out and flatten the paint, removing every last speck and dimple on the surface until it is satiny smooth, slightly reflective, and even.

You should give a few more coats of paint at this point and repeat the sanding process...again. For this project, I stopped after applying the second round of paint, allowed it to dry for a few days, and then did my final sanding.

The paint works by suspending tiny metallic particles on the surface, creating the glitter effect. Sanding this coat dulls those little metal bits, and they lose their sparkle. When applying metal flake paint, don't spray the surface of the work in two directions only. Rather, cover the surface by using a random combination of up and down and left to right motions. This helps evenly distribute the metallic glitter over the surface and prevent streaks and clusters of particles. Your last coat of lacquer should be as heavy as can be without causing pools or drips, and it should be allowed to cure for 48 hours. After that, a few heavy coats of a compatible clear topcoat should be applied.

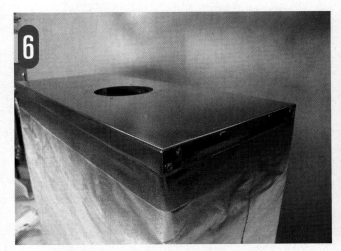

For the top panel, I used a lacquer-based "candy apple" metal flake paint from Plasti-Kote. Unlike the solid enamel color, metal flake should not be wet-sanded directly.

These clear coats must be wet-sanded with 600- to 2,000-grit paper until the surface is smooth, flat, and free of orange peel.

Step 7: Rubbing Compound and Finishing Glaze

It has been a few days, and you just can't stand to let the painted parts just sit around anymore, right? The last and final step is to use a rubbing compound and polishing glaze on the painted surfaces to draw out the beauty and shine that's hidden inside. The rubbing compound is basically like liquid sandpaper, but the abrasive particles are extremely fine, equivalent to about 6,000-grit. This removes the very fine scratches left behind by the 2,000-grit paper. Apply a small amount of compound (about the size of a nickel) to a clean terrycloth and begin rubbing a small section of painted surface with firm pressure in a circular motion. Keep rubbing until dry; then either flip the cloth over or use a clean one to remove the remainder of the compound.

You'll notice a bit of color left behind on the cloth, which is normal.

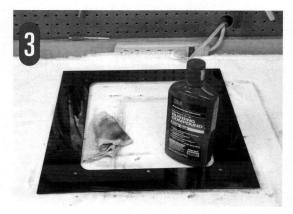

After the entire surface has been rubbed with compound, you should be left with a nice reflective surface. But it doesn't end here. Next comes the polishing glaze to create a deep, wet-look shine. With a cloth, apply the glaze to the entire surface and rub with a firm, circular motion. With a second cloth, buff the entire surface until it's clean and shiny.

As you can see, all that exhaustive wet-sanding and interminable waiting for paint to dry have paid off.

You can clearly see the mirror-like shine and the sharp reflections on the surface of the paint. Nice!

Step 8: Painting the Bezel

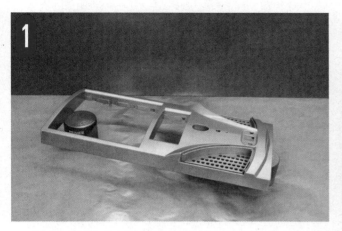

For the bezel, I had some Dupli-Color METALCAST blue in my paint cabinet and decided to use it up. The METALCAST paints simulate anodized metals in a two-part process. The first part is a ground coat of metallic silver paint, over which the color coat is applied. The color coat should be done lightly; too much paint and the ground coat is completely covered, ruining the effect. It's a pretty tricky paint to get used to, but with practice you can create an anodized look that can really fool people. I used this brand of paint on Mecanique (shown in Chapter 6, "Let There Be Lighting") and also for the front bezel of project Jujube (see Chapter 10, "Building the Ultimate Scratch-Built Mod").

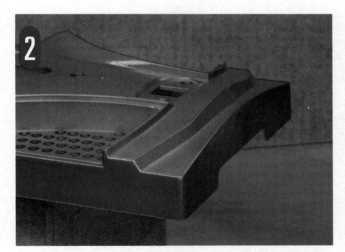

If you have the will and patience, you can get the same mirror shine on all the plastic parts of your case as well. Follow all the same steps as previously described, with the exception of using the sanding block. This level of detail should be done by hand, with small pieces of sandpaper.

Step 9: Admire, Gloat

For the photo op, I just had to throw in a few lights and a front bay fan controller with blue LEDs. I can now think of this project as a really cheap case with an expensive paint job. In the end, I think I succeeded in making this case look just a little bit better than it looked when it first arrived on my workbench. But just a little.

Easy-to-Do Airbrushing and Painting Techniques

Everyone has his own unique approach to case modding. Most modders bring their experience with various hobbies and professions. Model building, prop making, and prototyping have always been my passion, and it's pretty easy to see their influence in the pieces I create. If you've ever tried your hand at scale model building or even collecting *Warhammer*-type figurines, some of the techniques I use for painting the mouse pad in this chapter will be familiar to you. This type of painting I find extremely enjoyable (unlike wet-sanding case panels) and peaceful; it's also quiet and doesn't require a shop full of tools.

For this section, I'll illustrate straightforward airbrushing techniques from the perspective of a model builder. I'm by no means an "airbrush artist," but I've developed enough skills with the tool to get the results and effects I want. Those of you who might be intimidated by the airbrush, have no fear. It's just another tool, one that takes only a few hours to learn, and with practice you might just find a new hobby for yourself.

When I started case modding, I already had dozens of old model kits and boxes full of scrap parts in storage, waiting to be used in various projects. One of the earliest mods I made was the skull and serpent mouse pad (Figure 1). I had a mouse pad at the time with some sort of swiveling gel wrist rest built in, and the thing was annoying as heck. I eventually brought the pad to my worktable and carefully adjusted the wrist pad by ripping it off the frame and throwing the stupid thing in the trash. Did one of the industrial designers responsible for this mouse pad jump up at the meeting table one day and say, *"I have a brilliant idea! Let's create a mouse pad with a swiveling wrist rest that's totally uncomfortable and doesn't really work! We'll sell millions of 'em!"*?

I can't really blame the designers; after all, I was the sucker who purchased it. I did some kit-bashing and gap-filling on the mouse pad, attaching parts from a couple of Skillcraft-brand model kits—a life-sized human skull and a reptiles and amphibian kit. The stone texture is made from patterned plastic sheets by Plastruct, a company that makes scale and architectural model parts. I put a really quick paint job on this mouse pad at the time, but I was never happy with it. For this chapter, I decided to give the mouse pad a coat of flat black primer and start fresh.

Airbrush FAQs

What Can I Spray with an Airbrush?

Just about any paint or liquid can be sprayed with an airbrush, as long as it can be properly thinned. You can use them for

- Acrylic paints
- Enamels
- Lacquers
- Oil paints
- Inks
- Water colors
- Glazes
- Latex
- Textile paints
- Food coloring

What Are the Differences Between Single-Action and Double-Action Airbrushes?

When the trigger button (the air controller) is pressed on a single-action airbrush, the paint is mixed with air and sprayed at a constant paint flow rate, determined by an adjustment you make on a small valve. Single-action brushes are good for covering large areas such as murals and for spraying heavy fluids such as ceramic glazes and textile paints.

Double-action brushes integrate the air control and color/paint flow control into the trigger. Pressing down on the button releases only air; it's when you slowly pull back on the trigger that paint is gradually introduced into the mixing chamber and the color begins to flow. This type of airbrush allows you to control the width of the painted line and the intensity of the color without having to stop and make adjustments. For subtle fade effects, double-action is the way to go.

How Much Air Pressure Is Required?

Depending on the type of fluids being sprayed, the pressure needed to operate an artist's airbrush is fairly low: 20–40 pounds per square inch (PSI) at 1/2–1 cubic foot per minute (CFM) is sufficient for many brands.

Which Type of Air Compressor Should I Use?

Most airbrushes require only a small hobby-type compressor. The diaphragm compressor (like the Paasche D500 I use) does not have a holding tank for air; therefore, it's constantly running to produce the air pressure for the brush. Tank compressors store the air in a holding tank until the pressure is low, at which time the motor kicks in, charges the tank, and shuts off again. These are generally more expensive and, unlike diaphragm compressors, require oiling and occasional maintenance. A tank compressor can also be more versatile, allowing you to run automotive spray guns and pneumatic tools, as well as your airbrush. On both of these compressors, a moisture trap should be connected to the hose. These traps prevent water moisture from entering the air hose and fouling your paint.

Which Type of Airbrush Is Right for Me?

The best way to select an airbrush that's right for you is to visit an art supply store that has a knowledgeable staff. They can help you select an airbrush based on your painting needs, style, and budget. A good store will always let you try a particular brush right in the store. I strongly suggest getting a book and instructional video on airbrushing basics, or even signing up for a class in your area to help you get started.

Which Kinds of Safety Precautions Should I Take?

Glad you asked. As with any painting project, or anytime you're working with noxious chemicals, you should wear hand, eye, and lung protection. That means latex gloves, safety glasses, and a respirator. Everything I said earlier in this chapter in "Before You Get Started—Safety Precautions" applies here. Learn it. Know it. Live it.

Paasche VL Airbrush— My Weapon of Choice

The Paasche VL is a double-action airbrush great for painting models, t-shirts, and custom designs for automobiles and motorcycles. I like this general-purpose airbrush for its versatility, ease of use, and capability to spray many types of media. The double-action feature of this airbrush gives me the control I need to paint lines from 1/32'' to about 1'' without having to stop and make adjustments, as I would with a single-action model. Unlike aerosol paint cans, an airbrush is capable of laying down a very fine mist of atomized paint. It's the only tool that can create hair-thin painted lines, subtle washes, and color fades at the touch of a button. The airbrush is an extremely precise painting instrument; good results can be achieved only with meticulous care, cleaning, and maintenance. Take care of your tools and it will reflect in your work.

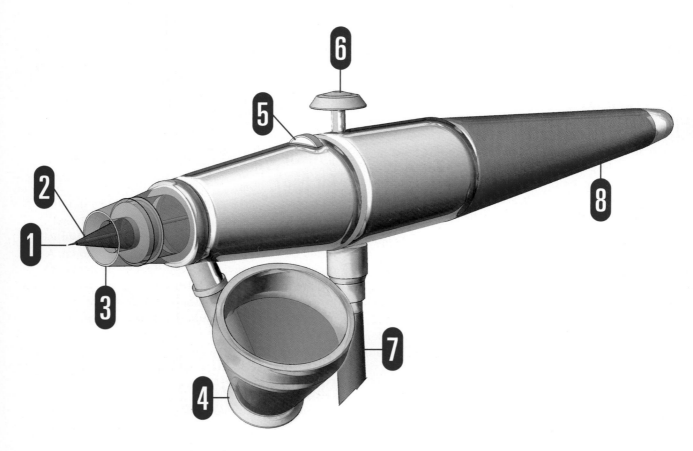

1 Needle

2 Cone tip

3 Air cap

4 Color cup

5 Line adjusting screw

6 Finger button (trigger)

7 Air hose

8 Handle

Tools and Materials for Our Airbrushing Project

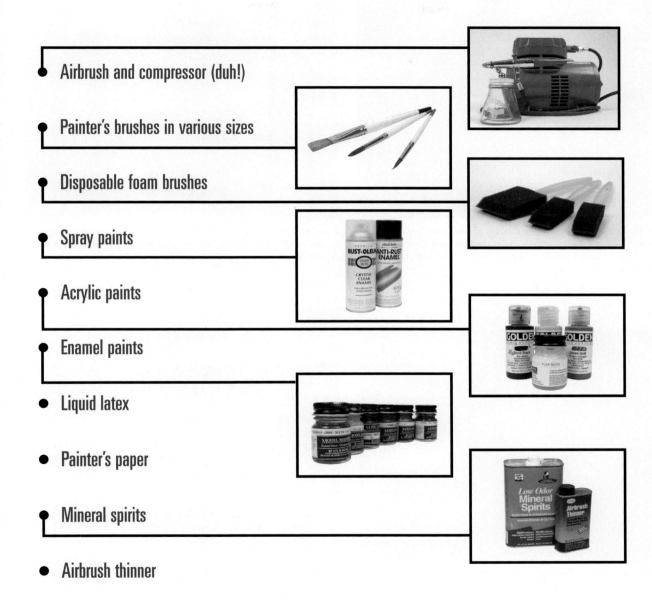

- Airbrush and compressor (duh!)

- Painter's brushes in various sizes

- Disposable foam brushes

- Spray paints

- Acrylic paints

- Enamel paints

- Liquid latex

- Painter's paper

- Mineral spirits

- Airbrush thinner

Step 1: Prepping the Mouse Pad

I gave the mouse pad a few good coats of flat black Krylon enamel, covering all the sins from my previous paint job. Even under good lighting conditions, I had a hard time seeing the detail and texture of the skull model.

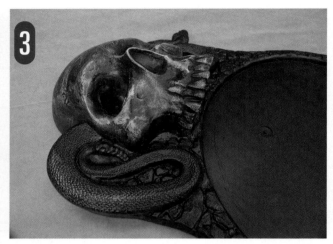

Because the base coat of black paint is enamel, I used a water-based acrylic paint for the dusting, which prevented it from mixing with and softening the enamel.

To help guide my airbrushing, I used a wide, flat artist's brush to lightly "dust" the surface details of the skull to make them pop.

Knowing the properties of the paint you're using is important, and one slip-up can destroy hours of work by using the wrong combinations. Here are the basics:

Acrylic paint over—Dried enamels, lacquers, and other water-based paint

Acrylic paint under—Enamels and water-based paints

Enamel paint over—Acrylics, enamels, lacquers, and water-based paints

Enamel paint under—Acrylics and water-based paints

Lacquer paint over—Some enamel primers, other lacquers, and unpainted surfaces

Lacquer paint under—Enamels, acrylics, and water-based paints

Step 2: Airbrushing for Shadow and Light

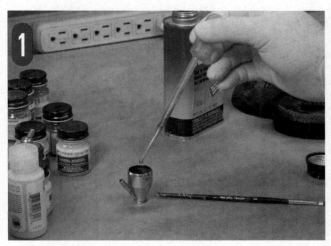

The key to getting even and consistent flow from an airbrush relies heavily on the careful thinning and mixing of the paint. The easiest way to judge the proper ratio between solvent and paint is to keep the mix about the same consistency as whole milk. Spattering, running, and dripping occur if the mix is too thin. If the mix is too heavy, the paint might not flow at all, or flow for a few seconds and quickly begin to clog the tip and mixing chamber of the airbrush. With some leather brown Model Master enamel paint in my color cup, I used a plastic pipette to add drops of thinner (mineral spirits).

To achieve the depth of color I wanted in the skull, I started with the darkest brown first. This is also a good method for just about any type of painting; start with the darkest colors and work your way to the lightest. This helps create depth and shadows where they might not exist on your model. I didn't cover the black base coat completely; I left certain areas thin or unpainted, such as the eye sockets and nasal septum to keep them dark and deep looking. Next, I returned a small amount of the brown from the color cup back into the jar and added a few drops of white.

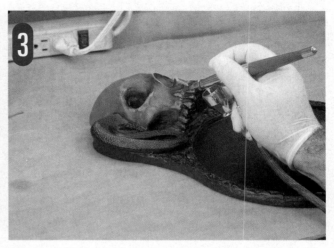

I then gave it a good mix with the handle of a paint brush, a habit I picked up many years ago, for some reason—maybe because the handle is just a darn stick and is convenient.

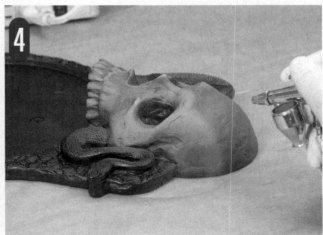

After a drop or two of thinner and another mix, I began using this lighter shade to highlight and outline the raised areas of the skull, particularly around the eye sockets, maxilla bones, and frontal bone.

5 I repeated the process again, going a few shades lighter this time and hitting the same areas but with a thinner spray pattern so I wouldn't completely cover my last shade.

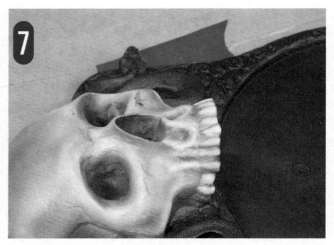

7 After I had the paint highlighting at a point where I was satisfied, it was time to get down and dirty and have some fun with a little glazing and sponge painting.

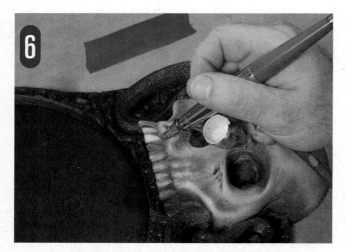

6 I eventually worked the colors up to an almost pure white and put a little of this on the teeth. With an airbrush, you can paint with the tool very close to the work because of the fine control of air pressure and color flow that you have.

Step 3: Sponge Painting and Glaze Effects

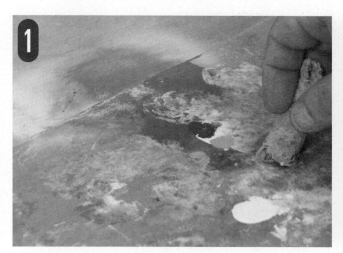

Sponge painting, or *stippling*, is a method of painting that allows you to lay down interesting textures and patterns of color on flat or sculpted surfaces. The method I like to use is to pour out several colors right on a work table covered with painter's paper and use it as a palette. You can see that I have some leather brown, yellow, and white enamel colors that I'm beginning to mix on my palette with a small piece of torn sponge. You can use any type of natural sponge, such as a sea sponge (large cells) or regular kitchen cleanup type (small, tight cells), depending on the scale of the texture and pattern you want. I first dampened the sponge with water to open the cells; then I gave it a dip in some mineral spirits.

Next, I began lightly applying the paint to the skull by tapping where I wanted a subtle effect, and heavier where I wanted a more solid coverage. The goal with the stippling was to blend the airbrushing I did earlier without completely covering it, allowing the brightest highlights and some of the dark areas to remain visible beneath this layer. I was careful not to wipe the sponge on the surface because this creates unwanted streaks of paint. Before I allowed the sponge painting to get too opaque, I began adding a clear enamel paint to my palette right from the spray can.

Getting the colors I wanted was a matter of dipping the sponge here and there—some brown, some white, a touch of yellow, and so on. I moved the sponge to a clean area of the palette now and then to test the color, the amount of paint on my sponge, and the consistency.

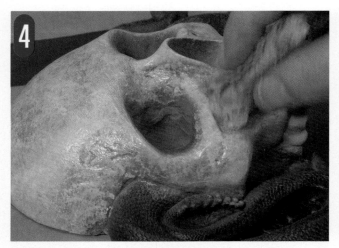

With a fresh, dampened piece of sponge, I mixed very small amounts of color paint with the clear to create a glaze. With this milky paint, I stippled the entire skull, further blending in the previous course of sponging and the underlying airbrushing. This translucent glaze gave all the layers of paint a nice depth of color and texture that accents light and shadow. For even better depth and spectacular highlights, you can repeat the process of stippling and glaze sponging until you achieve the results you want.

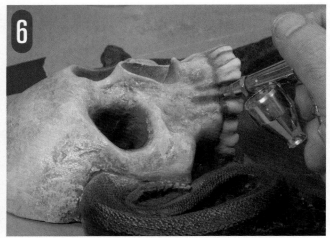

I thinned out some black acrylic paint and mixed it up in the color cup of my airbrush. I kept the paint viscosity a little heavier to prevent spattering as I began to paint in dark areas and details to the skull. I worked with the airbrush very close to the work to paint in between the teeth, nasal septum, and eye sockets. If my airbrushing got too heavy, I went back with a little glaze mix to soften and lighten it up. I continued with this combination of airbrush and glaze sponging until I was satisfied with the look. The goal wasn't necessarily to create a realistic-looking dried-out old skull, but to create sort of a caricature of one, bolder and larger than life. You can make your own painted mouse pad look like anything you want, and don't let anyone tell you otherwise. As an artist, you are in control of what you create, and to a plastic skull and serpent or any other piece, you are the supreme being. I put the piece aside for a few minutes drying time before I moved on to painting the serpent.

At this point, I let the paint settle and dry for about an hour under the warmth of my work lamp.

Step 4: Rubber Masking and Painting the Serpent

If you're intrigued enough to invest in an airbrush, you'll find that an entire world of helpful accessories is available. Airbrushing is all about the technique, and although a good eye and steady, practiced hand are very important, there are tools to help you along. Want painted hot rod flames on your case mod? No problem. Solvent-resistant airbrushing templates (also referred to as *shields* and *stencils*) are available that have precut patterns in many shapes. You'll find clouds, flames, skulls and bones, circles, flags, geometric shapes, and more. These are not just painting shortcuts for beginners; they

are the tools that just about every pro airbrush artist has in her bag of tricks.

The intricate airbrushed graphics you see on case mods, automobiles, and so on have all gone through a process of painting that uses many underlying layers. To protect each preceding layer, masking film (known as *frisket film*) is often used. This translucent, low-tack adhesive material is applied directly to the work and leaves no residue behind that can damage the surface. For razor-sharp lines and super-realistic detailing, there is no substitute.

Because I was painting a model here and not flowers and butterflies, I used liquid latex (to protect my previously painted skull from overspray). You'll find liquid latex in Halloween shops and at theatrical makeup suppliers for a few dollars. This brush-on liquid rubber is good for masking on irregular, textured surfaces, such as the separation between the skull and serpent.

With a disposable foam brush, I applied several layers of latex to the skull (only near the serpent) to build up the mask. I used a hair dryer to help cure the latex between coats.

With the skull protected from overspray, I laid down a base coat of color for the serpent. I did a Google search for some rattlesnake images (the model is actually a rattlesnake) and used them for inspiration and to get some sort of skin pattern going.

I then returned to my base coat color and added white, lightening it up to paint inside the white pattern. After that, I painted on a little burnt sienna and some more "organized randomness" to the pattern. I then was ready to remove the rubber masking.

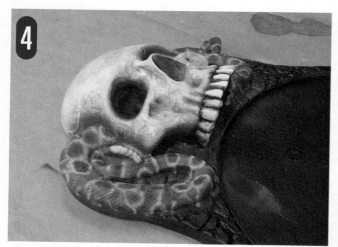

I started with pure white, creating patterns on the serpent with the airbrush. More than once I went back with a base coat color when I made a mistake or the pattern was just too heavy.

If your underlying paint is good and dry, you can peel the mask off without damaging or taking off the paint beneath with it.

The serpent model has a nice scale texture, so I took advantage of this and did some dry-brushing on it. Dry brushing is another classic model and figurine painting technique in which just the very tips and highlights of details are painted with a light color. The concept is easy to learn; however, it takes practice to get it just right and avoid overpainting the surface.

I began lightly scrubbing the model with the brush, leaving behind white paint on the scales without covering the colors beneath. If you have too much paint on your brush, you'll wind up smearing your previous paint job, while too little paint will not bring out the fine details. This technique, like glazing, is another way of creating lighting effects and fooling the eye with paint. By starting with darker colors and building up to the lightest, you can create incredibly subtle and realistic-looking objects with dry brushing.

I applied a small amount of white paint to a 1/2" flat brush and began removing most of the paint by scrubbing it on a clean part of my paper palette.

Next came all the little details, like the rattle on the tail, the eyes, and the mouth of the serpent. For these, I used a small, soft sable brush and painted directly from the jar, thinning where necessary. Now that the skull and serpent were painted, I went back and cleaned up all the overspray on the stone texture with black paint and a sable artist's brush. For the hard-to-reach areas, I thinned out the black paint until it was very loose and let the paint wash over the stone and into the cracks. The stone was painted using the dry brush technique with dark grays and a touch of green and was finished off with a light frosting of very light gray to make it pop.

Step 5: Admire, Gloat

To wrap up the project, I added some sheen to the serpent with clear satin enamel. I sprayed some paint right from the rattle can of clear paint into a tin can; then I transferred it to the color cup on my airbrush. Now I was able to carefully paint the serpent and avoid getting the paint on the rocks. After 3 years of sitting on a shelf collecting dust, this skull and serpent mouse pad might actually get used now that it has a respectable paint finish.

How the Pros Paint Cases

Learn how the pros at Smooth Creations turn an ordinary computer case into something extraordinary

Regular readers of *Maximum PC* are probably familiar with the spectacular paint jobs that adorn Falcon Northwest's gaming PCs. Indeed, the Medford, Oregon-based company actually commissions a professional auto-painting operation to provide the craftsmanship and customization that characterize Falcon PCs.

So, it should come as no surprise that we chose Smooth Creations to paint and decal our 2002 Dream Machine—a no-holds-barred celebration of the best a desktop computer can be (at the time, that is). We asked Kelt Reeves, Falcon Northwest's president, to take us on a guided tour of the PC's aesthetic transformation, from its humble beginnings to beauteous end. Follow along as the unassuming Cooler Master ATC-110 you see pictured here becomes the looker that was *Maximum PC*'s 2002 Dream Machine.

Our virgin case sans the paint and decals.

Step 1: Get Yourself an Art Department

DREAM Machine 2002

MAXIMUM PC   SPEED✓TESTED   *"Overclocked & Ready to Burn"*

Creating the basic design can be the most challenging part because practically anything you can imagine can be applied to a case. The inspiration for *Maximum PC's* Dream Machine was a BMW 2002 Turbo sports car, and our goal was to translate the classic car's aesthetic to a square-shaped box. *Maximum PC* made this step easy on us: Art Director Natalie Jeday created her own design in Adobe Illustrator, a vector-based drawing program, which is exactly what vinyl graphics shops like to work from.

Smooth Creations has executed case designs that range from a simple single-color paint job to any combination of vinyl lettering, graphics, airbrushing, and even embedded full-color photographs and artwork. The *Maximum PC* Dream Machine called for just paint and vinyl—lots of vinyl. Vinyl can be used for actual decals that are embedded in the paint or to mask areas of the case during painting. Because we were able to obtain vinyl in all the colors *Maximum PC* had specified, we decided to apply the vinyl to the case instead of having masks made.

Vinyl graphics are used on everything from street signs to race cars to those annoying decals of a peeing Calvin that you see on the back windows of pickup trucks. Luckily for us, Nick and Gary from Razor's Edge vinyl shop in Medford, California, can create all types of vinyl graphics. You, too, almost certainly have a vinyl shop in your hometown.

Vinyl graphics cutting is done on a specialized machine called a *plotter*. The plotter essentially draws a line between two points. But instead of using pen on paper, vinyl plotters use a wickedly sharp blade on paper-backed vinyl. Before the vinyl can be cut, the vinyl artist goes over every vector in the design to ensure that every line of every letter is complete and will cut properly. When the design is ready, it's then translated into special vinyl-cutting software. In this case, it's Flexisign Pro, a $5,000 program designed for sign makers. One of the unique features of this program is that it allows printing by color. Because the vinyl sheets have to be loaded and cut one color at a time, this software makes it easy to cut only the parts of the design that use the color you're currently working on.

Step 2: Off to the Vinyl Shop

Step 3: Cut the Vinyl Graphics

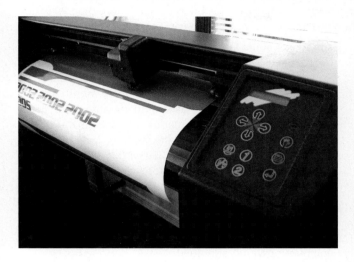

The vinyl itself is interesting stuff. It is waterproof; is fade resistant; and comes in hundreds of colors, metallics, and even reflective surfaces (as you've probably seen on emergency vehicles). The vinyl is actually a soft PVC film with an adhesive backing, mounted on silicon paper.

The plotter Razor's Edge uses is an amazing piece of precision equipment. Just the blades for this beast costs $30 a piece, and they typically last just 2 weeks. With tolerances literally down to millionths of an inch, the plotter can score the 2-millimeter thick vinyl just deep enough to cut it, without cutting all the way through its paper backing. One-millionth of an inch too shallow, and the vinyl won't cut. One-millionth of an inch too deep, and the paper will be cut through—outputting your job as a horrendous pile of confetti. Here we see the SummaGraphics plotter in action.

If you want to apply vinyl to your case, we strongly recommend you have it cut at a vinyl shop. Creating your own decal requires you to trace a printout using a razor blade knife. The vinyl itself is not printable with either an inkjet (remember, it's waterproof) or laser printer (it will melt and could catch fire).

We asked Nick why he was cutting out several copies of each vinyl graphic when the case design called for just one set. The answer became clear when Nick pulled excess vinyl from around the freshly cut graphics, a process called *weeding*. While the large stripes stayed put, fully one third of the small letters pulled off with the excess material. "Acceptable losses," Nick said. Evidently, in the vinyl game, you throw away much more material than you actually keep. Vinyl is very elastic, and thin pieces are easily pulled off (or stretched by accident) during weeding. For this reason, pinstripes of 1/8'' or less are nearly impossible to create with vinyl. And, as if that weren't enough, every center of every closed letter has to be painstakingly removed from the paper backing with a razor blade—by hand. Surprisingly, Nick still has his eyesight and most of his sanity.

As you might surmise, it pays to have your vinyl shop run off multiple copies of whatever you want to apply to your case. If you somehow stretch your decal or get it all stickied-up, you'll want a backup copy. We should also note that some shops won't even do single-logo jobs; minimum quantities vary.

Step 4: Weeding Sucks

Step 5: Get Yourself the Best Auto Painter You Can Find

We thought it was a crime to paint the beautiful aluminum Cooler Master cases—until we saw Jim's work. Jim (we'll just call him Jim because he's in the Witness Protection Program) is a Master car painter. I say *Master* with a capital *M* because that's actually a level in his trade. Jim has been painting cars for more than 20 years and has won many awards and car show competitions.

Jim works at the largest auto body shop on the West Coast. We'd give you the name of the shop, but it, too, is in the Witness Protection Program. This 40,000-square-foot shop paints more than 400 cars every month and has five car-size ovens for baking on the auto paint. Each of these thermal downdraft car ovens costs upwards of $250,000, has its own built-in life support system, and can bake a car (or PC) at up to 300°. After seeing the work Jim does on cars and motorcycles like this one, we knew he was up to the challenge of our PC cases.

You might be able to find an auto body shop in your area that will take on your job. Call around. Or finish reading this section, and decide whether you're ready to paint your own rig at home.

For the 2002 Dream Machine to remain true to its 1973 BMW 2002 Turbo inspiration, we needed an exact match of the classic car's original factory paint—Polaris Silver. But how do you match a car that hasn't been manufactured in almost 30 years? A specialized Sartorius ColorMix computer is used for the task. The machine contains a database of every color on every car ever manufactured and the color elements that comprise them. The computer tells the mixmaster which pigments to mix by weight, and he pours them into a can on a scale connected to the computer.

Because the Polaris Silver we mixed is an exact replica of the 1973 BMW factory paint, it's not as bright or metallic as paints made today. Evidently, in 1973, paint makers couldn't achieve the suspension of the courser metallic flakes used in today's metallics and pearlcoats. *Maximum PC* intentionally sacrificed some flashiness to be faithful to the original automobile.

Professional auto paints consist of chemicals that are much tougher and more beautiful than anything you can find at your local paint store. But they're also much more dangerous. For this reason, most professional paint stores do not sell to the general public.

Your paint options might be limited, but be sure to choose an automotive-grade paint or one that's recommended for the surface you're working on. A spray can is the recommended method of application in the absence of a professional spray gun.

Step 6: Smells Like... Brain Damage

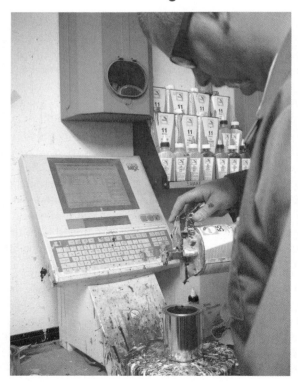

Step 7: Reduce Your Case to Pieces

Auto paints require intense heat to dry, and auto ovens can melt a plastic grill right out of a car if a painter neglects to remove it. So, a baked-on finish is not something to attempt with any plastic or plastic-fronted PC. Even the 2002 Dream Machine's all-aluminum ATC-110 has plastic fans, wiring, and LEDs that all had to be removed by hand to keep them from turning into a puddle of goo during the baking process. Here, Randy is using heavy-duty tape to secure each piece of the case to the spray tables.

Obviously, if you decide to have a plastic case painted, baking is out of the question.

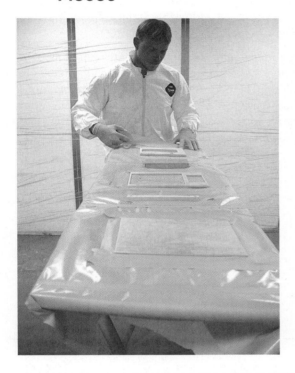

If you want to make a new paint job stick, you have to first strip off all traces of its original finish. You'll notice the painter is working with rubber gloves. Any salts or acids from your fingers soak into aluminum (a very porous metal) and can ruin the paint later. A fingerprint can show through 15 layers of paintwork, so wearing gloves is critical.

An orbital sander and sandpaper is another way to take the finish off a metal case. On a plastic case, your concern is cleaning the surface of release agents (chemicals used to release the case from its mold). For this, stick to a Scotch Brite pad and soapy water.

Step 8: Totally Ruin a Fine Finish

Step 9: Fun with Acid

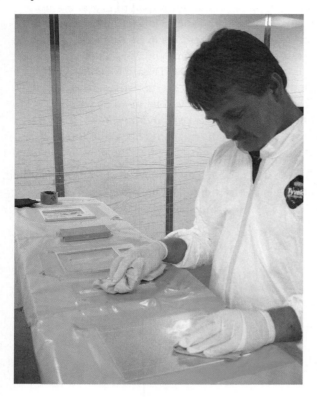

Please add phosphoric acid to the list of products "our lawyer says we can't recommend you use at home." This lovely substance is a light acid wash Jim used to rub down all the painted surfaces. The phosphoric acid eats away a tiny bit of the aluminum, removing microscopic corrosion already present in any exposed metal. It provides good, clean metal for the paint to bond with, and without this vital step, the paint won't adhere correctly and can flake off.

A product such as Jasco Metal Etch contains phosphoric acid and is suitable for prepping metals before painting. It costs about $4 a bottle and can be purchased at most hardware stores. Follow the safety instructions, and be sure to rinse the case's surface with water when you're done.

Our panels were finally ready for the first of the 15 layers that would be applied to them. The first layer was zinc chromate, known more commonly as aluminum etch. This yellowish goo provides a layer of corrosion protection for the freshly exposed aluminum. Yes, aluminum rusts, but it's not the normal reddish-brown rust. Aluminum oxidization actually looks like fine white powder, and it ruins a paint job.

Because it's a highly toxic substance, zinc chromate cannot be found just anywhere. In California, for instance, its use is strictly regulated. So you might just want to play it safe and substitute zinc chromate with a couple layers of sprayed-on primer (be your case metal or plastic).

Step 10: First Layer . . . and It's Still Not Paint

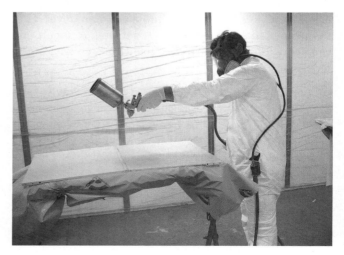

Step 11: Let's Mix Toxins!

We mentioned before that the Polaris Silver brew was just the pigment. Next, Jim mixed in the chemicals that would turn it into paint: reducer and activator. Jim, an avid *Maximum PC* reader, explained that the "reducer is like the PCI bus; it carries the paint through the system to its destination." The activator is a hardener that quickly dries the paint layers and makes them tougher. It does this via a process called *gassing out*—essentially, the solvents vaporize, leaving behind a tough layer of pigment. The whole concoction was loaded into Jim's Satajet 90 pneumatic spray gun, which he uses specifically for base coat jobs.

It's unlikely you'll have access to professional acrylic-urethane paint, so you'll probably be using enamel paint in a spray can. Although enamel isn't as strong or chemical resistant, it also doesn't need to be baked.

Many colors require just two base coats to achieve the desired shade, but silver is very transparent. So, three layers were necessary for a proper coating. Between each layer of silver base coat, Jim let the paint gas out for 5–7 minutes. If the solvents aren't allowed this time to evaporate, the paint will eventually blister and pop where the gas has been trapped.

With enamel, your paint should gas out for at least 30 minutes between coats. When applying coats, use smooth, even strokes that go in the same direction. Multiple thin coats are better than a single thick coat. Always gas out in between.

Step 12: Apply the Base Coat

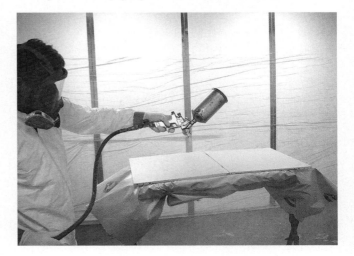

Step 13: Clear Coat Can Kill

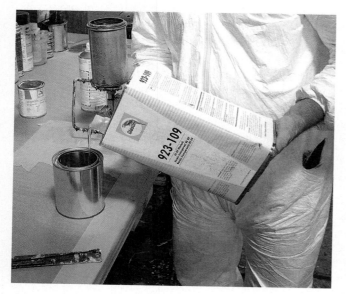

You might remember the Jonestown massacre in 1978, wherein a cult leader killed more than 900 followers by giving them Kool-Aid laced with isocyanate—a deadly poison if ingested. Because paint manufacturers seem to love deadly chemicals, they use isocyanate in making high-solids acrylic urethane, or *clear coat*. The fact is, clear coat makes all paint jobs look better; it gives both cars and Falcon PCs that gorgeous sheen. It's perfectly safe after baking, but in its liquid state it must not be touched, inhaled, or mixed with Kool-Aid because it can kill you.

In fact, isocyanate vapors can permeate your skin, causing the whites of your eyes to turn yellow, cirrhosis of the liver, and internal bleeding. Jim said that many old-school car painters refused to use the carbon filter gasmasks that allow safe use of isocyanates. Because your body cannot purge isocyanates, after you've inhaled enough of this stuff over the years, a mere whiff of it will make you vomit. According to Jim, a lot of the older guys doing car pinstriping today were once painters who inhaled too much isocyanate and can no longer tolerate being near the stuff.

But clear coat looks really sexy, so we decided to use lots of it. We started by applying clear coat over the base coat to give our vinyl graphics a perfect, smooth surface to adhere to. There would be much more clear coating later. For the clear coats, Jim used a different spray gun, a SataJetRP. It provides very quick atomization of the acrylic urethane as it's ejected from the spray gun, and this prevents clumping.

You can buy cans of enamel clear coat at the same shop where you buy your enamel paint. The two substances work fine together, but for best results you should stick with the same manufacturer for both your paint and clear coat. To be extra safe, do a test run on a small area (such as a drive rail) to ensure your paint and clear coat work well together.

After the first clear layer had been applied, the finish needed to be baked on. For standard paintwork without vinyl graphics, we would have applied three layers of the clear coat and then done the baking. However, the vinyl graphics needed to be applied to an already baked, "finished" paint job. So, after applying aluminum etch, three layers of base coat, and the first layer of clear coat, we put our parts into the oven.

Although we do know of a few readers who've baked painted PCs inside their kitchen ovens, we can't recommend you go down this dubious path. Also, most do-it-yourselfers use enamel paint, so baking is therefore a nonissue.

Step 14: Preheat Oven and Bake

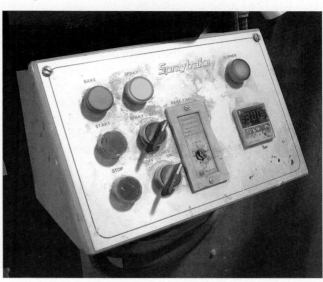

Step 15: Lay Down the Vinyl

When our clear coat was ready, we needed to lay our vinyl stickers in the approximate positions dictated by *Maximum PC's* art director. To position the decals accurately, we applied tape as guides to keep our lines exactly straight and used application fluid—a slippery substance that allows the decals to be moved around a bit after their sticky backing has been exposed. You can also use soap and water for this stage. Many of our graphics, such as "speed tested," were actually multilayered. The black layer went down first. We let it dry a bit, and then the white layer was wet down and placed on top. Lastly, we soaked the transfer paper so it could be carefully peeled away.

When you apply two layers of vinyl to a case panel, the vinyl naturally sticks above your paintwork in places. This vinyl has to be protected by submerging it in clear coat until the surface of the case is once again smooth and perfect. We did this with five more layers of clear coat. After two or three new layers of clear coat had been applied, they again needed to be baked. You can't do too many layers of clear without baking them on because they start to pool and get uneven if applied too thickly when wet. So, after we baked our second layer of clear coat, another two layers of clear coat were added and the PC was baked for a third time.

Step 16: Sweet, Sweet Clear Coat . . .

Step 17: Mmmm . . . Fresh-Baked Viper!

Because Jim's oven burns $100 worth of electricity every time it's run, the Master painter usually bakes our parts along with a car he's working on. In this shot, you can see *Maximum PC's* case baking alongside an $80,000 Dodge Viper! (Let's hope the owner of the car understands the honor he was bestowed.)

After all the larger pieces of the case were decaled, there was still some detail work to attend to. It turned out the vinyl stripes we had made for the front air grill were exactly the width of the grill, but we needed that color to wrap around the edges a bit so no gaps would show when it was installed. Jim therefore had to match tiny bits of blue, purple, and red paint to the color of the vinyl, and he used a small artist's airbrush for this detail work. Here we see Jim carefully masking and painting half of the tiny reset button where a stripe crosses it.

Step 18: Finish Up

Step 19: How to Scratch That Beautiful Clear Coat

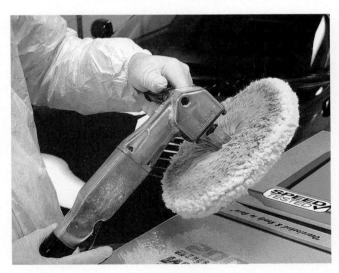

Despite Jim's precision gunning, clear coat is never 100% perfect at first. It will have a few broken bubbles and imperfections that need to be sanded out. For this, Jim uses the application fluid again and a fine-grit sandpaper.

Once sanded, the clear coat's imperfections are gone, but the sandpaper makes it look hazy due to the thousands of fine scratches just made. To bring out its brilliant shine, Jim used 3M's Perfect-It rubbing compound. Rubbing compound is basically very fine-grit liquid sandpaper. He applied it with a pneumatic polisher and two different grades of foam discs (one soft, one really soft) and polished it to a gorgeous shine.

Just like any other fine automobile finish, the Dream Machine looks best when you can see your reflection in the shine. To achieve this effect, Jim applied a thin layer of car wax. Not just any car wax, mind you. New paint jobs are "soft" for about their first 6 months of life. Tiny bits of solvent gas out of the finish during this time, hardening the paint to a tough protective shell. It's important during the first 6 months that these solvents not be trapped in the paint, lest they cause blistering and cracking. So, be sure to use a wax that's labeled breathable or that's specifically intended for new paint jobs.

Step 20: "He Never Drives It, Ferris. He Just Polishes It with a Diaper."

Master painter Jim Saling will take questions regarding home projects at his website, at www.smooth-creations.com (oops, did we just blow his cover?).

Step 21: Enjoy!

And Sometimes Even Paint Need Not Be "Paint"

Jerami Campbell's case-modding exploits have appeared in many issues of *Maximum PC*. But the creation you see on this page—the Mini LAN Party Rig, chosen as our Rig of the Month in April 2003—might be most remarkable for its paint job that...well...doesn't look like a paint job.

The rig's well-worn appearance comes courtesy of an iron-based paint Jerami mixed himself. That's right—iron-based paint. Jerami followed the initial painting with an application of a solution that *rusts* the iron. He then applied a seal that protects against potential rust stains and toxins. Jerami explains in greater detail:

"It takes a lot to make the case rust 'naturally.' Sometimes you can see brush strokes, or the color of rust is too strong or not strong enough. Plus, it's hard to get the same tone of rust throughout the entire case. Once I was happy with the rust, I had to spray-seal the entire case. This darkens the rust, sometimes dramatically, but you have to seal it because rust is toxic and it stains."

Jerami advises us that a company called Modern Options (www.modernoptions.com) now sells "antiquing solutions" that can give new objects the look of old—everything from authentic rust to a "verdigris patina."

The Mini LAN Party Rig is an all-in-one party companion that includes storage for a keyboard, mouse, and headphones. Jerami needed to extend the case by an inch to fit in everything he wanted. To do this, he took a Dremel tool to a couple of old Asus motherboards and then constructed a new case face by joining the mobo pieces together with copper channeling and a soldering iron (á la stained-glass assembly).—J.P.

All packed and ready to go, the rig weighs in at a manageable 35 lbs. The box is 13.5" tall, 7.5" wide, and 18.5" deep.

A custom-built cubby holds Jerami's Virtually Indestructible Keyboard, his Microsoft Intellimouse Explorer, a Nostromo game pad, and a pair of headphones.

The computer power supply, network hub, and monitor all plug into a power strip that resides inside the case, keeping things nice and tidy for easy transport.

This square of mobo was home to a processor back in the day. Now it adds flourish to a custom fan vent.

Chapter Five

Fans, Fans, and More Fans

We show you how to make your case blow...

David Prudenti's "Pyramid PC" was *Maximum PC*'s October 2004 Rig of the Month and was built to resemble the Egyptian pyramids. Prudenti refers to his mod as "an artistic tribute to radical beliefs" and is a to-scale Plexiglas replica of Giza's Great Pyramid.

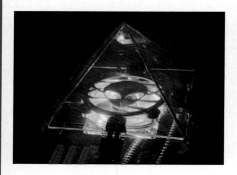

The pyramid is guarded by alien-head fan grills and includes a vented, detachable capstone at the tip of the pyramid, which allows an interior fan at the top of the case to pull hot air up and out of the case. Each side of the case has a decal bearing the image of an actual crop circle. Much like we explain in Chapter 1, "Prep Work: Laying the Perfect Foundation," Prudenti first conceptualized his design in an illustration program and then built a cardboard mock-up before he began building.

Bill Owen modified a wheel from an R/C truck to fit inside the center of this 80mm laser-cut grill.

This Bill Owen-designed aluminum fan sports a custom-designed laser-cut acrylic grill. Laser-cut grills are available off the shelf, but they are limited to fairly uninteresting designs.

Bill Owen constructed the Nemisis9 turbine from some very clever parts, including a 4"–3" PVC closet flange pipe and a 1 3/4" R/C plane prop spinner. After shaping the bodywork, Bill applied Datsun 280Z Orange Mist factory paint with an airgun.

These are not the jet turbines of some new military aircraft engine but close to it. Bill Owen has perfected the art of the fan mod, using model aircraft *spinners* to create the look of power and speed. The 120mm aluminum framed Panaflo fans are from a pair of extinct '80's-style IBM server power supply units. You can find instructions on making your own incredible fan mods (and lots more) on Bill's website at www.mnpctech.com.

This Bill Owen-designed 120mm fan was fitted inside a 3 7/8" fan duct, capped off with an 1 3/4" propeller spinner, and finished with metallic blue paint.

The 92mm rings on this fan were cut on a computer numerical control (CNC) milling machine by Bill Owen and modeled after an aircraft fuel filler assembly. A Proline R/C Truck spinner was attached to the top.

The art and practice of PC case cooling has long been a topic of, dare I say, *heated discussion* among hardcore enthusiasts. While doing the research for this chapter, I focused my sights on articles, whitepaper studies, and discussions pertaining to the most basic of cooling apparatuses—the humble case fan. You can easily spend many hours (like I did) pouring over the charts, comparisons, and collected data regarding the physics and theory behind case cooling with 12VDC fans. When the back-and-forth arguments on several well-respected community forums left me with more questions than answers, I sat down with a cup of coffee and a few whitepapers. To my surprise, I found some very interesting reading hidden among the jargon and technical data offered by these engineering notes.

Some of the information I found can be helpful in planning future cooling strategies. To better understand the fundamentals of case cooling, let's turn to the enclosures themselves. The basic advanced technology extended (ATX) standard PC case is designed with the necessary architecture in mind to bring outside air into a case to cool off the components and then exhaust the warmer air. The principle of this case design usually relies on fan intake at the front of the case, airflow across the components, and fan exhaust out the back. This is not by any means a streamlined process considering that components like AGP and audio cards, not to mention wires, cables, and even RAM, are great at blocking airflow and creating turbulence. In the end, this forced convection method of cooling does work and seems to be the best option that current case design offers.

Because every design and interior layout of a PC case is different, there really isn't a "one-size-fits-all" solution for cooling with fans. It boils down to striking a balance between adequate air movement, noise levels, and (of course) aesthetics. Following are the basics of DC fan cooling that you should consider for your own case modding projects.

Positive Pressure, Negative Pressure, and Neutral Pressure

Several schools of thought exist regarding the best methods for cooling the typical PC enclosure— whether to create a positive pressure, a negative pressure, or a neutral pressure environment inside the case:

• **Positive pressure**—In a positive pressure fan setup, air is forced into the case at the front, creating (very slight) atmospheric pressure inside the case. It is then forced out the back through the vents (or any openings, for that matter).

• **Negative pressure**—A negative pressure (or *evacuation*) cooling environment is achieved by placing exhaust fans at the back of the case and drawing outside air into the cabinet from vents toward the front or, again, any custom opening you care to chop out of it.

- **Neutral pressure**—In a neutral pressure setup, a fan (or fans) is placed at the front of the case and one (or more) at the rear. Typically, you have an equal number of fans (or equal CFM rating) at the front and rear.

All these methods work perfectly fine. However, each has a few pros and cons you should consider. In a negative pressure setup, for instance, it's more difficult to place a filter on an exhaust fan to prevent dust from entering through cracks and crevices in the case (the drawback to filters, though, is that they cut the fans' efficiency). In a neutral pressure setup, using filter material on the front fans decreases their pressure and efficiency, therefore allowing dust to enter the exhaust fans through cracks and crevices. It seems, then, that a positive pressure method of case cooling wins the cup. However, even that has a quirk: The slight heat generated by the fan itself is forced into the cabinet. When building a custom case, it is very important to remember that your case cooling strategy should be among the first design decisions you consider carefully.

See "Properly Positioning Case Fans" later in this chapter.

Cubic Feet per Minute

A fan's capacity to move and exchange air inside your case is measured in a rate called *cubic feet per minute (CFM)*. This rate varies greatly between manufacturer, type, and size of fan. To measure the CFM ratings of fans, testing labs and technicians use a handy little device called a *thermoanemometer*. Although its name is a mouthful, it works fairly simply. A small fan blade built in to the device measures the velocity of air coming from a fan, and the built-in sensors return an accurate reading in feet per minute. Pretty neat, huh? Sure, but what does all this CFM stuff mean for you and your case cooling needs? Let's use a simple formula that gives a pretty good estimate of the kind of air movement you can expect from your fans.

For example, let's take an *empty* mid tower case 17" high × 8" wide × 19" deep.

When you divide those numbers by 12 and then multiply them, you get a measurement inside the case of 1.50 cubic feet of air. Here's the math:

17÷12=1.42
8÷12=.67
19÷12=1.58
(1.42×.67)×1.58=1.50

If your case is fitted with two 30CFM case fans and a 30CFM exhaust fan on the power supply unit, you have a total rating of 90CFM (30+30+30). Now divide the total CFM of the fans by the volume of air, and you have 60CFM (90÷1.50). With this setup, the fans are exchanging the air inside your case 60 times per minute, or once every second. It's not rocket science, but it can help you to know this stuff.

When overclocking your system, you need to move and exchange large volumes of air to compensate for the extra heat generated when fans are your primary source of case cooling. If you frequently throttle your system between high performance and stock, using fan speed controllers is a big help in reducing noise during the idle times when less heat is generated. See "Fan Speed Controllers," later in this chapter.

For Whom the Bel Tolls

With all this air moving and motors spinning, the noise level of your rig becomes the next important consideration. Case fans also carry a decibel (expressed db, or one tenth of a bel) rating, which is a logarithmic unit of sound intensity, or *sound pressure level (SPL)*. The range of human hearing is measured in decibels from a reference point of 0db, or the threshold of hearing. Decibels also come with a *frequency weighting* measurement. Frequency weighting, such as dbA, dbB, and dbC, measures sound in relation to its effect on people. The dbA measurement is the best at describing the damaging effect of sound on human hearing.

Your average PC noise level is about 30–50db when you calculate the combined levels of the case fans, CPU cooling fan, graphics card fan, and the like. When noise levels start climbing over 85db, hearing loss or ear damage can occur pretty rapidly. In short you don't want a lot of these bad boys. When fans are installed inside your case, the overall decibel level drops, considering that fans are tested and rated outside of cases. Most of the noise, it seems, is generated not by the aerodynamics of the spinning rotor itself, but from the type of bearing assembly, which we discuss in more detail later in this chapter.

In an effort to reduce noise, some case manufacturers are moving away from the smaller, faster spinning fans and making room inside for the larger ones. An 80mm case fan with a 36CFM rating at about 34dbA is a good average. A 120mm fan has a typical rating of 53CFM and a rating of 28dbA. Big difference, yes? The larger 120mm fans spin at a lower revolutions per minute (rpm) rate, reducing noise from the motor and bearings, yet they move more air with their bigger blades.

Sleeve Versus Ball-bearing Fans

There's one other specification you might want to look into while shopping for fans, and that's the bearing type. Attached to the rotor (or *impeller* or *blade*) is a shaft that rides on these lubricated bearings. The types you'll most commonly come across are the oil-impregnated sleeve bearings and the ball-type bearings. Each type of fan bearings generates its own distinct frequency, and ball-type bearings can be slightly noisier. In the past, I've had ball-bearing fans fail prematurely when dropped, so handling becomes an issue with this type. You also might notice ball-bearing fans growing steadily noisier with age.

Engineers generally agree that sleeve-bearing fans have shorter operating lives (and are much cheaper to manufacture) than their ball-bearing cousins under the same operating conditions. Ball-bearing fans are much better performers and more reliable at higher temperatures. For system-critical applications such as CPU

cooling fans, ball-bearing is the way to go, unless you're like me and are always under the hood changing parts around.

Fan Type Comparison Chart

Criteria	Ball Bearing	Sleeve Bearing
Fan longevity	Longer life	Shorter life
Heat endurance	Higher	Lower
Mounting options	Vertical, parallel, perpendicular	Vertical
Noise levels	Quieter at high speeds	Quieter at low speeds
Parts	Precision	Non-precision
Lubricant	Less evaporation	More evaporation
Price	More expensive	Less expensive

A basic sleeve bearing fan, cracked open. Here's how it works: When DC current is applied to the fan, a sensor mounted on the PCB switches the current to the different stator coils (the copper windings) at the appropriate time, bringing the magnet in the rotor (also known as the *fan blade*) along with it in the alternating magnetic field that is created.

1 Rotor shaft
2 Magnet

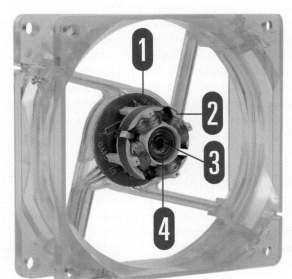

1 Printed circuit board
2 Motor stator
3 Bearing
4 Oil ring

Properly Positioning Case Fans

With CPU speeds exceeding 3GHz, hard drives hitting 15,000rpm, and videocards generating enough heat to deep-fry an Arkansas pickle, the flow of fresh, cool air through case interiors is becoming increasingly important—especially if you're tricking out a custom mod. Heat causes instability and instability causes blue screens of unhappiness.

> Regular readers of *Maximum PC* will recognize this section as having appeared in a 2002 edition of our magazine. We're presenting it here again because it beautifully illustrates the importance of proper fan placement, especially if you are building a nonstandard rig or adding aftermarket case cooling. The hardware examples used in this article are dated, to be sure, but the ideas illustrated apply to any PC.

But how do you promote the best airflow possible? How do you know whether your fans should be sucking air in or blowing air out? How do you determine if you should have a fan mounted on top? And what about drive-bay coolers? We decided to find out.

To help us determine the best fan placement spots, we pumped "movie fog" into two computer cases and observed exactly how each rig's interior fans affected the flow of the smoke within. If the smoke wasn't properly whooshing past critical components, we knew we'd need to reevaluate fan placement. Our first case study focused on a home-built dual-Celeron rig. It was loaded with a bazillion fans and wrapped in a SuperMicro full-tower case. Our second case study involved a factory-built Dell rig featuring a 733MHz Pentium III. It came with a default two-fan configuration.

Getting Started

For our experiments, we bought a sheet of Plexiglas, a Plexiglas cutter, duct tape, 5 feet of flexible heater vent tubing, and a smoke/fog machine. The device works by vaporizing a fog fluid mixture into superfine particles.

First, we cut sheets of Plexiglas to replace the case sides and used the duct tape to seal leaks all around the edges of the Plexi. After some experimentation with different methods of introducing smoke into the systems, we found that we got the best results by feeding smoke into the cases via a heater hose. The hose was connected to the smoke machine on one end and to a cardboard box on the other end. We then fitted the cardboard box over the PCs' front air intakes.

We filled each system with smoke to make airflow patterns visible. While we were able to clearly see distinct patterns emerge when we turned on the smoke-filled PCs, the photographs in this section don't illustrate the patterns very well, so we've added arrows to highlight our observations.

Anyone can conduct airflow tests at home. Just be aware that there's always risk associated with pumping any kind of vapor into an electrical device. Electric shock is certainly a consideration, and you can also destroy your delicate electronics. For this reason, you might want to eschew home-testing and just use this article for general advice.

Case Study 1—SuperMicro SC-750A

To see how airflow works in a full-tower rig, we performed our first test on SuperMicro's SC-750A case. Twin 8cm fans were mounted in the front bezel, a 10cm fan sat above the power supply (complementing the existing power-supply fan), and three fans served the motherboard's chipset and two CPUs. An 8cm case fan for blowing air onto the CPU and a 4cm fan mounted on the back of the case (directly behind the CPU) were

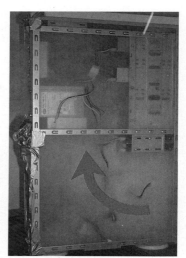

Air entered the 750A's case along the arrow's path but was not sufficiently vented through the area around the power supply.

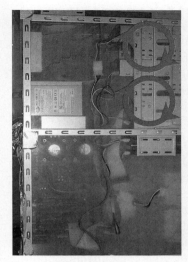

Though the 750A's optical drives are staggered for better airflow, they could still benefit from the optional drive bay fans. In their current config, the drives suffer from dead air zones.

notably absent. We chose this elderly system because it was positively stuffed with peripherals, including three hard drives, two optical drives, four PCI cards, and a smoking-hot (at the time) GeForce DDR videocard warming the AGP slot.

The first thing we noticed about the SC-750A was that the triple CPU/chipset fan combo created massive air disturbance. The fans threw up small funnels of smoke as they sucked air down onto their respective chips. This, of course, doesn't necessarily aid in cooling; such a system might simply blow hot air to other parts of the case. Also, for the smoke to exit, it had to flow from the front of the case, through the turbulent air above the CPUs, and into the power supply where it was evacuated—a convoluted, inefficient course. Moral of the story? If you want to really cool your CPU and chipset area, you should install an exhaust fan behind the CPU, below the power supply. This pushes hot air out of your case and into the room at large.

Our test also confirmed the need for the svelte cables provided by rounded IDE cables or Serial ATA. Our 750A hid a veritable rat's nest of SCSI, IDE, and floppy ribbon cables that acted like a wind drogue, blocking the flow of air from the two front fans. Serial ATA's I/O cables, which are about 1/4'' in diameter and more than twice as long as current IDE ribbon cables, are a welcome change for PCs.

Another problem we encountered concerned dead air surrounding peripheral cards. Because the I/O cables prevented bezel fan air from blowing directly onto the PCI cards, air movement in the PCI card area was stilted at best. Although the SC-750A alleviates

some of this by including passive vents near the PCI cards, we didn't find them adequate for cooling today's hot peripherals. So we added a PCI exhaust fan to better evacuate the air near the PCI slots.

The SC-750A was properly configured in respect to its placement of storage devices. The two optical drives were wisely mounted with plenty of room between them, encouraging airflow. If you have problems cooling drives, the 750A actually lets you mount fans on both sides of your drive bays. If your case has that option, we recommend installing the fans, particularly if you're running a lot of hot, high-speed drives.

We didn't expect the auxiliary fan mounted above the power supply to do much good because we thought the power supply fan would steal most of the air before it reached the top of the case. To test our theory, we ran the system both with and without the top fan enabled. Surprisingly, airflow was reduced considerably when the top fan was disabled, causing the air to

A rat's nest of drive cables in the 750A blocks almost all the air flow from the two front bezel fans.

bog down in the lower half of the case. When the top fan was on, air moved well from the lower intakes and over the drive bays before it was blasted out of the system. To see if we could mimic this action for those of you with mid-tower cases, we shut down the top fan and added PC Power and Cooling's Turbo Cool 2X, an additional fan that screws to the back of the power supply and is purported to increase the airflow through your system. The Turbo Cool's high-velocity fan made quite a difference in clearing the smoke, working almost as effectively as the auxiliary fan that lives above the power supply. Unfortunately, this fan also sounds like a DC-3.

Case Study 2—Dell XPS B733r

In the Dell's case, cool air is sucked in past the hard drives, making a beeline for the wind tunnel, where it is vented. However, a massive dead spot covers the PCI cards.

The second system we ran through the grinder was one of our old Dell test rigs. It used the standard Palo Alto case employed by Dell and a number of other OEMs, a 733MHz Pentium III, 128MB of RDRAM, and just two fans. The Palo Alto is designed for power users who don't need a ton of expansion capabilities. Like most OEMs using the Palo Alto case, Dell relied on a custom-fitted wind tunnel that reaches from the CPU to an 8cm fan mounted inside the back of the case. The wind tunnel design has the advantage of directly venting air from the CPU rather than just moving it around inside the case. It also allows the use of larger fans that spin at lower rpms—and thus produce lower decibel levels.

With only the wind tunnel fan and the power supply fan aiding exhaust, how well does this system work when compared to a system with a zillion fans? It turns out that the wind tunnel performs much better than we expected. In the Dell, smoke moved at a good clip from the lower front bezel, past the hard drive, and out through the gaps in the wind tunnel. The pattern was much clearer than the wind chop that affected the configuration on the SC-750A case. As is to be expected in a case with few fans, there were several dead-air spots, specifically around the lower PCI slots and drive bays. We recommend installing a PCI exhaust fan, a supplemental external power supply exhaust fan, and a hard drive cooler to wipe out excess heat in the trouble areas.

What to Do at Home

Every PC case is different, so we don't recommend that you immediately tweak your PC based on what we learned from our two case studies. Instead, grab a thermometer gun (such as the Raytek MiniTemp) and set up your own tests. Measure the temperature around typical hotspots (memory, CPU, 3D accelerator, and hard drives); then tailor your cooling solution to fit your case's needs.

As a general rule, we found that having more intake fans than exhaust fans can actually impede airflow. If anything, you'd do well to have extra exhaust fans to complement your puny power supply fan (which also exhausts air, but at a meager pace). The extra exhaust fans actually draw a small amount air into the case as a natural part of their functionality; then they scoot out all the hot air generated by your components. Bottom line: It's better to blow air out than to suck air in.

If you have a hot AGP card or PCI cards that generate excess heat, some form of active cooling around the expansion slots could benefit your case's climate. Consider a fan that fits into a spare expansion slot. Any type of device that can get air moving in this area is good.

We can't wait for Serial ATA to become common. Until then, consider using zip ties or Velcro straps to lash down the cables in your case. If you have lots of ribbon cables floating around your system, consider buying some presplit IDE cables that are a little more aerodynamic. Also check www.plycon.com for more information on rounded IDE ribbons.

Unless you have a proper exhaust system, CPU fans do little more than blow hot air around your case. So, if you have an unused fan mount behind your CPUs, take advantage of it by adding another fan that blows air out. If you don't want to fool with adding more fans, consider picking up a power supply equipped with a better fan. We recommend something from PC Power and Cooling.

If nothing else, our little experiment proved that brute force isn't necessary when cooling your PC. A well-designed cooling scheme using 2 fans is just as effective at ventilating your case as adding 15 fans but not having any overall plan.

The most common case fan sizes, from left: 120mm, 92mm, 80mm, and 60mm.

Fan Gallery

Many companies make fans, but we recommend you stick with makers that have a solid, established reputation, such as Pabst, Evercool, and Vantec. Case fans generally range is size from 60mm to 120mm.

Case Fan Sizing

120.000 millimeter [mm]	*equivalent to*:	4.72440''
92.000 millimeter	*equivalent to*:	3.62204''
80.000 millimeter	*equivalent to*:	3.14960''
60.000 millimeter	*equivalent to*:	2.36220''

Evercool Aluminum Frame Case Fan

Dimensions—120×120×25mm

Airflow—79.14CFM

Noise level—36dbA

Voltage range—7VDC–14VDC

Nominal voltage—12VDC

Bearing type—Ball bearing

Connector—3 pin

Pabst 4412F 120mm Fan

Dimensions—119×119×25mm

Airflow—55.3CFM

Noise level—26dbA

Voltage range—7VDC–14VDC

Nominal voltage—12VDC

Speed—1600rpm

Bearing type—Sleeve

Connector—3 pin

Evercool Case Fan

Dimensions—80mm×80mm× 25mm

Airflow—32.40CFM

Noise level—25dbA

Voltage range—7VDC–14VDC

Nominal voltage—12VDC

Bearing type—Ball bearing

Connector—Molex

Vantec Stealth Fan

Vantec 80mm Stealth fan

Dimensions—80mm×80mm×25mm

Airflow—27CFM

Noise level—21dbA

Voltage range—7VDC–14VDC

Nominal voltage—12VDC

Bearing type—Double ball bearing

Connector—3 pin

Vantec Tornado

Dimensions—80mm×80mm×38mm

Airflow—84.1CFM

Noise level—55.2dbA

Nominal voltage—12VDC

Bearing type—Double ball bearing

Connector—Molex

The notorious 80mm Vantec Tornado is one of the most powerful CPU fans you're likely to encounter with a rating of 84.1CFM. It's also one of the loudest, with a decibel level of 55.2. Expect near water-cooling temperature levels with this screamer when paired with a monster heatsink like the Swiftech MCX64 series. Just have your PC in another room, or at a relative's house in a different state if you can.

Fan Speed Controllers

Before modders were able to purchase front bay fan speed controllers, the more industrious and electronically gifted among them were busy rolling their own. Now that we have all these nifty controllers available, the rest of us can take advantage of the features they offer. These controllers are powered by a single Molex connector and distribute 12VDC to each channel for up to four fans. By regulating the voltage output and lowering the fan's rpm, peace and quiet is just a turn of the knob away. Front bay devices also add color and pizzazz where there would otherwise be a blank 5 1/4'' or 3 1/2'' drive bay bezel.

The Nexus Fan Controller from Vantec connects up to four fans and allows you to manually adjust their speeds and, thusly, the noise levels inside your case.

The Nexus NXP-301 Fan and Light Controller combines fan control and cold cathode light activation into one 5 1/4" drive bay unit. It offers three fan control channels that can be adjusted from completely off to full speed.

Fan speed is adjusted by four potentiometers that vary the voltage from 7VDC to 12VDC. Each channel supports 15-watt to 18-watt fans; however, this type of controller is not recommended for CPU or other mission-critical fans. This Nexus Controller unit fits in a 5 1/4" drive bay and is available in black or silver finish, both with blue LED illuminated knobs.

Also built in to the unit is an onboard inverter for controlling two CCFL lights for on/off or sound activated modes.

The Matrix Orbital MX211 5 1/4" PC bay insert is one of the most feature-rich digital devices you can install on the front of your rig.

Why the Matrix Orbital MX211 Is Our Fave...

How do we love thee? Let us count the ways:

• All system temperatures are gathered via the motherboard and software.

• The display can report hard disk space, RAM use, system uptime, and frame rates for games.

• Even better yet, the display can alert you to new email, headline news, stock quotes, weblogs, and other information from websites that offer rich site summary (RSS) syndicated feeds (requires an Internet connection, of course).

• It monitors Winamp information, such as title, track, and remaining time. You can also scroll through music titles using the built-in seven-button keypad.

• The unit can control up to three 12VDC fans or LEDs using the onboard general-purpose output (GPO) connectors.

• It provides speaker volume control.

• A memory chip stores all the previous settings so a power loss doesn't result in a total loss of those settings.

• The screen can display custom text either horizontally or vertically. Also, it features software-controlled text speed, startup screen, line wrapping, scrolling, contrast, backlight, and time-out setting (up to 180 minutes).

This USB-controlled LCD panel is a software-controlled, visual gateway to everything that's happening inside your system.

The Cooler Master Aerogate 2 combines speed control for up to four fans with temperature monitoring of system components. A single lighted dial controls all four fans independently, while the backlit panel displays fan speed and temperature readouts from four temperature probes, or thermistors.

Other features include up to 18 watts per channel and a built-in 40mm fan for cooling hard disk drives that are mounted in the same 5 1/4" drive bay. See Chapter 8, "Building the Ultimate Off-the-Shelf Mod," for an example of how I used this very controller to dress up my ultimate off-the-shelf mod.

Fan Accessories

The following pages contain an assortment of accessories and gizmos you might find useful while modding cases. We present them here in hopes of offering you some additional flexibility when it comes to planning your wicked mods.

Fan Adapters

Fan adapters enable you to retrofit CPU heatsinks and cases with larger fans for increased cooling. Common sizes are 60mm–80mm, 70mm–80mm, and 80mm–120mm.

Vibration Dampening Kits

Rubber gaskets like these from Vantec help prevent noise-causing fan vibration from being transferred to the case. They can be found in 120mm, 92mm, 80mm, and 60mm fan sizes.

Fan Filters

Fan filters are the best way to trap and reduce the amount of dust that can foul the inside of your case and components over time. You'll even find removable and washable filters built right in to some higher-end PC cases.

Ducting Mods

Ducts like this one from Thermaltake move the fan away from the CPU heatsink in an effort to eliminate the dead spot caused by the rotor hub of the fan.

Temperature Probes

This flat-style temperature probe can be mounted with clear tape anywhere in your case for monitoring system temperatures, and it comes included with front panel devices like the Cooler Master Aerogate 2. They are also thin enough to be mounted on the bottom of the CPU and graphics card heatsink block right next to (but never on top of!) the processor die. The readings from thermistors and front panel devices are not 100% accurate, but they give a pretty decent estimate.

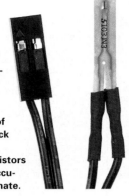

Hard Disk Coolers and Bay Coolers

When you can't place hard disk drives in the path of cool incoming air, a hard disk cooler can help keep temperatures in check. This unit has two 40mm fans mounted on an aluminum bracket that screws to the bottom of the hard disk. The extra room the cooler takes up prevents you from using the space directly above or below it, though, depending on how you mount the drive.

Bay coolers are another option for sucking air into your PC, although they often make your PC sound more like a vacuum cleaner than we'd like.

Slot Coolers

Fan cards are mounted in an available PCI slot to help cool any PCI or AGP card surrounding it. This cooler from Vantec is made from UV-reactive plastic illuminated by eight LEDs and has a sliding fan speed controller on the bracket.

Painting Your Fan

Sooner or later you're going to create a mod that calls for a custom-painted fan. When basic black or the flashy colored plastic of an LED fan just doesn't fit your theme, it's time to throw a little paint on them. As far as I know, paint has no ill effect on the delicately balanced mechanisms of a fan—so long as you disassemble the fan and paint only the paintable parts! However, painting does call for some microsurgery and a gentle hand to disassemble the fans. Let's crack one open and take a look.

Not all fans can be disassembled. Some are permanently sealed and therefore not very good candidates for painting. So be sure to examine your test subject fan closely before you start prying it apart.

These fans might work for some mods using similar color schemes, but in most cases, they're just too garish to match most mod schemes. Never fear, though, because with a little patience and some skill, you can transform one of these neon fans into something that matches your mod.

Step 1: Exposing the Fan Bearing

This not-so-pleasantly colored Vantec LED case fan just gives me the shivers, but it's nice and bright and makes a good photographic subject for dissection.

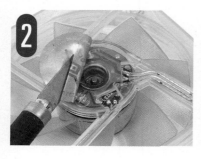

On the exhaust side of the fan, remove the protective sticker and save it for later use. The sticker prevents dust from entering the bearing, so you'll want to put it back on when you are finished painting.

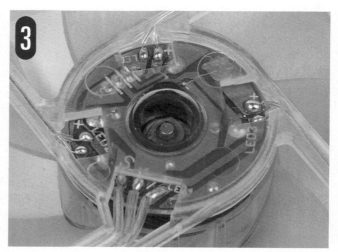

Some fans have a small rubber cap protecting the bearing opening, so save this part as well if yours has one.

Step 2: Removing the Retaining Ring

Gently remove the fan blade assembly and set it aside.

This sleeve-bearing fan has a small split retaining ring made from nylon on the shaft that holds the rotor in place. I was able to carefully remove this one by cautiously grabbing and twisting it with a pair of precision tweezers. You don't want to damage (or lose) the retaining ring at all; otherwise, you'll have trouble holding the rotor on properly.

Be aware that a ball-bearing fan can have a small spring on the shaft that helps keep the rotor in the proper position. When taking one of these apart, don't lose the spring!

With the fan blades removed, you can see the coiled copper wires of the stator assembly as well as the printed circuit board. For this project, I didn't paint the frame of the fan, but if I had, I would have used some masking tape to protect the stator assembly, LEDs, and circuit board.

Step 3: Masking Off the Magnet and Shaft

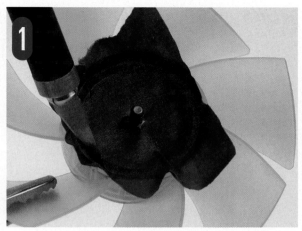

To prevent paint from getting on the magnet and shaft (a bad thing), I cut a small hole in a piece of blue tape and used a sharp hobby knife to remove the excess from around the hub.

Make sure you closely examine your masking job before you start painting. It's very important that paint not get into the magnet and shaft because it can gum up the works and make the fan inoperable.

Step 4: Painting the Fan Blades

I first painted the rotor with DupliColor METALCAST silver ground coat and let it dry for 30 minutes. My trusty helping hands device, with the alligator clips on the end, came in handy for holding the rotor as I painted.

Before I started painting, I couldn't resist adding a little detail piece to the rotor hub. I fashioned a piece of acrylic in a hemispherical shape and glued it to the fan. I used just a small drop of epoxy on the hub and placed the hemisphere in the center; then I put the rotor back on the frame temporarily. By spinning the rotor, I determined whether the hemisphere was centered and made slight adjustments where needed. After 10 minutes, the epoxy was set and I could mask it off and paint.

When I returned to the rotor, I gave it a few light coats of yellow anodizing color paint and let that dry overnight. I reassembled the fan, snapping the nylon ring back on the shaft and placing the protective sticker back on the hub. See Chapter 4, "Painting Cases," for more information on spray painting techniques. Be sure to follow the safety precautions I point out there.

Step 5: Admire, Gloat

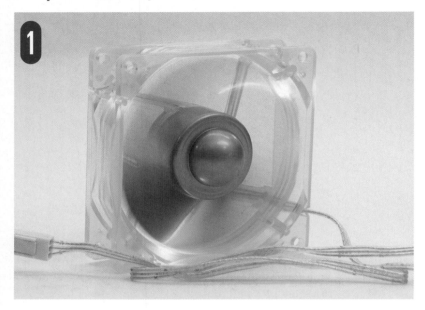

Once it was reassembled, I tested the fan outside of a working PC, letting it run for quite a while to ensure I hadn't damaged anything during my painting adventures.

I'm not quite sure if I made this fan look better or worse. I might just go back and paint that frame after all!

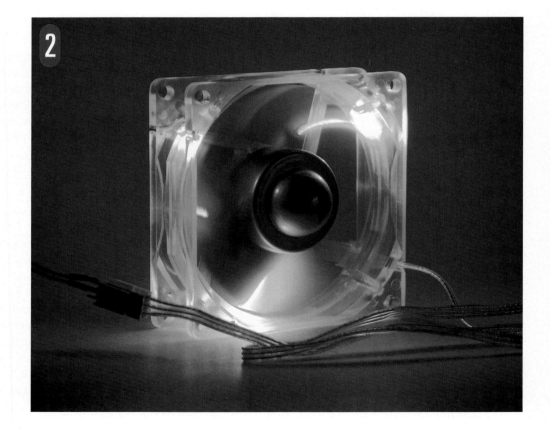

Making Your Own Fan Templates

If you get bitten by the modding bug, sooner or later there will come a time when you'll want to mount a fan in a spot not normally reserved for it. To do this, you might need to create your own fan template. Here are the steps:

A great way to put all that scrap metal from window cutouts (see Chapter 3, "Making a Case Window") to good use is to make a set of fan templates from them. After you have a set of the most common sizes, positioning and marking your case for fan blowholes is a breeze. Here I took a piece of scrap aluminum and marked it with a sharp pencil, using a fan as a guide.

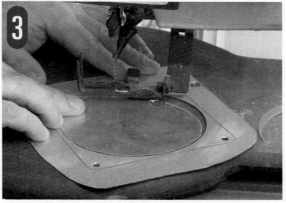

First, I drilled the fan mounting holes with my drill press. Next, I drilled a hole in the center and then passed the blade of the scroll saw through to begin my cutout. You can also use a rotary tool and metal cutting disk, jigsaw, or hole saw for this part.

To mark the mounting holes, I used a drill bit and lightly tapped the end with a hammer. You can also use a fan grill to do this if you have one in your stash.

After some edge cleaning with a hand file and sandpaper, I had a nice, accurate 120mm fan template I can use over and over.

Cutting Blowholes

When you need a little extra cooling in your case, it's time to punch a few holes and install some extra fans. For the cleanest round cuts in metal, I like to use the proper-sized hole saw and a variable speed power drill. You can also use a jigsaw fitted with a metal cutting blade, or go old school and use a rotary tool with cut-off discs. *Whichever tool you choose, safety glasses must be worn.* Even a small metal particle in the eye can mean a trip to the hospital for an all-day affair, or worse. Steel splinters can be even nastier because they begin to rust as the hours pass in the waiting room and can quickly rot out your eyeball. The doctor will see you now, but you might not see anything ever again. See Chapter 1 for all you need to know about proper safety precautions.

Tools Needed for Our Project

- Power drill with hole saw, jig saw, and metal cutting blade, or a rotary tool with a reinforced cutting disc
- Drill bit set
- Counter sink
- Straight edge
- Tape measure or combination square
- Drop cloth or newspaper
- Fine hand file
- Safety glasses!

Fan/Approximate Hole Saw Sizing Chart

60mm	2 1/2'' hole saw
80mm	3'' hole saw
92mm	3 1/2'' hole saw
120mm	4 1/2'' hole saw

Step 1: Measure Twice, Cut Once

Use a tape measure for positioning the fan on the center of the case.

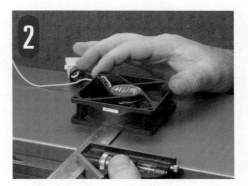

Using a combo square in place of a tape measure is easier than using a tape measure.

I traced around the edge of the fan with a pencil to mark where I planned to cut the case.

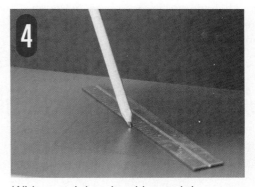

With a straight edge, I located the center of the square. *X* marks the spot!

Whichever tool you decide to use for cutting your blowhole, try to keep as much debris and metal chips out of the case as possible. Use newspaper or a drop cloth to protect the inside of the case. Another trick is to loosely drape a few strips of masking tape inside the case just beneath your marking to catch the shavings as you cut the hole. A good-sized metal shaving can wreak havoc later by shorting out the motherboard or other components.

Step 2: Cutting the Hole

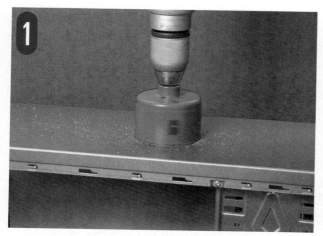

Place the hole saw's pilot bit on your center mark and begin drilling slowly until it penetrates the metal. Slow to medium speeds and an even pressure on the hole saw make a nice clean cut and prevent the blade from wobbling.

Hole saws tend to make a slightly beveled cut, so be careful of the sharp edge until you file it.

Step 3: Marking Screw Holes and Filing

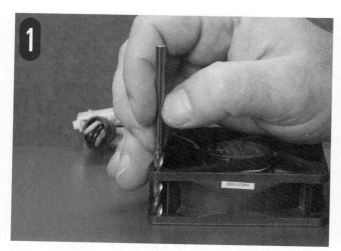

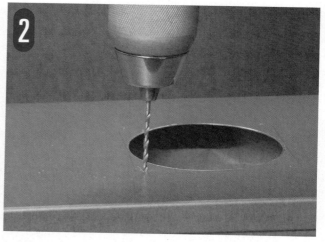

Here I marked the fan screw holes by spinning a drill bit a few times that was passed through the fan housing. You can also use a fan grill and pencil if you have a spare.

To prevent the drill bit from "walking" across the surface and scratching it, lightly tap the pencil marks with a center punch and hammer. I started off with a smaller drill bit to pilot the hole and then finished drilling it with the proper size for the screw.

A counter sink removes the burs and polishes off the hole from the outside and inside.

Square off and dull that sharp edge carefully with a hand file. There's never a need to put any sacrificial blood into your work.

Step 4: Mounting the Fan Grill

Once the hard part is over, paint your fan grill if you desire, let it dry, and then carefully mount it in your nearly installed blowhole.

Do this right and people will question whether you added the fan or your case came that way from the factory.

Fan Bay Excess, Thy Name Is RagE

Yeah, I know what you're thinking: This mod won the September 2001 Rig of the Month contest because it bears such an elaborate paint job. Well, indeed the artwork is certainly incredible. But for the purposes of this chapter, I'm highlighting A. Dale McLean's Tower of RagE mod because it contains no fewer than 23 internal case fans. Let's spell that out for you: twenty-three. And each fan is integrated very well into the Supermicro 750a server tower on which Dale based his project.

When we received the submission, we had to ask the question you're undoubtedly asking yourself now: Does the case truly require that much cooling, or was Dale just having fun? The craftsman (who has a degree in electronics engineering) explains:

"This case was built around everything I'd learned from building the last one—what worked and what didn't. Then I kind of 'amplified' everything that did work. Normally, I run with only my 'primary intakes and exhausts' on. That means that I turn on three 80mm side intakes, four 80mm intakes cooling the drive bays, the front bay blower, and one 120mm YS-Tech that performs exhaust duties in the back. Meanwhile, four of the 120mms and two 80mms are rarely used.

"With only these fans running, my case temps are room temp—even after a full night of fragging. I have a thermal sensor attached to the wall outside the machine to measure room temp. The only time I find it necessary to run the 'secondary intakes and exhausts' is after I've shut down the other fans for a time—usually in order to talk to my wife. I designed this thing to be the meanest, loudest, air-cranking mofo going."

Cool, dude. And, yes, we do mean *cool*.—J.P.

Dale built his fanbus/baybus from scratch (though he gives due credit to Cliff Anderson of Fanbus.com because the original concept was his). The bus's LEDs are bi-colored and, when the switch is turned on, they change from red to green to indicate the status of the fan.

The tower's artwork was inspired by Nazareth's 1979 *No Mean City* album. As Dale says, "I'd been using the skeleton dude with the straight razors as a logo in OGL for some time."

Let There Be Lighting

All the world's a stage, and all the men and women merely players.
—William Shakespeare

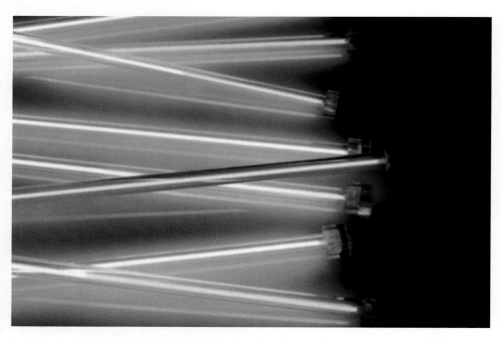

If you want your PC to look as fast and furious as possible, we recommend custom case lighting. It doesn't do squat for boosting actual performance, but it does give your rig that mean and hungry look.

Y ou've spent countless hours rehearsing and planning for your big show, and the audience is restless, playbills in hand waiting for the curtain to rise and the story to unfold. During the production, you've worn many hats: director, producer, prop master, technician, and lighting designer. The stage is set and dressed, your actors costumed and anxious to show their stuff. You take a deep breath, cross your fingers, and click the Submit button, posting the final photos of your case modding creation to the Web.

Case modding is not unlike a stage production where every aspect of the presentation from the enclosure (the "stage") to the components and accessories (the "actors") have to be considered to successfully create the drama you've intended. Case lighting is no small part of that production and will most likely be the first impression your rig makes. One of the easiest ways to understand and master proper lighting techniques for your case mod is to use the stage and film analogy. So, let's rig it, flip the switches, and light 'er up.

Case lighting is one of the areas of modding that can be the most enjoyable, where you can

Case lighting comes in a variety of colors and sizes. Larger lights can be used for full-size mods, while smaller lights are perfect for lighting small form factor cases and shuttle mods.

apply the finishing touches that set your project apart from the crowd. The key to good lighting practice is experimentation, and you'll be glad to know that there are only a few rules and very little technical mumbo jumbo. A good sense of style and theme, careful placement, and color coordination are all it takes. With dozens of easily installed lighting products available, there's endless opportunity for creative lighting. As with any craft, knowing your tools and materials and how to use them properly are paramount, so let's take a look at some of these.

Finding just the right lighting color scheme for your case mod is a matter of experimentation, and having fun. Mecanique is a Danger Den water-cooled case mod with an anodized red paint finish and industrial look. With a scratch-built cooling tower, the radiator was brought outside the case for enhanced thermals. The round window was water-cut from a slab of 1/4" aluminum by the fine engineers at customwatercuts.com.

The Classic Cold Cathode Fluorescent Lamp

Cold cathode fluorescent lamps (CCFLs) are the flood lights of the case lighting world, giving the brightest and widest possible illumination inside or outside your case. The technology is fairly simple: It's a gas discharge lamp in which a phosphor coating inside a glass tube is electrically stimulated by electrodes. The *cold* refers to the type of electrode on each end, and unlike traditional lamps, they don't use filaments that heat up and lead to excessive temps inside your case.

CCFLs for case modding are designed to run off the 12-volt rail from your systems power supply unit. A CCFL kit includes one or two lights, an on/off switch, and a small box called an *inverter* that adapts the power from your PSU to suitable voltage for the lamps. CCFLs come in several colors: red, blue, purple, yellow, green, ultra violet, and white.

For broad lighting, a single 12'' stick inside a small- to medium-size case will do the trick. The smaller 4'' lamps are ideal for mounting in tight spaces such as drive bays and even beneath components like your VGA card. Lamps are also available in 6'' and even a whopping 24'' in length for the largest of cases. The inverters are available in single and dual output, allowing for one or two lamps, respectively. One drawback of these lights is the length of the wires on the lamps themselves. Generally, the length of the wire from the lamp to the inverter is limited to about 7''–8'', due to the specific and predetermined load necessary to power the lamp. In this case, lengthening the lamp wire results in a dim or nonworking light. The good news, though, is that you can lengthen the power lead to the inverter as much as you need to reach the far corners of your case without consequence.

CCFLs are among the most common lighting products you'll find on the shelves of your favorite modding store.

Color and saturation quality vary greatly between brands, so online research and experimentation is a good idea when designing a lighting scheme with cold cathodes.

Power inverters for cold cathode lighting. These typical dual output modules allow you to connect two lamps at a time. These inverters usually have specific voltage outputs, so mixing and matching brands is not a good idea. Molex power connectors come standard in most kits.

Mounting Lights

Finding just the right spot for a CCFL stick, inverter, and switch depends on the architecture of your particular case and the placement of any side panel windows. A good lighting rule of practice is to place the lamp where the stick itself won't be seen: Indirect lighting is much more pleasing to the eye and in turn won't spill unnecessarily from the window.

Every case mod has a sweet spot where the viewing angle is best for appreciating the design of the interior lighting effects. To find this, mount the lamps temporarily (always power off your PC first!) with a few strips of tape, dim the house lights, power up, and stand back a few feet. If you can see the bare bulb, search for another spot where it would be less conspicuous but still provide a nice, warm glow.

Cold cathode lamps come protected inside an acrylic tube. The square mounting blocks on each end can be removed with a sanding drum for fitting the tubes in tight spaces. You shouldn't remove the glass cathode from inside the acrylic tube because you risk breaking the fragile wire inside or, worse, shorting it out.

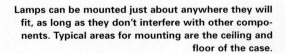

Lamps can be mounted just about anywhere they will fit, as long as they don't interfere with other components. Typical areas for mounting are the ceiling and floor of the case.

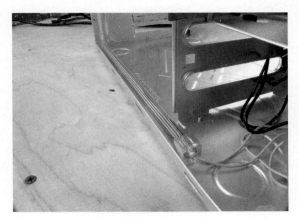

When installing lamps, double-stick tape does the trick, or you can use a few drops of clear silicon adhesive for difficult areas.

Mounting Lights Continued

CCFLs are housed in acrylic tubes to protect the glass and are quite durable, so repositioning them while lighted is okay. You can easily redirect the light from the CCFL if necessary by cutting a 1/4'' strip of foil tape (basically, automotive pin striping) and wrapping it on the tube. This is a good method for concentrating the light on hard-to-reach areas inside your case.

If you've found the right spot for the lamps, your next step is to mount the inverter and, if you choose, the on/off switch. There's no doubt that the inverters are pesky components to hide, and they can come in less-than-pleasing factory colors. If you find yourself with one of these ugly sky blue boxes, it's a good time to get the spray paint out and give the inverter a more suitable color. Lamps and inverters can easily be mounted with double-stick foam tape, zip ties, or clear silicon adhesive. With a life span of about 20,000 hours, there's little need to worry about permanently mounting the sticks with adhesives.

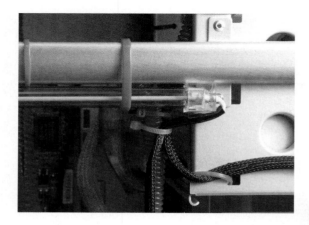

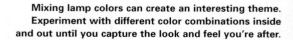

Use the case chassis for mounting lamps. Zip ties are another mounting alternative and can be easily removed for repositioning.

Mixing lamp colors can create an interesting theme. Experiment with different color combinations inside and out until you capture the look and feel you're after.

Indirect lighting makes for a much more pleasing glow inside. The blue lamp is nicely hidden on the ceiling of the case.

Changing Lamp Colors Without Changing Lamps

You're not alone. I've yet to find cold cathodes that produce just the right color (or *color temperature* for you techies) out of the box. If you're faced with this dilemma, help is just a trip to the greeting card store away. Lighting technicians for film and stage rely on gels to control and correct color. These durable, specially made sheets of thin plastic are placed in frames and mounted in front of lighting equipment to produce the effects needed.

You can make your own inexpensive colored gels by using translucent acetate wrapping paper purchased wherever holiday and occasional goods are sold. With a rainbow of colors to choose from, you can cut lengths of it to wrap the CCFL tube, using clear tape to hold it in place. Experiment with the colors, using white lamps with colored acetate and any combination of colored CCFL you like. You now have the power to light it up like a pro!

Stage and film lighting technicians use expensive gels for special effects and color balancing, but these cheap rolls of gift wrapping acetate can be found at card stores.

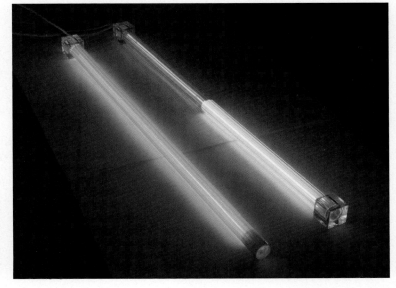

Changing the color of any lamp is as easy as cutting a strip to length and using clear tape to hold it in place. You can create interesting lighting effects by wrapping a single light with two or more colors.

Lighted Fans: Keeping Your Rig Cool and Stylish at the Same Time

Case fans are no longer the aesthetically ignored, purely functional devices they used to be. Where they once occupied dark little corners of a case, happily going about their spinning, whirring business of keeping your case cool, they have since become front and center lighting attractions. These illuminated fans are another example of early case modder ingenuity and imagination that was picked up (or, quite possibly, ripped off) by manufacturers and mass-produced.

There are two basic lighted case fan designs—those that use LEDs (light emitting diodes) and their more expensive brethren, the cold cathode fan. The former incorporates several miniature LED lights into the body of a clear plastic fan, usually aimed at the blade. You'll find them in many flavors, including green, red, and white, and in combinations of colors. Cold cathode case fans have a thin, ring-shaped tube mounted on the face of the fan. The cathode ring is reversible, for use as an intake or exhaust fan. Lighted fans look best when placed behind a grill or mesh, creating a really slick, futuristic look. Some fans are so bright that they can also be used as a primary lighting source inside cases with windows and in blow holes on top or on side panels.

LED-style fans typically do not have separate power leads for the lights, but rather draw power from the hub of the fan, eliminating extra wires that can cause clutter inside your case. CCFL fans, on the other hand, require an inverter to power the lamp and need a bit more management to tame the tangle of wires. A good feature of CCFL-lighted fans is that you can remove the light tube and use it anywhere in your case, opening up lighting possibilities way beyond its use on the fan. You can use the CCFL ring to illuminate logos and blow holes, and it's thin enough to mount under your case for cool-looking ground effects.

This CCFL lighted fan can provide a serious amount of illumination inside your case. The drawbacks of this fan design are the crazy amount of wires that have to be managed and the necessary inverter box. The cathode ring is very thin and also removable, allowing you to use it just about anywhere it will fit.

LED lighted fans, though not as bright as cathodes, incorporate a single power wire for lamp and fan operation. Made from an ultra-violet (UV) reactive plastic, these fans glow nicely when powered up.

LED Lights: A Powerful Punch in a Puny Package

LED technology and development is growing by leaps and bounds. They are weaving their way into everyday life and devices, slowly edging out the ancient incandescent as king of the lighting hill. LEDs are about five times more energy efficient than their incandescent cousins (including neon and cold cathodes, for that matter). The next time you stop at a traffic light, chances are that the old filament lamps have been replaced by super-bright LEDs. This type of lighting might someday replace those in your home and office fixtures.

With their low power consumption, high brightness, and growing range of colors available, LEDs are making their way into case mod lighting products not only as accent lights, but also for entire lighting schemes. Several ready-to-use LED products are available for your case mod. The LED Lazer-type light is a small fixture with three bright LEDs. Installation is simple using a Molex pass-through connector directly to your power supply. These fixtures are best used as spotlights to illuminate dark areas under components and hardware.

Beyond the three small pinpoints of light they produce, they simply don't provide enough coverage to illuminate an entire case, but as detail lights they are superb. Their small size enables them to be squeezed into really tight places such as drive bays, under the case lid, between disk drives, and on doors. Decorative LEDs are also showing up on sticks of RAM, CPU heatsinks, motherboard components, and case feet.

Another product is the Antec brand light tube, an array of six ultra-bright LED lamps encased in a plastic tube. These 12-volt powered fixtures include a control module with a dial controller for adjusting sensitivity to sounds and music and even a flashing mode. Other brands, such as Sunbeam, boast twice as many LEDs per stick and special effect modes such as pulsating, fades, chases, and more. Both of these brands have built-in on/off switches mounted on a PCI bracket, eliminating the need to install your own. Unless you're creating a '70s disco theme, these lights are best used discretely and sparingly: Too many flashing, pulsing lights can cheapen an otherwise great rig.

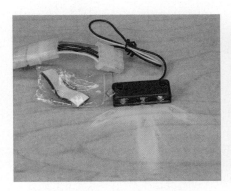

Ready-made LED goodness. This little unit incorporates three ultra-bright, narrow-focused LEDs that can be used as spotlights to illuminate the dark areas inside your case. There's nothing to stop you from removing the plastic casing and using the lights just about anywhere.

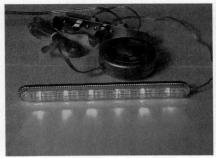

The LED light stick does more than just light up. The kit comes with a sound-activated module that can pulse, flash, or flicker the lights to music or ambient noise.

LEDs are showing up just about everywhere. The very cool indicator lights on these sticks of RAM fluctuate with system usage. Also note the LEDs on the North Bridge cooling fan.

LED Facts: The Diode Demystified

An LED generates light photons directly from the energy of electrons; unlike an incandescent lamp, it does not rely on heat to light up. This gives LEDs the benefit of turning on and off in an instant. They can be flashed several hundred times a second or even used as strobe lights with the proper circuitry. Most LEDs require a very low voltage, somewhere between 1.5 and 4 volts. The red and yellow-green colors usually require less voltage (around 1.8 volts), whereas the aqua, blue, and white colors require more voltage (around 3.6 volts).

You can lower the voltage supplied to an LED as much as you like—to set the brightness to whatever you desire—but don't give it more voltage than it is rated for. If you do, it will burn up almost instantly. The reason for this is that, unlike most electronics, LEDs decrease their resistance as they heat up. So, if you start flowing too much current through an LED, it overheats, allowing even more current to flow through it in a death spiral until it burns up. You can power an LED at safe voltages by simply putting a resistor inline with the LED to keep the current flow below the maximum level. In the following table you will find some common LED colors and voltages, along with the resistors needed to operate them off of 5-volt and 12-volt sources.

LED Color	LED Voltage	Resistance Needed at 5 Volts	Resistance Needed at 12 Volts
Red	2	150	500
Yellow	2.1	145	495
Green	2.5	125	475
Aqua	3.3	85	435
Blue	3.6	70	420
White	4	50	400

Alternatively, you can calculate the resistance needed for your own application with the following formula:

$$(Vsource - Vled) / Aled = Rled$$

When broken down, the formula looks like this:

Vled = The recommended voltage of the LED

Vsource = The supply voltage

Aled = The recommended current of the LED, in amps (divide by 1000 if rated in mA)

Rled = The value needed for the resistor

LEDs are rated for brightness in microcandela (mcd), and you'll find that the higher the mcd of an LED, the brighter it is. A note of caution: Some manufacturers play a sneaky trick that takes advantage of the way mcd is measured. They give the LED a narrow beam that projects the light in a spotlight fashion, thus giving the LED a very high mcd rating; however, it isn't much good for lighting up a case. Always check the viewable angle of the LED to ensure that it is the proper width for your needs. 10° is considered small, and something around 25° is average, with 40° being wide.

12-Volt DC: Automotive Accessories to the Rescue

As a busy case modder, I'm always on the lookout for easy solutions to design dilemmas. When it comes to case lighting, some terrific modders are experts in electronics, and some modders can't tell an LED from a BLT.

Regrettably, I lean far toward the latter in terms of electronic prowess. For the ohms law–challenged among us, there are sneaky ways around these design problems. It's no secret to modders that automotive lighting accessories are, for the most part, compatible with the 12-volt power supplies in rigs. I frequently stop at local auto supply stores and browse what I like to call their *Wall of Wonder*—an entire aisle dedicated to lighting accessories. I look at every single peg-hooked product and *wonder* how I could use it for modding.

Auto supply stores often carry CCFLs, neon lights, ultra-bright LED lamps, EL (electro-luminescent) wire, and many other 12-volt-powered goodies that can easily be retrofitted for case mod use. The cigarette lighter adapters that are common on these lighting components are removed and replaced with inline switches and Molex connectors. Automotive cold cathode lighting, in my opinion, has the best-looking reds, yellows, and greens I've seen, and they are considerably brighter (for their respective size) than those sold at computer shops.

The LEDs I've found at these stores are super-bright, come in several colors, and are ready to use—provided you install the proper resistors for 12-volt power. Expect to pay a few dollars more for these lighting supplies. Buying mod parts at an auto supply store isn't the most frugal approach. However, for ease of use and installation, these products can't be beat. You can also find some themed lighting parts here, too, such as small metal skulls and dragons with blinking LED eyes, adjustable strobe lights, and more. If you haven't yet tapped this resource for case mod lighting, you just might find some useful products here.

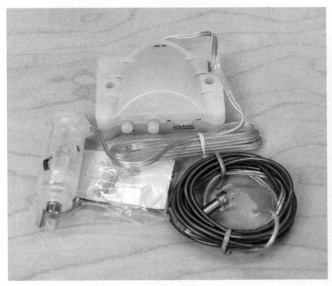

This EL wire kit from an automotive store can be easily modified for use inside your case. Simply remove the cigarette lighter adapter and solder on a spare Molex connector.

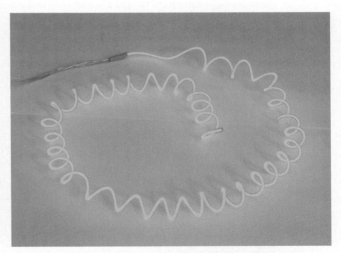

While not extremely bright, EL wire is flexible, holds its shape, and can fit into small spaces.

Turn-ons: Switches

While planning your case lighting design, you should consider the type of control you need for each fixture. You can hard-wire the lamps for always on, powering them up along with the system. As an alternative, you can have more than one lighting theme for your case by installing multiple fixtures and controlling them with individual switches. For daytime, you might want to punch up all the lights; at night, you might want to flip a few switches and have a slightly more subdued theme. Switches can be found in many shapes and sizes, from round rockers to toggles at local electronic stores and online retailers. The only specification to consider with switches is the maximum DC voltage rating: Anything 12 volts and above is suitable for case mod lighting.

Switches are commonly installed for easy front panel access in any spare 5.25'' or floppy drive bay by drilling the proper-size hole in the plastic bezel. For more discreet switching, you can always mount miniature switches on a spare PCI bracket on the rear of the case. Illuminated switches with built-in LEDs can add some pizzazz to your theme by putting a little color in just the right spot.

Mechanical switches for case mod lighting come in a variety of styles and sizes to fit any case mod theme. From left: miniature rocker, round rocker, illuminated oval rocker, illuminated toggle, and military-style flip switches. Make sure the switch you choose is rated for 12 volts or better.

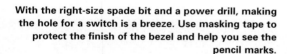

With the right-size spade bit and a power drill, making the hole for a switch is a breeze. Use masking tape to protect the finish of the bezel and help you see the pencil marks.

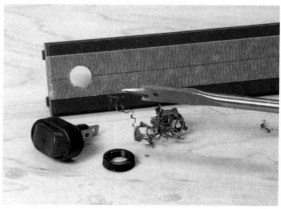

The front of your case can become a stage lighting command center, adding interest as well as function to your rig.

Maximum PC Fave!

Black Lights . . . for the Dark Arts?

Please don't be frightened, children. Mark Ray, the creator of this mod, swears that the Latin containment spells inscribed on the side of his case window are not be feared. In fact, he says, the spells are there to keep evil spirits away—not to invoke their presence.

This May 2003 Rig of the Month winner, nicknamed Jackal-in-the-Box, is a potpourri of awesome craftsmanship. It's got water-cooling and twin fan buses, among other neat flourishes. But we chose it to cap off this chapter because Mark's containment spells are "summoned," if you will, by the rig's unique lighting scheme.

Let us clarify: To create the rig's ethereal illumination, Mark used a combination of high-intensity blue LEDs and black cold-cathode lighting—and the inscribed spells appear only when the black lights are flipped on. According to Mark, so-called "high-intensity" LEDs can be 10 times as bright as their cheaper LED counterparts. Cold cathodes provide even greater illumination but have their own issues: Any more than two sticks requires a larger power supply—100W more than what a system typically requires. And if you decide to go the UV route, Mark says, you should bear in mind that acrylic tends to block about 70% of a UV light's intensity.

Mark replaced the sides of his case with custom Lexan panels, with standoffs and cutouts providing added dimension. He firmly believes that a table saw is far superior to the "score and snap" method when cutting acrylic. To prevent scratching, he says, leave the protective backing on the plastic until the cutting is done. And if scratching does occur, Mark swears by Novus Plastic Polish.—J.P.

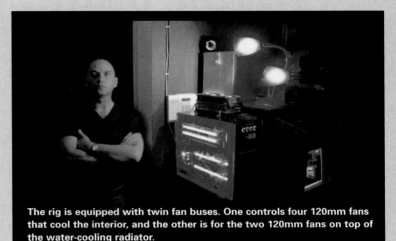

The rig is equipped with twin fan buses. One controls four 120mm fans that cool the interior, and the other is for the two 120mm fans on top of the water-cooling radiator.

Here we have "the stack." This is the pet name for the radiator assembly that protrudes from the case's top. Dig the twin 120mm fans.

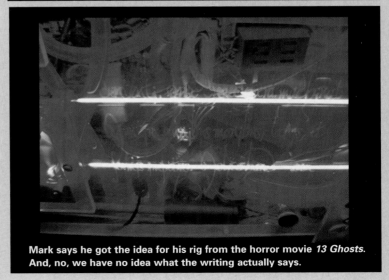

Mark says he got the idea for his rig from the horror movie *13 Ghosts*. And, no, we have no idea what the writing actually says.

Chapter Seven

Laying Cables

Who says your rig's cables can't be sexy?

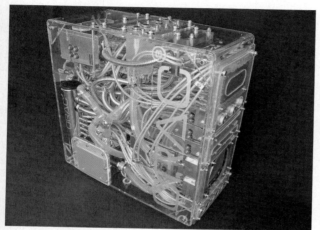

The vintage British sci-fi-inspired Orac^3 mod by Peter Dickison (a.k.a. G-gnome) features a clear case and possibly the most inspired cabling we've ever seen. G-gnome's cable sleeves were made from a variety of offbeat materials, such as shower hose and aquarium tubing.

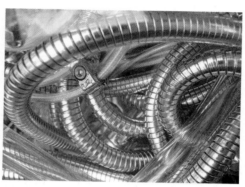

We'll never look at an ordinary, garden-variety chrome shower hose the same way again after seeing Peter Dickison's Orac^3 mod.

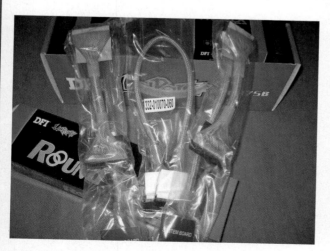

The rig's DFI LanParty motherboard boasts day-glo orange accents (perfect for folks who want that "modded look" out-of-the-box). But DFI also goes one step further by bundling in UV-reactive, rounded IDE cables. See, the modding craze really has penetrated every nook and cranny of the market.

Why go with standard PC cables when you can shroud them in dark, dank industrial tubing for that *City 17* look-and-feel? This close-up not only shows off Piloux's cabling savvy, but also gives us a clear shot of the orange Plexiglas shards that embellish the case interior.

In addition to some of the freakiest cabling we've ever seen, the infamous Orac^3 mod enclosure was made from chrome, neon green perspex, polished stainless steel, and clear acrylic.

Piloux's *Half-Life 2* mod is much, much more than a mere exercise in creative cabling. In fact, it's a mélange of highly advanced case-modding techniques discussed elsewhere in this book. Nonetheless, this rig—commissioned by Valve founder Gabe Newell himself—illustrates exactly how trick cabling can add extra texture to a complete, comprehensive, case-modding gestalt.

With side panel windows and clear acrylic cases opening up the inside of our rigs for all the world to see, it's a given that you should learn how to tame and conceal the oodles of wire that bring power to hardware and components. Cable wrapping and *sleeving*, as its called, have developed into somewhat of an art form, with case modders spending many hours performing wire management magic.

The culprit most responsible for every day being a "Prince Spaghetti Day" of tangled and twisted wires inside your case is the power supply unit. Even the best PSUs come out of the box with long lengths of unruly wires. Although some manufacturers offer units that are "presleeved" at the factory, the more discerning case modder is not satisfied with the lack of color choices. A few industrious online retailers have caught onto this and offer custom sleeving services with your choice of colors and materials. Another interesting product is the modular PSU, in which you plug only the power cables your system needs directly into "jacks" on the PSU housing.

Besides the PSU, some wires and cables on other components could benefit from a little sleeving lovin'. Power leads from fans, switches, temperature probes, and lighting fixtures are among the other parts that are good candidates for dressing up and organizing. It's not uncommon to find every wire and cable color matched and organized inside a custom PC these days. Good cable management (or lack of) is guaranteed to be the first thing your audience notices when the side panel is removed from your case.

The materials case modders are using to spruce up the wires inside their rigs are borrowed from several industries. Wire sleeving and protective products are available for just about every environmental condition you can think of—from intense heat and corrosive chemicals to the absolute zero temperature of outer space. Although case modders can seem like Jet Propulsion Laboratory technicians at times, it's unlikely that we'll need *that* level of specification (or expense) for our own projects. Expandable braided sleeving and wire (split or spiral) loom are quite popular and are available as kits or sold by the foot. In the following pages, we'll take a look at the basics of using both of these materials.

Lastly, although this chapter shows only the mechanics of some basic cabling setups, I do show some actual custom cabling in Chapter 8, "Building the Ultimate Off-the-Shelf Mod." There, you'll see how you can use the simple tricks I show you here to dress up any off-the-shelf PC.

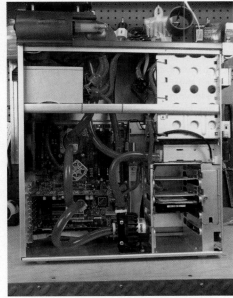

Wire management and sleeving help give an open, airy feeling to any PC interior, especially to those areas exposed by a side window.

Up Close: The Tools and Materials

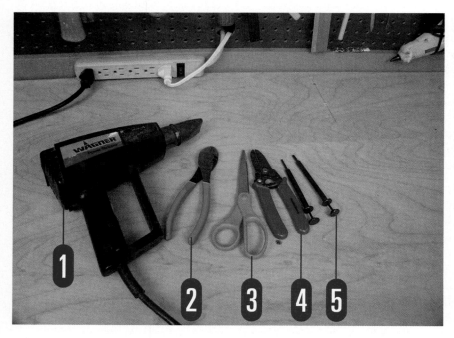

Before you start your cable dressing adventure, there are several important tools of the trade you'll need on your bench. For setting heat-shrink tubing, a favorite tool is the heat gun. Generally used for stripping paint, if you have one with low, medium, and high temperature settings, it can be used safely with shrink tubing. Angled cutting pliers provide accurate cuts when removing zip ties and cutting wires. A sharp pair of scissors is also needed to cut wire-loom and braiding to length. Wire strippers are a must for removing sheathing when, for instance, you're shortening power cables and resoldering them. Molex extractors are specialty tools that make quick work of removing both female and male connectors.

1 Heat gun

2 Angled cutting pliers

3 Sharp scissors

4 Wire strippers

5 Molex extractors

You can find cable dressing supplies at automotive supply stores, electronic retailers, and online modding shops. Split-loom tubing comes in many colors and in diameters from 1" to 1/4". Expandable braided sleeving is the most popular for case mods and is found in many flavors, including bright silver and ultraviolet reactive colors. Heat-shrink tubing is the cleanest method of terminating the ends of split-loom and braided sleeving and comes in several diameters and color choices. Colored zip ties are good for attaching your dressed cables to the interior of the case. PVC (electrical) tape is another option for terminating the ends of your sleeved wires, but the ends have a tendency over time to become frayed and unglued. Expandable braided sleeving is another type of cable dressing that is easy to use and makes a world of difference. Chrome wire looms make tucking away wire bundles a snap. Take a look at the work being done by other case modders on the community forums for even more interesting ideas, materials, and methods of cable dressing.

1 Split-loom tubing

2 Heat-shrink tubing

3 Braided cable sleeving

4 Zip ties

5 Electrical tape (PVC)

6 Chrome wire looms

Step 1: Taming the Nest of Snakes

If it's your first time taking on the task of dressing cables on your PSU, be prepared to spend several hours doing so. Even for the more experienced case modders, this part of the project takes time and patience for the best results. Right out of the box (photo left) the power supply is an unsightly piece of hardware that has no place in a custom PC. Your first step should be to separate the cables into individual lengths at the point where they sprout from the PSU.

With a pair of angled cutting pliers, you can snip off the factory installed zip ties if you find that they might interfere with your sleeving. Your next step is to determine which power leads you need for your particular custom rig and those you do not need. If you don't plan to use the 3.3v floppy drive power cable, for instance, you can easily remove it to make your wiring that much neater. In the next step, I show you how.

Carefully clip the factory-installed zip ties

Step 2: Removing Molex Connectors

Molex extraction tools are simple but handy devices to have in your case modding toolbox. There is a tool available for male, female, ATX main power, and floppy connectors.

The tool is inserted in the Molex connector, where it compresses the tiny metal barbs that prevent the wires from pulling out. A plunger mechanism built in to the tool then pushes the connector out and free of the plastic housing.

Up Close: Wire Configurations

It's very important that you take note of the wire configuration before you start removing connectors. If you connect things in the wrong order, you can short out your PSU, wreck your mobo and other components, and even turn your rig into a toaster oven if you get it wrong. Always, always, always consult the PSU manufacturer's documentation or website to ensure

that you get this right. For general reference, we've provided the basic wiring configuration of the connectors found on industry-standard ATX power supplies. Note that some manufacturers use a proprietary wiring scheme that differs from the industry standard. Be sure that your PSU isn't one of those PSUs that uses a different configuration.

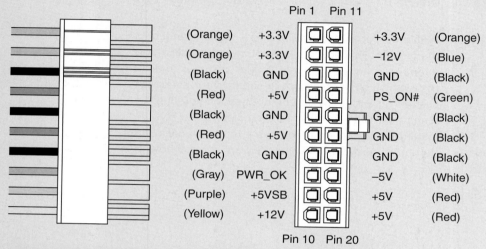

	Pin 1		Pin 11	
(Orange)	+3.3V		+3.3V	(Orange)
(Orange)	+3.3V		−12V	(Blue)
(Black)	GND		GND	(Black)
(Red)	+5V		PS_ON#	(Green)
(Black)	GND		GND	(Black)
(Red)	+5V		GND	(Black)
(Black)	GND		GND	(Black)
(Gray)	PWR_OK		−5V	(White)
(Purple)	+5VSB		+5V	(Red)
(Yellow)	+12V		+5V	(Red)
	Pin 10		Pin 20	

ATX 20-pin main power connector (Molex 39-01-2200)

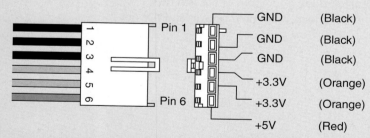

Pin 1	GND	(Black)
	GND	(Black)
	GND	(Black)
	+3.3V	(Orange)
	+3.3V	(Orange)
Pin 6	+5V	(Red)

ATX auxiliary power connector (Molex 8993)

All power supply pinout illustrations courtesy of Scott Mueller, Upgrading and Repairing PCs

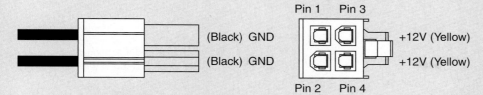

ATX 12v power connector (Molex 39-01-2040)

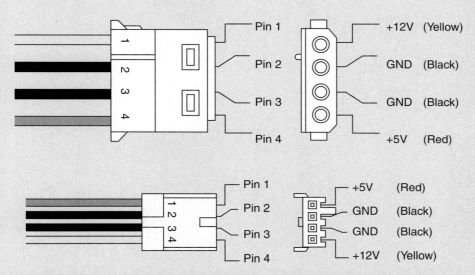

Peripheral and floppy connectors (AMP 1-480424-0 and AMP 171822-4)

For much more on the topic of connectors, pinouts, power supplies, and PC hardware in general, be sure to check out Scott Mueller's *Upgrading and Repairing PCs, 16th Edition*, from Que Publishing. At nearly 1,700 pages, this is the definitive PC hardware guide that no serious PC hardware maven should be without.

Also, it's very important to note that some older Dell PCs use motherboards and power supplies with non-standard ATX wiring. If, for any reason, you are modding a PC containing a proprietary Dell motherboard and/or power supply, be *very* careful when futzing with the wiring on either of these connectors. In fact, we recommend you consult Dell for the exact pinouts of these devices. Connecting a standard ATX power supply to one of these nonstandard Dell motherboards, or connecting a nonstandard Dell power supply to a standard ATX motherboard, could spell disaster—usually in the form of smoke and fire. You might be in the mood to bathe your PC's innards in a fiery glow, but we're pretty sure actually torching your rig isn't what you had in mind.

Step 3: Removing Unwanted Power Connectors

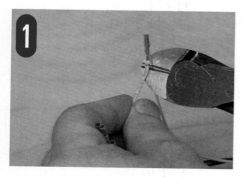

After you've removed the Molex connector from the wire lead, you can easily remove that unwanted 3.3v floppy power connector. With a pair of angled cutters, snip the wires one at a time *as close to the pin as possible*; this is very important for preventing exposed wires from peeking out of the Molex connector and causing a short.

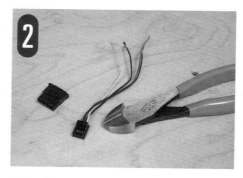

After the connector is removed, you can save it for use on another project.

If you decide to leave those floppy drive power connectors, removing the connector is easy. With a sharp, pointed instrument, carefully compress the metal barbs while simultaneously pushing forward.

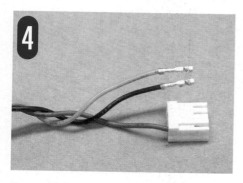

Be careful to take note of the colored wire configuration for replacing the connector later (see "Up Close: Wire Configurations," earlier in this chapter).

It's easy to dig into your power supply's wiring harness and start making modifications, but we'd be remiss if we didn't tell you to carefully think all of this out beforehand and be sure you know what you are doing. If you think there's even a chance that you'll want to use the floppy connector—or that you might want to give (or sell) the power supply to someone else later—we recommend you not remove the power connector. Instead, tuck it away and zip tie it out of sight.

Also, if you're not 100% comfortable jacking with wiring, we recommend you don't. Not only can you damage your hardware if you make a mistake, but you could set your PC, your house, and maybe even yourself on fire. Lastly, you can turn your expensive power supply into a nifty paperweight with just a few snips.

As always—and if you're a regular reader of *Maximum PC*, you already know this—contain all your wiring work to the outside of your PSU. Mucking around the inside of PSU is dangerous and should be left to the pros. Even an unplugged PSU can carry enough stored electrical charge to injure or kill you.

Step 4: Installing Split-Loom Tubing and Heat-Shrink Material

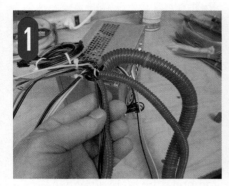

Installing split-loom is as easy as cutting the tubing to size and then slipping the power wires carefully inside through the split that runs down its length.

Heat-shrink tubing cut to about 7/8'' long pieces can now be slipped over the tubing on each end. You should replace the Molex connector at this point, paying close attention to the proper configuration of the yellow (12v), red (5v), and black (ground) wires.

After the Molex connector is on, push the heat-shrink tubing against it. With your heat gun on a low to medium setting and about 6'' away, shrink the tubing a little at a time until it begins to form and shape to the split-loom tubing. Keep the heat gun moving back and forth—never in one spot—to prevent melting the split-loom. Repeat the process for the opposite side of the cable where it comes from the PSU.

If you find the power wires popping out of the split-loom, you can always solve this problem with a small color-matched zip tie.

These large end caps (left) make a clean and good-looking termination for your split-loom sleeved cables.

The finished product is now an organized, color-coordinated addition to the project.

Step 5: Applying Expandable Braided Sleeving

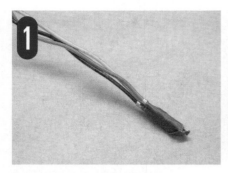

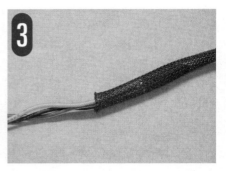

Expandable braided sleeving is another type of cable dressing that is easy to apply. Kits are available from Vantec that come with several feet of sleeving, color-matched heat-shrink tubing, and even zip ties. Before inserting the wires inside the sleeving, you should tape them together as one piece; this also helps prevent the barbs on the pins from catching and snagging on the braiding.

After the plastic braiding is cut to length with a pair of scissors, use a lighter to cauterize the end and prevent fraying while installing the wires.

Once the wire is inserted, push it as far as it will go before it catches on the braiding. When this happens, compress the braiding until it expands and, at the same time, grab the end of the wire and inch it along.

When the end is through, follow the same procedures for installing the heat-shrink tubing and Molex connector.

As you can see, this type of sleeving is a more elegant cable dressing than split-loom, and it gives a much slimmer appearance.

Step 6: Mounting and Hiding Cables

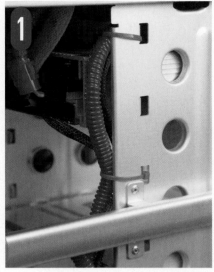

Every case is different, and each has its own ways in which you can mount the cables inside the system. A little clever use of the cases' architecture can provide just the right solution for keeping those wires neat and out of the way. Here, I used zip ties and secured the split-loom cable sleeving to the case chassis.

Use braided cable sleeving and color-matched zip ties to tidy up the inside of your case.

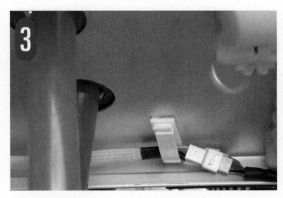

Wire management clips can be found in many shapes and sizes for organizing all types of cables. These self-stick types can be found at electronic and hardware stores. They can get fairly unsightly themselves, so use them sparingly. They have a tendency to loosen over time, but you can help prevent this by removing the foam tape from them and using a fast-setting epoxy instead.

Here, I was able to use one of the chassis support rails as a hiding place for this cable run.

It's the Thought That Counts

We concede that Michael Johnson's Matrimony Mod doesn't look like the work of an experienced craftsman. It's neither polished nor particularly, well…*good-looking*. But in some ways, Michael's mod—*Maximum PC*'s choice for the April 2004 Rig of the Month—might be the "purest" case mod in this entire book. For Michael Johnson didn't create this mod to win a contest or even to draw simple praise from other hardware hackers. No, he created the mod to win the heart of his beloved. That's right: He *proposed marriage* with the computer you see on this page.

Michael says he spent every lunch hour for three weeks in his parents' garage, working on the mod where his girlfriend wouldn't discover it. Yes, you have to love the mini-ribbon roses and "lacy wedding-ish stuff" that accent the case. But what makes the Matrimony Mod most noteworthy (as a craft, at least) is its cabling. Michael covered every cable and wire with white-wrap heat-shrink, along with intertwined stringed pearls, which he bought from a crafts store. Not your typical radioactive waste-green tubing, indeed.

As for his hand-Dremeled case window, Michael etched, "Will you do me the honor?" The words are just barely visible in the photo we have here, but the question was answered with an affirmative, apparently, because a wedding is planned for the summer of 2005. Of course, maybe it didn't hurt that Michael placed a good-sized rock into the top-tier of the hand-crafted faux wedding cake that sits atop the PC.—J.P.

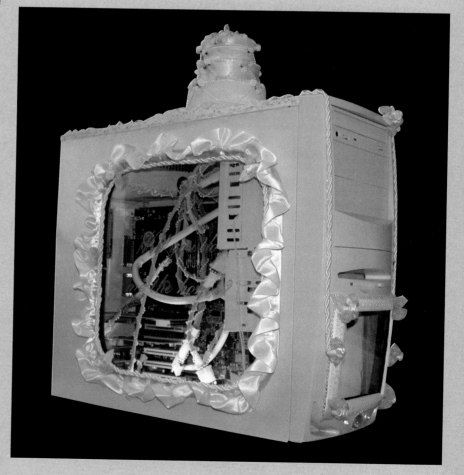

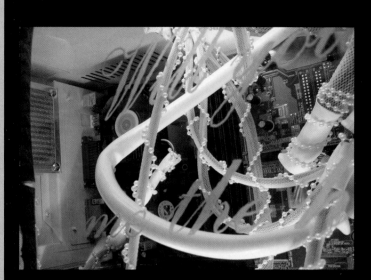

Quaint, yes, but the matrimonial cabling sends just the right thematic message. As for the window etching, Michael taped a Photoshop document to the inside of the case to serve as an etching guide. "My hand kept falling asleep holding the Dremel steady, so I had to take breaks to get the blood flowing again."

Let this rig be a reminder to all budding case modders: The best ideas are always born from personal inspiration.

This is where Michael hid the ring, all of which begs the question—how did he lure his girlfriend into his computer room to even *see* the mod? Maybe it was something like, "Honey, you'll never believe this! I just downloaded a cracked beta of Doom III!"

Is Rachel more interested in modding, now that she has been honored with a mod of her own? "Yes, but probably just as a spectator," says Johnson. "Will we be the first husband-and-wife modding team? Probably not."

Chapter Eight

Building the Ultimate Off-the-Shelf Mod

Turn any unassuming, garden-variety PC case into a work of art. We show you how!

While not a traditional case mod per se, Steve Ferris's Wider View setup is a dream come true for flight sim fans everywhere and is a great example of what a determined hardware hacker can do. Steve's cockpit earned him Rig of the Month honors in our September 2003 issue.

Doug Donakowski made us salute when we saw his patriotic prefab design with custom marking, painting, and decaling. Doug's effort not only confirmed his love for his country, but also earned him first place in our July 2003 Patriotic PC Contest. Ten hut!

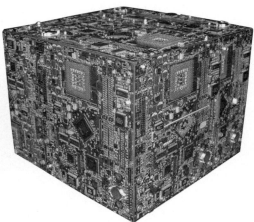

Chris Gair proved that even without a custom-cut window, you can still see his hardware. Chris used numerous dead motherboards to trim the exterior of his prefab case. His masterpiece was featured in *Maximum PC*'s December 2003 Coolest PC Case Modding Contest.

W hen you have the know-how to build and troubleshoot computer systems, it's only a matter of time before your skills will be called upon by tech-challenged friends and frantic family members. Like having a doctor (or, better yet, an auto mechanic) in the family, the computer savvy are invariably asked to test, diagnose, and dole out prescriptions for good PC health—and always when you're eating dinner. One such call came during the writing of this book from a very good friend of mine named Bill, only his request was for help in putting together a new rig.

In addition to being a master model builder and filmmaker, Bill is also a detective with the Technical Assistance Response Unit of the New York City Police Department. On the job, he's expert with high-end video-editing and surveillance equipment used to help catch bad guys, but for home he wanted a custom-built system he could use to edit his films and create digital effects. Of course, we would also have to turn up the cool factor a few notches by adding some readily available performance parts and accessories.

It's fun to spend other people's money, but before my friend could part with the cash, we had to come up with a plan based on the features and functionality he was looking for. Only a few years ago, the hardware necessary to capture, edit, and tweak digital video was beyond the reach of the average hobbyist. These days, though, with the availability of multimedia-enhanced hardware, even those on a modest budget can assemble a powerful system that was once found only in Hollywood editing suites. We made a checklist of the features he was interested in, and afterward we balanced a budget based on those needs.

Here are the key things Bill wanted from his creation:

- CPU muscle power
- A reliable, feature-rich motherboard
- Quality RAM for stability
- Onboard video capture for DV and analog sources
- Plenty of fast hard disk space for storage
- A good-looking, premodded case with room to grow
- Quiet operation for a studio environment

Starbucks? Who needs 'em? Nik Pelis certainly doesn't. He can stay properly caffeinated while fragging his buddies at LAN parties using the coffee maker built right in to his Caffeine Machine. Nik's coffee maker, er, PC won our hearts and was named *Maximum PC*'s Rig of the Month in September 2002.

We scoured the shelves of my workshop for the parts I already had in stock, and for the rest we hit the streets of Brooklyn in search of hardware. I was surprised to find a good selection of case mod parts at a new store just a few blocks away from my home, and at prices competitive with online discount retailers. For me, the local shops are worth paying a few extra bucks just to have the goods in hand walking out of the store. As a frequent customer, I can usually get them to rush deliver products they don't have in stock—a plus for the impatient shopper like me.

After a morning of shopping, we finally settled on the parts to use for the custom video-editing rig. There really is an enormous amount of premodded parts available to fit just about any theme, and it's easy to overdo it. Sometimes it takes only a few well thought-out mod accessories to create a case that makes a bold statement but still has that customized look. For light and a bit of color, we chose two front bay devices that were easy to find and fairly inexpensive.

Before light and fan control units were mass-produced, hardcore modders were kept busy creating circuit boards and homemade front bay devices to do the same. These folks are the true pioneers of case modding, and I'm sure their incredibly clever designs are responsible for the products we see on the market today. Our goal for this project was to create, in a single afternoon, a good-looking, easy-to-build PC complete with a few performance parts and mod accessories.

Kevin Schulthies was one of many *Maximum PC* readers who showed his pride in our 2003 Patriotic PC contest. Kevin's design uses a prefab case and a technique known as *case wrapping*. This technique involves printing a high-res image on a mesh-type material that allows the onlooker to see both the image and what lies beneath it. Kevin was awarded runner-up honors in our contest.

Hands-on How-to: Doing It All with Prefab Parts

Getting dirty with off-the-shelf parts

Materials Used for Our Project:

Case:
Antec P-160 Performance One Series

Processor:
AMD Athlon 64 3200+ 1MB cache

Motherboard:
MSI K8T800 NEO-FSR

RAM:
Corsair DDR400 PC3200 1GB

Graphics card:
ATI All In Wonder 9800 Pro

Audio:
Sound Blaster Audigy 2ZS

Storage:
System disk: Western Digital 36GB Raptor 10000rpm SATA drive
Capture disk: Western Digital 160GB 7200rpm SATA drive RAID 0 array: Dual Western Digital 160GB 7200rpm IDE drives

Power supply:
Antec Smart Blue 350W

CPU cooling:
Swiftech MCX6400-V

Front bay devices:
Cooler Master Musketeer Controller Panel
Vantec Nexus 4-Channel Fan Controller

OS:
Windows XP Professional

Miscellaneous:
Zip ties
Various types of heat-shrink tubing and braided cable sleeves

Tools Used for Our Project:

Standard Phillips screwdrivers

Molex removal tools

Lighter

Wire cutters

Needle-nose pliers

Xacto knife

Estimated Time Commitment:

5 hours

There's an incredible amount of modding accessories you can easily add to a new or existing PC. Parts such as high-end CPU coolers give a pro look and help boost performance when overclocking. Bay bus devices like fan speed controllers not only look great, but also help keep your rig's noise down to a comfortable level.

The Antec P-160 Performance One Series case is good-looking, well-made, and a pleasure to work on. With features such as a removable motherboard tray, quick-release hard disk drive rails, stealthy optical drive covers, and a digital temperature display, it's hard to beat for the price.

Step 1: Building the Beast: Taming the Wild Wires

Before you start adding braided cable sleeves and heat-shrink tubing, be sure to read Chapter 7, "Laying Cables."

Probably one of the most tedious tasks for any case modder is cable dressing; however, it's also the most rewarding (Figure 1). When you put the extra effort into the small details, they become a big part of a well-made case mod. If you open a case and see a nice, tidy interior, you can tell that many hours were spent organizing what would have been a snake pit of wires and cables. The Antec P-160 case comes with a nice premodded feature on the front in the form of a swiveling control panel. On the panel are two USB ports, one 1394 FireWire port, a dual temperature sensor display, two audio jacks, and power/reset buttons. The entire case was broken down to the frame to make the job of wire management a bit easier.

The next step was to organize all the wires connected to the control panel using braided cable sleeving and heat-shrink tubing to terminate the ends (Figure 2). Braided sleeving can be quite stiff, so for the power, reset, and LED activity light wires, I like to leave about 3/4'' of bare wire at the end of the sleeving. This allows me to bend them easily and make a sharp turn to connect them to the headers on the motherboard. We decided not to use the audio ports on the control panel, so rather than coil them and take up precious space inside, we removed them completely.

The power supply unit was the next to undergo some plastic sleeving surgery. I decided to use split loom tubing on the PSU leads for a quick and easy dressing job (Figure 3). The more power supplies you dress up, the less tedious it becomes. After a few dozen of them, consider yourself an expert! I purchased a few packages of blue-colored split loom from an auto supply store, along with the plastic collars used to terminate the ends.

Based on the hardware and components in this rig, I snipped off any power leads that weren't needed, such as the power connecters for the floppy drives (Figure 4). There's no rule that says you can't mix split loom tubing with braided sleeving on the same PSU. Every wire dressing job is different, so use any material you find appropriate to the design and installation.

If you're antsy about opening your PSU—and you should be very careful because power supplies do hold a dangerous charge, even when unplugged—leave the power supply in its original casing until you are sure you understand the dangers posed by power supplies.

Unused power supply cables, such as the fan controller and auxiliary cable, can be coiled up and zip tied (Figure 5).

Choosing the Right PSU for Your Mod

Beware of the craptacular power supplies that ship with most cases. Although there are always exceptions, most cases ship with low-quality PSUs that don't actually meet their advertised power ratings when running above normal room temperature. That's right: As the temperature inside the power supply rises, the actual power output of the supply goes down. And when power output goes down, you run greater risk of system crashes. Also, today's hot-running CPUs and videocards frequently heat the air *entering* the power supply to above 100°F, and the resulting decrease in power output starves these power-hungry components. Without plenty of clean power, your PC will crash. This is a bad thing.

Now, all that said, we've found that the power supplies that come with small form factor cases are usually decent. Why? Because these small form factor cases are engineered within an inch of their lives, and their manufacturers put a lot of focus on electrical and cooling issues. Also, these small cases

offer scant upgrading opportunities, so the manufacturer can easily predict the maximum number of new components an upgrader might add and then reliably calculate the maximum draw on the PSU. If you get a small form factor case for your mod, be sure it has a top-rate power supply because the PSUs for these wee dealies are difficult to upgrade.

If you can't trust the wattage rating of a preinstalled PSU loaded into a cheapo case, what options do you have? We recommend sucking down the extra cost and purchasing a high-end supply. After all, if you're going to spend $2,000 or $3,000 on PC components, you don't want to fry them because your bargain-basement PSU surged when it should have sagged. We think that PC Power and Cooling (www.pcpowerandcooling.com) makes the best power supplies available today, but they aren't cheap. We've used PC Power and Cooling supplies for every annual Dream Machine project ever built for one simple reason: Their power supplies are *hardcore*.

Every Dream Machine *Maximum PC* has ever built has included a PC Power and Cooling power supply. Here's a PC Power and Cooling Turbo-Cool 510 Deluxe that was used in the 2004 Dream Machine.

For this mod, we're using Antec's SmartBlue power supply, which gives you a modded look without that annoying death-by-electrocution problem posed when trying to mod an off-the-shelf power supply. Its two blue LEDs shine through a 92mm clear plastic fan. This PSU also sports a braided ATX cable.

In fact, we've run puny 250W supplies from PC Power and Cooling that have eaten cheapo 400W PSUs for dinner. That's right: The 400W jobs have let us down, while the PC P&C supplies—saddled with a 150W disadvantage—have given us blissfully uneventful stability.

PC P&C's Silencer series supplies are perfect for most machines. Silencers come in 310W and 410W ratings and use slow-moving, large fans to keep components cool without making too much noise. Now, if your system boasts a full magazine of power-hungry components, consider upgrading to the Turbo-Cool 510. It is, without a doubt, the best power supply money can buy. It produces 650W peak and 510W continuous, which is more than enough juice for even the beefiest workstation.

Fanless power supplies that stay cool with just a massive heatsink (instead of a fan) are relative newcomers to the power supply world. In fact, they're so new that we haven't actually gotten one into the *Maximum PC* Lab yet. But their principle is simple: Instead of using a noisy fan to pull air through the PSU

and out the back of your case, these "passively cooled" PSUs uses a series of heat pipes (metal rods that transfer heat from one place to another) to transfer heat to a large heatsink that sticks out the back of your case. Passively cooled power supplies aren't for neophytes, and there's one very important thing to consider before purchasing one: Because you won't have a PSU fan venting the hot air that builds up in your case interior, you'll need to vent the hot air your CPU produces some other way. In real-world terms, this means you either have to mount a fan behind the CPU or go with a more exotic cooling method—such as water-cooling. We trust that if you add a passively cooled power supply to a system with a basic water-cooling rig, you'll be just fine (and you'll also have a fanless, almost perfectly quiet PC!).

Like a good case, you should be able to use your power supply for more than one upgrade. Money spent on a high-quality PSU will save you from having to constantly replace frizzle-fried parts.

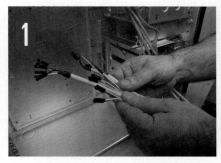

For cases that come with mod features such as front panel devices, you'll have cables that need dressing up and organizing. You should break down the entire case by removing the side panels and front bezel. This not only helps to gain access to wires that need dressing, but also helps to familiarize you with the features of the case.

A few feet of braided colored cable sleeving and some heat-shrink tubing gave these wires a clean look, ready for installation. You can find kits that come with sleeving, color-matched heat-shrink tubing, and zip ties. For big jobs, you can even purchase wire sleeving by the foot in many colors.

Dressing the wires on a PSU is a necessary evil. Nothing says "customized" better than the work you put into the smallest details. For this project, colored split loom tubing from an auto supply store was used. These were available in 1/4", 1/2", and 3/4" diameter sizes. The collars to terminate the ends and the matching zip ties were sold separately.

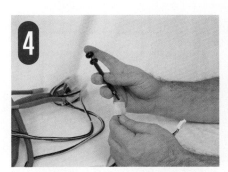

With a Molex tool, I removed the leads we wouldn't be needing, such as the floppy drive power connectors. You can just as easily coil these leads up with a zip tie and tuck them out of the way if you might need them for future upgrades.

The split loom was terminated at the PSU with a 3/4" plastic collar. A couple of zip ties were used to secure the bundled wire harness together. The auxiliary power connector was simply coiled up, zip tied, and later tucked away above the PSU after it was installed.

Step 2: Installing the Motherboard and Processor

The first major piece of hardware to be installed was the motherboard. The removable mounting tray feature of the case made this part of the build a lot easier. After the motherboard was mounted on the tray, the processor was dropped into place (Figure 1) and locked down. A drop of thermal grease about the size of a grain of rice (Figures 2 and 3) was squeezed out and spread very thinly over the surface of the CPU. There is a lot of debate about the correct amount of thermal grease to use, and the only good answer is the *proper amount*. When you consider that the role of thermal grease is to fill the microscopic imperfections in the metal of the heatsink and on the CPU, a thin film is all that's necessary.

See Chapter 11, "Exotic Cooling," for more on cooling techniques and Chapter 12, "CPU Overclocking," for recommendations on thermal grease and general overclocking tips (assuming that you plan to milk every last drop of performance from your off-the-shelf mod).

Advice from the Editors at Maximum PC

Because this book's focus is to cover PC hardware hacking and overclocking, we didn't have room to tell you to build a PC from scratch. The steps provided in this chapter show you how to build a specific, off-the-shelf mod using high-performance parts, but this chapter does not tell you how to choose the right equipment for your needs or give additional details about how each of the components works. For that, you need to pick up a copy of a pure PC building book. We suggest *Maximum PC Guide to Building a Dream PC* by our very own Will Smith. Sure, we're biased, but we don't believe you could pick another book to better complement the one you're holding now.

Forget the Thermal Paste? Call 911.

Whatever you do, don't forget to properly apply thermal paste before mounting your heatsink fan assembly. Doing so is not only a direct violation of at least one *Maximum PC* credo, but is also a good way to melt down your processor and possibly set fire to your wicked cool mod. Where's the fun in that?

A removable motherboard tray is a nice feature to look for in a stock case, and it makes installation of other components, such as the CPU and heatsink, a breeze. Carefully line up the pins on the bottom of your processor with the holes in the socket. The CPU fits in the socket from only one direction, so don't force it! When the processor is in place, gently push the socket lever back into place, locking the CPU to the socket.

A small drop of thermal grease (also called *paste* or *compound*) is applied to the CPU and spread thinly on the entire surface. Here, I'm using the thermal grease that came with the processor. The overclockers in the crowd might want to use a performance paste, such as Arctic Silver. The net effect is likely to be the same, but some overclocking enthusiasts swear by higher-end thermal pastes.

The film created by the thermal paste fills the microscopic imperfections on the metal surfaces of the CPU and heatsink. Made from thermally conductive ceramic particles (and in some brands, micronized silver), it's extremely efficient at transferring heat.

Step 3: Installing the Heatsink and Fan

The Swiftech MCX6400-V is a monster CPU heatsink for AMD 64 socket 754 processors. This high-performance cooler has 405 helicoid pins made from aluminum alloy buried in a polished block of copper and is designed for the enthusiast/overclocking crowd—perfect for this off-the-shelf mod (Figures 1 and 2).

Mounting the Swiftech MCX6400-V heatsink and fan was our next step. This monster heatsink is favored by enthusiasts and overclockers for its exceptional cooling performance when used with low- or high-output fans.

The stock coolers included with CPUs can't compare to the performance of hardcore hardware like the Swiftech, although it's always wise to do your home-work ahead of time and make sure that the aftermarket cooler you are considering is specifically rated for your CPU. The stock coolers generally work well as long as you are operating the CPU within its rated parameters, but they're generally not the best choice if you plan to overclock.

Be Careful Installing the Heatsink

The specific directions for installing heatsink and fan assemblies vary from manufacturer to manufacturer. Some heatsink and fan units are built in to one unit, whereas others are installed individually. Some are mounted using clips that connect to the CPU socket; others use support rails that first mount to the motherboard and then allow the heatsink to be snapped in, thus supporting the weight of the heatsink and fan. The bottom line is that you should do your homework before buying and installing any heatsink and fan. Make sure that the heatsink and fan you buy are rated for the CPU they're intended to cool and that you follow the directions to the letter. Failure to do so can result in all sorts of swearing and general mayhem, including (but not limited to) loss of performance, broken hardware, and hardware that burns brightly when powered on.

Step 4: Making Connections to the Motherboard

After the heatsink was mounted on the motherboard, the tray was installed back into the case (Figure 1) so I could begin routing all the cables and wires.

The leads from the front control panel of the Antec case (Figure 2) were the first to be sorted out and zip tied to the interior. The architecture of every case is different, but all of them have ways that you can cleverly and neatly rout the various wires to their destinations. One advantage of an aluminum case is that you can easily drill small holes for zip ties just about anywhere you need to. If you are drilling holes, be sure you clean the metal shavings (balled up masking tape works well for this) and debris meticulously from the case to prevent electrical shorts and to keep disaster from striking later.

Because the control panel has two probes, I decided that these would monitor the CPU and graphics card processor temperatures. The case was turned on its side for removal of the Swiftech CPU heatsink. When the cooler was off, I could see by the stain (Figure 3) left on it by the thermal grease that good contact was being made with the processor. This also indicated to me how close I could mount the thermal probe for more accurate temperature reading. A small strip of clear packaging tape was cut and used to mount the tip of the probe right onto the copper base of the cooler (Figure 4).

Nice and easy: The motherboard tray was reinstalled into the case. If it were up to me, features like this would be standard on all enclosures. There's nothing worse than trying to snake your hands into a small, dark space to tighten screws and mount hardware.

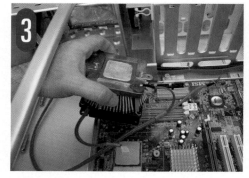

The wires from the Antec's front control panel were the first to be routed to their destinations and zip tied in place. Use the architecture and frame of the case itself to help neatly organize wires and cables.

The CPU heatsink was temporarily removed so the temperature probe from the control panel could be taped in place. You can clearly see the impression of the CPU in the thermal grease, a clear sign that good contact is being made. Keep the thermal probe clear of any areas where it might prevent proper seating of the heatsink.

After the CPU cooler was back in place, the cable for the thermal probe was zip tied to the case. Be sure to make this cable accessible in the event that you have to remove it or reinstall it in the future.

Step 5: Mounting the Drives and Drive Bay Components

When this was complete, the hard drives were mounted (Figures 1 and 2) to their removable rails and the SATA cables were folded, zip tied, and prepped for installation.

For fan speed adjustment, a Vantec Nexus four-channel controller was installed in one of the two 3 1/2'' floppy bays (Figure 3). This controller has blue LED lights behind each knob, fitting in with our overall blue and silver theme. Next, the ATI graphics card was installed, as was the sound card so I could rout the necessary cables to each. For the graphics card, the second temperature probe from the control panel would have to be installed first. I removed the mounting pins (Figure 4) from the graphics card heatsink with needle-nosed pliers; then I flipped it over to simultaneously squeeze the clips (Figure 5) and push the heatsink off the card. The tip of the probe was taped in a safe area (Figure 6) of the heatsink, where it wouldn't interfere with the processor die.

The remaining parts to install included the 5 1/4'' drive bay components (Figure 7) such as the DVD burner and the nice-looking Cooler Master Musketeer. The Musketeer has three needle-style indicator gauges and two slider controls. The sliders regulate the speed of a single fan, and the VU meter measures (in decibels) the strength of the audio signal output of your sound card. The first needle gauge on the unit indicates the fan voltage from 6 to 11 volts; the second gauge indicates sound input; and the third gauge indicates temperature via the supplied temperature probe, which I hooked up to monitor ambient case temperatures. Overall, the Musketeer has very limited functionality; however, with the retro analog look and illuminated gauges, it seemed a good fit for the case.

Choosing a Fan Speed Controller

Sunbeam's fan controller has a clean face adorned with four fan-throttling knobs and accompanying LEDs. The knobs themselves are standard fare: Turn them clockwise to accelerate the fans; turn them counterclockwise to slow down the fans. It's the LEDs that make this controller really interesting. Each LED has dual colored diodes to visually indicate its fan speed. Check this out: If you throttle up a fan, its LED shines blue. Turn up the fan beyond 7 volts, though, and the LED turns red, letting you know that the fan's really starting to blow (in a good way).

If Sunbeam's controller doesn't cut it, might we suggest the Nexus Controller? With its sci-fi etchings and blue button halos, the Nexus is one of the most handsome fan buses around. And with four fan dials on its fashionable black (or silver) faceplate, the Nexus is also robust—capable of handling even the biggest, baddest air pushers. (It's rated at 19 watts per channel, which is powerful enough to accommodate even fast 92mm fans.) Although it would've been super-cool if the relative speed of each fan correlated with the relative intensity of each knob's LED, that's unfortunately not the case. Each ring gets fully blue regardless of how much power its associate fan is using. But we must admit that it does look purty. If you're one of those *Star Trek* nuts with a computer known affectionately as the Enterprise, this fan controller is a must-have for your fleet.

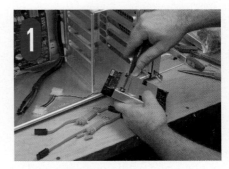

The hard disks were mounted to their removable trays using the screws provided with the case. Rubber grommets on the trays help isolate vibration from the drives and make for a quieter system—a nice feature of the P-160 case.

The SATA cables were folded and zip tied after measuring how much slack was needed on them to reach the motherboard.

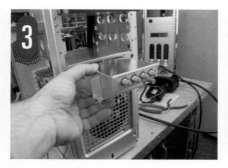

The Vantec Nexus controller has four backlit knobs to control the speed of case cooling fans. Each channel can output 7–12 volts at 1.5 amperes and is good for high CFM (cubic feet per minute) fans. This model is not recommended to control CPU fans or those fans that come with built-in thermal controllers, though. Make sure you read up on the specs of any mod accessory you plan to use in your system.

To attach the thermal monitoring probe to the GPU heatsink on the graphics card, it first had to be removed. The heatsink on this ATI All In Wonder card is held in place by small plastic pins that are easily removed with pliers. Put the pins in a safe place!

After the pins were removed, the card was turned over. A squeeze on the plastic retaining post with a pair of pliers and a little push released the heatsink from the card.

The same rule applies for this thermal probe as with the CPU: Attach it in a place that won't interfere with contact between the VPU die and the heatsink.

The remaining 5 1/4'' bay devices, such as this Cooler Master Musketeer and the DVD burner, were installed. The drive rails included with the P-160 case make for quick and easy installation and removal of components.

Step 6: Installing the Power Supply

The power supply unit was bolted on (Figure 1); next came the routing of all the power lines to the various components. Extra cable can be tucked away in nooks and hidden from view (Figures 2 and 3) to give a clean appearance inside the case. The rest of the hardware, such as RAM, case fans, and the RAID controller card, were installed just before I was ready to close up the case and fire up the rig. Overall, I think the inside of this case (Figure 4) looks neat and clean, thanks to hours of work and attention to detail.

There are just too many options for modding accessories and hardware to mention, but you should have an idea now of how the functional and not-so-functional-but-good-looking can come together to make a nice-looking mod from easy-to-find parts. Your best bet is to read the online reviews of accessories, get tips and tricks from this book, and just go for it. I did happen to make a case modder out of my friend Bill, who, after working with me on this system, has caught the bug. His first project will be to cut a custom window from the side panel and install some CCFLs. Cool.

After the power supply was installed, it was time to get down to routing all the power lines and connectors for the components. Any extra cables can be coiled up or slipped inside an empty pocket away from view.

The remaining hardware, such as the sound and RAID controller cards, was installed and hooked up.

To connect the front panel FireWire cable to the sound card (an onboard 1394 controller is a feature of the Sound Blaster Audigy card), I did a search online to find a diagram for the proper pin connections. The two SATA cables (in orange) were hidden from view behind the disk drive cage.

Things started to look orderly inside our video-editing system. Spend as much time as you need inside the case until you are completely satisfied with the look. Don't be afraid to snip off a few zip ties and rearrange the cables if it's not looking quite right inside your own rig. The next (and final) step was to double-check the connections throughout the entire system, hook up a monitor and peripherals, and fire this baby up!

Project Juggernaut—The Finished Mod in All Its Glory!

Project Juggernaut, as named by my friend Bill. With a definite *NYPD Blue* theme, the clean looks and sleek style of the stock Antec P-160 make for a classic off-the-shelf case mod.

A black DVD burner was chosen to complement the silver, chrome, and black accents of the stock case.

The addition of the Cooler Master Musketeer was a modding choice based purely on style, overlooking its limited functionality. There are so many choices for case styles and modding accessories available that deciding on the right ones for your project should be a matter of personal taste and experimentation.

Behind the three illuminated air intake slots on the front, a removable (and washable) fan filter helps keep the dust build-up inside to a minimum. Bill really caught the modding bug, so I installed a switch on one of the blank bezels to encourage him to get started on a window cutout and design the interior lighting.

Off-the-Shelf Gear

Adding a Little Bling-Bling to Your Off-the-Shelf Mod

Just because you're building your mod from parts picked from the rack doesn't mean you have to settle for second best. The editors in the *Maximum PC* Lab routinely review modding accessories—everything from cathode lighting, fans, and cables, to just about anything else you can image. Here, we highlight a few of our faves.

Decorative Thumbscrews

At a passing glance, these shiny nubs of metal could easily be mistaken for the faux gold teeth of a rap star—bling bling. But closer inspection reveals they're flashy renditions of commonplace computer screws. And you don't even need a screwdriver to use them. Besides allowing your case panels, drives, and cards to be hand-tightened into place, the screws come anodized in just about every color, so you're sure to find the perfect complement for your design theme. You should also be on the lookout for look-alikes of the screws that Cooler Master uses in its high-end cases. These screws have a Phillips top, so they can be either leisurely tightened by hand or fastidiously fastened with a screwdriver if you're the extra-cautious type.

Acrylic Power Supply Mod

A power supply isn't all that much to look at, what with its lackluster casing and staid FCC sticker. And its uninspiring appearance can be downright irksome when your PC's interior is on constant display through a modded case window. Indeed, the PSU can totally disrupt the feng shui of your PC's innards. But if you have the huevos to crack open your ATX power brick (unplugged, of course), you can swap your PSU's original steel enclosure for a much hipper, colorful acrylic jobbie from Directron. Prying eyes will be treated to an array of PSU internals as seen through a sturdy, tinted shell. Available in configurations for most power supply formats, these PSU case mods come in about every color imaginable.

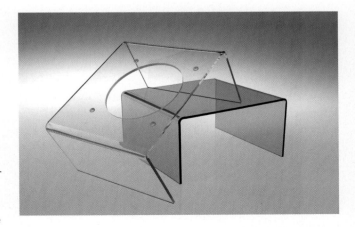

Neon Maxx Blacklight Accent Paint

When viewed under normal light conditions, PC Toy's blacklight spray paint is completely invisible. But flip the switch of some UV cathodes, and suddenly your case is Studio 54 (albeit much smaller, full of wires, and without all the cocaine). The neon paint is an obvious adornment for components like fan grilles and heatsinks, but ambitious modders might go so far as to craft custom stencils for more elaborate paint jobs. The paint is available in red, green, hot pink, white, blue, yellow, purple, and orange. But please don't use all the colors on a single case—unless you're going for a Tammy Faye motif.

Electroluminescent Tape

Only a mad scientist could have thought this up: Cross-breed adhesive tape with the visual flair of a cold cathode tube to produce the marvel that is EL tape. Thin and flexible, the tape is the most form-fitting of all PC lighting solutions. Wind it around case edges, across windows, and over just about anything the sticky backing will adhere to. Trim the tape any way you want, but be aware that the included inverter has connects for just two pieces of tape. Don't expect the tape to glow brighter than cathodes; however, it is perfect for places where other lighting won't fit.

Black Hole BlackFlash Power Onyx Plus

Heavy-duty PC equipment looks that much more impressive when it appears to be sucking major wattage from your wall. The BlackFlash Onyx Plus power cable is an Amazonian boa constrictor in a yard full of AC earthworms, and its hefty 10-gauge wires are capable of knocking back a whopping 10 amps at 250 volts. To top it all off, each 10-foot cable is sheathed in a jet-black mesh covering, making it the slickest power supply cable around.

SuperBright LED Lights

CrazyPC's LED spotlight is hard to notice when it's off: The small silver pod sits discreetly inside your case, minding its own business. But when power surges through its housing, the trio of LEDs come to life. The three distinct beams of light are more focused than other lighting solutions, thanks to the lens they travel through. Use the light nodule to highlight specific pieces of hardware or to knock out a patch of gloom your cold cathodes can't reach.

Black Hole BlackFlash Special Edition Loomed LAN Cable

Jack into a LAN party hub with the BlackFlash cable, and you'll be the envy of every geek in attendance. The armored gigabit cable is sheathed in aluminum braided hose that looks like a race car's steel brake lines. Each slinky piece of metal cable is hand-tested and finished off with gold interconnects for corrosion resistance. Your ping times won't drop, but the cable's cut-resistant sheath ensures that your network lifeline stays up during LAN party hustle and bustle. We haven't seen a better looking piece of CAT-6 yet.

DDRMaxx Copper Memory Heat Spreader

If you didn't spring for performance DDR RAM, it's likely you're sporting unsightly naked DIMMs. For shame! With a little fashion help from some copper covers, you can have those bad boys looking sharp. The covers are intended to tame RAM temps, but the adhesive padding is a bit thick, in our opinion. We suspect they won't cool your RAM to any helpful degree. The real reason for throwing a heat spreader on sufficiently cool DDR is to appease the eye. Mounting these smooth, reflective copper spreaders is the easiest way to dress up raw, drab RAM chips.

North Bridge Maxx Chipset Cooler

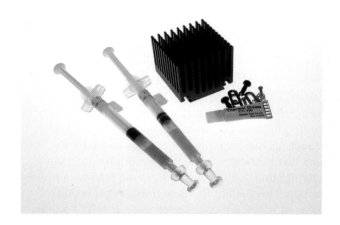

Some motherboards have fans on their North Bridge chips, and some have heatsinks. Then there's the kind of motherboard that has neither, and looks the worse for it. Place this shiny, blue porcupine of a heatsink on your bare North Bridge chip to cool it off a few degrees and increase your mobo's pimp factor tenfold. The heatsink is passive, meaning it should provide enough cooling without a dedicated fan. Be warned: When the thermal paste goes on, the aluminum heatsink ain't coming off.

Cathode Sound Module

People tap their feet and clap their hands to the sound of music. But PCs just sit there, lame and inanimate despite the irresistible kick and snare drum in Britney's new Top 40 hit. How'd you like to see your PC do the *Running Man* while cranking out the tunes? Well, that's not gonna happen. But the sound-sensitive cold cathode controller is the next best thing. Plug it in and your PC's lights get all jiggy wid it, flashing on cue with low-frequency beats. The microphone sensitivity is adjustable so you can sync it up just so and then sit back and enjoy the show.

Security Case Screw

Paranoid PC users, rejoice. These chromed security screws make unauthorized parts removal impossible—without the included key, that is. Taking the place of standard screws, the security screws can keep LAN party competitors from messing with your compo-nents. They can also securely lock down your drives and PCI cards. Because they look so good, you'll be tempted to use the screws throughout your case, inside and out. But don't be overzealous. If you switch parts regularly, you'll find that these screws take a bit more time to tinker with than the regular variety. One more hint: Don't lose that key unless you're prepared to run your current parts indefinitely.

Crystalfontz LCD Display Kit Model 632 USB

With the Crystalfontz LCD display, you'll be able to appraise your PC's status at a glance. Set up the backlit screen to report a number of useful stats in the highest of style. We've set up our LCD to show CPU utilization, email subject headers, MP3 track names and numbers, and EQ settings. It's perfect for managing MP3s without the aid of an overly conspicuous 21'' monitor. Available in blue, yellow, and white backlights, with black or silver bay mounts, there's a Crystalfontz LCD display out there that's sure to match your lifestyle.

Military Switch

When the firefight gets underway in *Battlefield 1942*, wouldn't it be cool to sound a red alert and throttle up your auxiliary fan array with a simple flip of an honest-to-goodness military switch? That's just one of the many possible uses for this all-purpose, heavy-duty case switch that's indeed approved for use by the U.S. armed services. A finer toggle you will not find. A bright red safety cover prevents misfires and, by throwing it into its prone position, the underlying switch is kept safely off. We'd like to see a row of these switches complementing a custom camouflage paint job for the ultimate ready-for-action aesthetic. Set the switches up to control any of your accessories. Just make sure you have a drill, a 15/32'' bit, and a soldering iron for proper installation.

Sunbeam Cathode Fan

Here's an interesting twist: You don't necessarily want to highlight the gear in your box. Rather, you're hoping to detract attention from the dust bunnies and disorder inside your PC. When it comes to case fans, you can't get any more eye-catching than the extra-strength lighting of a cathode. We weren't thrilled by the added cable clutter of the cathode and the power inverter, but the truth is, you barely notice it (or any other imperfections) amid the fan's blindingly bright lights. The downside? The fan grill is thick enough to make traditional mounting locations tricky.

From the Shelves of a Bygone Era

Saying that Scott Clark's Industrial Revolution mod is based on off-the-shelf parts is like saying a custom-hacked hot rod is based on a stock factory chassis. Indeed, this mod (which Scott describes as "neo-industrial—part Thomas Edison, part twenty-first century") is anything but stock. No, what we have here is a triumph of case-modding creativity that's much, much greater than the sum total of its various parts.

Nonetheless, this October 2003 Rig of the Month winner proves you can base a spectacular theme PC on a stock enclosure. In fact, Scott's case is so generic that it didn't even come with a name and model number (it was just a cheap eBay find, says the modsman). The gigantic "evaporative cooling tower" is handmade, but the rig's water-cooling system is powered by another prefab part, the Dangerden MAZE 2 copper water block.

The lesson here is that it sometimes pays to purchase off-the-shelf parts. The time you save in fabrication can be parlayed into other, more important handcrafted details. After all, you don't hand-assemble video cards on your kitchen table, do you?

Without a doubt, the rig's various bits of vintage instrumentation (all purchased on eBay) create the lion's share of the project's charm. We can't decide whether they qualify as "found objects" or "off-the-shelf parts from a bygone era," but we're mighty impressed that each instrument serves a functional purpose. It's the perfect marriage between technologies past and present.—J.P.

The rig's various electrical subsystems can be controlled either individually or via a single master switch.

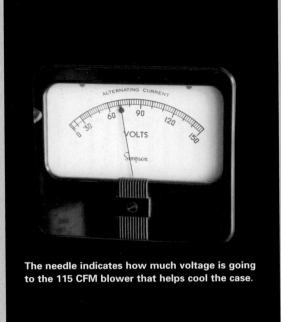

The needle indicates how much voltage is going to the 115 CFM blower that helps cool the case.

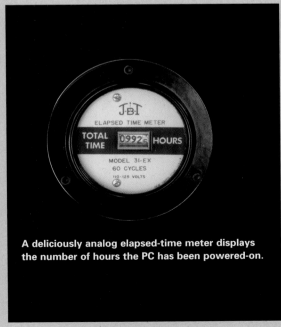

A deliciously analog elapsed-time meter displays the number of hours the PC has been powered-on.

Chapter Nine

Building the Ultimate Found-Object Mod

Turning damn near anything into a PC

Alex Wiley proved that a found object mod can be stylish and classy, while still delivering top performance. Wiley's Marantz 2220B Receiver Mod was *Maximum PC*'s May 2004 Rig of the Month and is the definition of smooth.

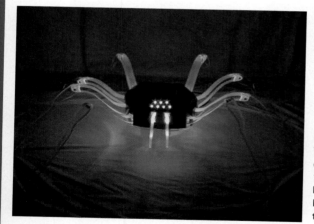

Part found object, part built-from-scratch, Alex Wiley's Spidercase made our skin crawl with its creepy good looks, lighted fangs, and general "arachnidness." Fashioned from an old square oil bucket, some fiberglass, plastic, and a lot of Bondo, the Spidercase is testimony to the fact that you can stuff a PC into just about anything.

Joshua Driggs's (a.k.a. ZapWizard) Radioactive Computer is built in a military ammo box. The multipin connectors were custom-made by Driggs, and the vacuum fluorescent display is capable of running system stats, WinAmp visuals, or a sine wave, as pictured here.

If you ever have the pleasure of visiting the home or workshop of a case modding enthusiast, some of the most remarkably engineered mods you might encounter are the ones you walked right past without a second glance. You might even find your host busy in the kitchen burning his or her latest mixed music CD in the toaster. No, seriously.

Not since a tiny surveillance camera was sewn into the stuffing of a teddy bear have we seen such attempts at a covert cover-up of personal computing hardware in the home. From the whimsical and weird to the downright practical, found object modding is the ultimate in stealth and integration. Whereas one aspect of modding is to make the computer blend into an environment by using select materials, colors, and paint schemes, found object modding takes this idea to a whole new level. From household appliances to old stereo equipment and toys, no object is safe from a modder with a plan to turn one of them into a fully functional PC.

Creating PCs from found objects is probably one of the most fun and challenging hardware hacking projects. Typically, the goal of the modder is to skillfully integrate all the hardware and components into a stealthy, unassuming enclosure—for instance, an old stereo amplifier (see Alex Wiley's Marantz 2220B Receiver Mod shown in this chapter). Original buttons and knobs become power and reset buttons, even volume and fan speed controllers. With some electronic prowess, old analog volume meters become dancing hard drive activity displays. The best examples of these mods use, to some degree, the original mechanical and aesthetic elements of the object being transformed.

What I find interesting about these mods is that they're a pretty neat indicator of shrinking desktop hardware technology. You can bet that when the next smallest motherboard or hard drive is released, it will shortly thereafter find its way into an everyday item by the hands of a mad modder. The hardware of choice for the smallest of these projects is the Mini-ITX

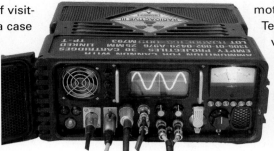

Joshua Driggs used green active cold-cathodes to give his custom rig an eerie glow; Driggs didn't sacrifice speed for style either. In fact, this puppy packs an AMD Athlon XP 2700+ proc, an nForce Micro-ATX mobo, an ATI Radeon 9200 videocard, a full-size hard drive, a DVD drive, and (get this) nine fans.

motherboard made famous by Via Technologies, with its integrated video, audio, and CPU. Measuring about 7'' square, these boards fit into relatively small objects such as tabletop humidors, hardcover books, picture frames, and gaming systems.

Although the Mini-ITX-based projects are excellent for Internet surfing, file serving, and media boxes, they fall short (with currently available consumer hardware) on the requirements of serious PC gaming and other power-hungry applications. For the found object mod in this chapter, I wanted a powerful and relatively compact gaming system that was stealthy, stylish, and portable. With that in mind, my alternative to the Mini-ITX motherboard was the larger Micro-ATX (MATX) board. These boards pack many of the features and functions of their larger ATX cousins into a smaller package by sacrificing several PCI slots and using tighter design engineering.

My found object victim is an interesting hard-shell backpack I spotted someone wearing at a LAN party. What I at first thought were more suited for a turtle/human hybrid, these great-looking backpacks, upon closer inspection, have a lot of modding potential. The shell is made from acrylonitrile butadiene styrene (ABS) plastic, the same tough material bike helmets and protective gear are made from, and in my eyes, the perfect enclosure for a PC.

Charles Thomas used an ammo container to create his Binladenator rig, winning runner-up honors in *Maximum PC's* July 2003 Patriotic PC contest.

Hands-on How-to: Creating a Found-Object Mod

Sweet Swedish Inspiration: The Ultimate Portable Rig

Tools Used for Our Project:

- Rotary tool
- Utility knife
- Hacksaw
- Metal snips
- Combination square
- Power drill
- Hand tap
- Soldering iron
- Bench vise
- Ball peen hammer
- Label-making machine
- Spade drill bit
- Sanding drum
- Sandpaper (100- to 800-grit)
- Artist's brushes

Materials Used for Our Project:

- Boblbee hard-shell backpack
- AMD 64 3200+
- MSI M-ATX K8T800 motherboard
- ATI X800 Pro
- 1GB Corsair RAM
- Panasonic Slim DVD/CD-R Combo
- Western Digital 36GB 10k RPM Raptor hard disk drive
- Windows XP Professional
- AGP right-angle adapter card
- Cooler Master Aerogate controller
- 80mm and 60mm case fans
- Swiftech CPU cooler
- Sheet styrene
- Krylon Fusion paint (gloss black and burgundy)
- Masking tape
- Door weather stripping kit (aluminum rails)
- Stock aluminum
- Socket head screws
- Thumbscrews
- Generic case screws
- Brass motherboard standoffs
- Gap-filling super glue (Zap brand or others)
- Denatured alcohol
- Self-sticking wire management clips
- IDE cable adapter
- Zip ties
- Modder's wire mesh
- 5-minute epoxy
- Split-loom tubing
- Heat-shrink material

Estimated Time Commitment

- 150 hours (although it might take you less now that you can follow my lead)

When the Boblbee backpack arrived and I was able to take a closer look at it, a certain sense of uh-oh befell this humble hardware hacker. Was it in reality too small to accommodate a Micro-ATX-size computer system? Before purchasing the backpack, I did as much research as I could (short of calling the manufacturer in Sweden) to find the dimensions and specs for this model, and from those careful calculations, my hardware should fit.

I closed my eyes, took a deep breath, and then panicked a little more before I began to open the boxes of hardware for the intended project. Somewhere there was an audible drum roll as my heart skipped a beat and then rejoiced as the MATX motherboard fit nicely inside the backpack with room to spare. It was most assuredly going to be a tight fit, but for now all was well in the world of modding. You might find yourself in the same situation when purchasing items sight-unseen, but in the end careful research pays off.

This sporty hard shell backpack from Boblbee caused a double-take when I first saw it at a LAN party. Built tough from ABS plastic and sturdy nylon, it's great for transporting laptops and other sensitive items. It also turned out to be a great contender for a found object mod.

When the backpack arrived at my door, my first impression was that it would never fit the hardware I had planned for it. After a bout of modding panic, I checked the largest component—the motherboard—for fit. With a sigh of relief, I had passed the first hurdle in transforming the Boblbee backpack into a stylish and portable gaming PC.

Step 1: Mocking Up the Hardware Housing

Before I even purchased the backpack, I gave a lot of thought as to how I would design and integrate the hardware into it. The factory finish on the backpack was a nice pearl burgundy, and having to repaint it was a task I didn't want to include in the modding plan; my goal was to keep it as close to the manufacturer's original design as possible. With this in mind, creating a kind of framework to mount the hardware to appeared to be the best solution. Sheets of polystyrene plastic (similar to ABS plastic) and aluminum stock were to be the materials for the project, so I took a trip to the plastic supply store and to my local airline hangar-sized home store for supplies.

I jumped right in by sketching out in pencil and then cutting four rough shapes from sheet styrene with a utility knife. This plastic is easily cut by first scoring several times and then carefully snapping. With a bit of practice, you can create accurate cuts using this low-tech method—not to mention you lessen the dust and mess created with power tools. With strips of masking tape to hold the housing together, the next couple of hours was spent carefully marking and shaving the plastic to fit snugly inside the backpack (Figures 1 and 2). When the shape and size were acceptable, I used a gap-filling super glue to bond all the parts together.

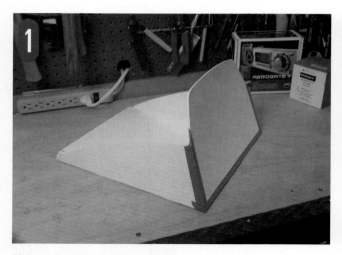

Using sheets of sturdy polystyrene plastic, I mocked up a simple housing that could be slipped inside the back-pack.

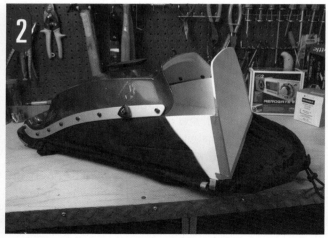

Getting the angle just right on the front was an important factor in achieving a good look and fit. Several accessories inside the case had to be removed, such as a zippered notebook folder and pen holder. One of my goals was to keep the backpack as original as possible.

Step 2: Mounting the Motherboard and Videocard Inside the Plastic Housing

Now that I had the proper shape and size for the plastic housing, the plan was to mount all the hardware within the given area inside it. Starting with the motherboard and ATI X-800 graphics card, I positioned them in various ways to find just the right spot for them to live. In this photo, you'll notice the graphics card is not mounted in the standard vertical position in the AGP slot, but horizontally (Figure 1). To save space inside this housing, I borrowed a little technology from the server industry in the form of an AGP right-angle adapter card. This nifty device can be had for about $15 and comes in several heights and configurations for positioning AGP cards on the motherboard.

To give the project a more engineered and professional look, I designed a simple rail system for mounting a

removable, sliding motherboard tray (Figure 2). It also served another purpose by allowing me to mount a slim, laptop computer–type CD-RW drive beneath the tray. For the railings, I found these great extruded aluminum parts at the home store that were part of a door weather-stripping kit. The extrusion has a U-shaped channel that enabled me to make a sliding rail together with other stock aluminum parts.

Next I made a tray, again from sheet plastic, using the brass standoffs that came with the motherboard (Figure 3). The motherboard was placed on the plastic sheet; then all the mounting holes were traced on with a pencil. A small pilot hole was drilled in the plastic, and then a 6/32" hand tap was used to thread the holes for the standoffs.

With the motherboard in place, it was obvious that the videocard would have to be mounted horizontally to conserve precious space. To do this, I purchased an AGP right-angle adapter (AGP 8x–compatible) that is primarily used in stacked server-type cases. Because I had no plans to use the PCI slots on the motherboard, it was no problem to have them covered by the videocard as a result of using the adapter.

To give a nice engineered look to the project, I built a sliding motherboard tray from aluminum parts. Raising the motherboard up also gave me a spot to mount the slim CD-RW drive for the system. These extruded parts were found in the weather stripping aisle of my local home hardware store. You never know where you'll find great parts for your own mod, so keep a sharp eye out for just about anything.

A motherboard plate was made from styrene, complete with brass standoffs for mounting. A nice feature of sheet styrene is that it's easily tapped and threaded to accept screws and bolts.

Step 3: Creating an I/O Bezel

Putting the motherboard tray aside for now, I concentrated on creating a I/O (input, output) bezel for the front of the housing. The front of the housing was angled about 15° to match up with the shape of the backpack, so some tricky pieces of framework had to be cut and glued into place (Figure 1). Unlike a standard layout for a PC, all the wired inputs and devices had to be located on one single panel. Using sheets of paper to make pencil rubbings of the various components, I was able to plot out all the necessary holes, slots, and openings. Having that angled front piece made for a very challenging but fun part of this project (Figure 2).

For some added interest as well as function, I decided to put a fan speed and temperature monitoring device

on the front as well (Figure 3). I started with a Cooler Master Aerogate controller, first removing the small 40mm fan that was mounted on it. I then made a rectangular housing from styrene to hold the device. Instead of having all the system fans connected directly to the power supply unit, I now had a central hub that required only a single Molex connector, making the system slightly more compact.

Because of the cramped space I had to work within, I was concerned about effectively cooling the AGP card, especially because I had to mount it with a right-angle adapter. Using a small piece of styrene, I was able to create a housing for a 40mm fan that created an exhaust system for the AGP card (Figure 4).

The front panel of the housing turned out to be very sturdy due to the complex framing I had to do in plastic. The best glue for styrene is any type of gap-filling super glue, such as Zap! Brand or Flash brand. I also used a super glue *kicker*, which is a spray-on drying accelerator specially formulated for cyanoacrylate adhesives. I applied the glue as if welding, filling the corners of each joint with a thin bead of adhesive.

Here you can see how nicely the slim CD-RW drive fits beneath the motherboard tray. For this project, every square inch had to be accounted for and used to some degree for components and basic design structure.

Front bay devices like this Cooler Master Aerogate are a convenient hub for connecting system fans. I removed the small fan that was to the left of the LCD display (originally meant for hard drive cooling) to save space. The remaining hardware was mounted in its own box made from styrene. The temperature sensors for the CPU, hard disk, case, and videocard provides at-a-glance monitoring of system performance.

I was a little concerned with cooling this ATI X800 Pro card efficiently now that it was to be mounted using an AGP right-angle adapter. I was able to fashion a small piece of styrene and mount it on the adapter and, using the 40mm fan from the Cooler Master Aerogate, created this exhaust system.

Step 4: Creating the Skeleton

The front panel of the housing now became a structural element, made quite strong now by the intricate bracing and many plastic pieces required for the I/O area. A support brace was made for the PSU from aluminum stock and fastened to the front panel with small socket-head bolts and tapped holes (Figure 1). With the last of the plastic fabrication behind me, the next step was to mount the motherboard tray and create aluminum framework, or *bones*, to hold all the remaining hardware securely in place. The method and madness were fairly straightforward—using aluminum bar, I would angle and cut pieces bent into various shapes that would fit into the given space (Figure 2). I found myself repeatedly assembling and then breaking down the parts to get them to fit

properly. More than several aluminum pieces wound up in the scrap heap; however, each time I made the same piece the result was a clean bend with a nice fit. Spare case screws really came in handy for this part of the project, so keep those pesky little parts in a nice big box for later use. Thumbscrews were a nice finishing touch for parts that had to be disassembled often, and they made the job a bit easier (Figures 3, 4, and 5).

A final test fit of every component was done to double-check clearances inside the backpack. When I was absolutely sure my Rube Goldberg-like contraption would work, it was time for a thorough cleaning of each part—plastic and aluminum—in preparation for painting.

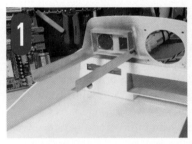

These two rails for mounting the power supply were connected to the front panel using socket head screws. Because the panel is multiple layers of plastic, it became strong enough to attach hardware. Aluminum angle stock like this can be found at hardware stores and home centers in many shapes and sizes.

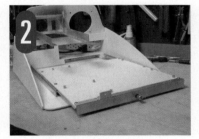

The removable, sliding motherboard tray helped a great deal during the many times the hardware had to be installed—and removed—during construction. It also adds a spark of simple engineering interest to the project.

Forming the skeleton that would hold all the components was a trial-and-error process. Aluminum stock was measured and then bent by hand in a bench vise to form the proper shape. A ball peen hammer was also used to "persuade" the metal into shape.

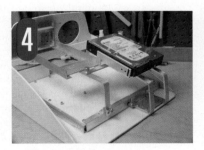

What looks like a Rube Goldberg contraption is actually a pretty well-designed structure for holding all the PC hardware.

The screws used to connect the framework were all leftovers from stock cases. The aluminum and plastic were threaded to accept the screws using a hand tap.

Step 5: Breaking Out the Paint

Every time I create a mod, I hope to finish it off by discovering new methods and techniques for building the next one. With this project, that discovery came in the form of a relatively new paint product. Painting plastics with traditional coatings has always been a challenging task for industrial designers, model makers, and now case modders. It seemed that no matter how careful we were with the cleaning, preparation, and priming, there was always a certain amount of anxiety about the durability of the final finish. Alternatives to plastic painting, such as special dyes that stain the plastic permanently, are available. Although they're more durable than paint, the color selection is limited and the process labor intensive. If that's not your cup of tea, there is always having your pieces sent to an auto body painting specialist to have them apply a coating. This is great for a PC chassis, and the results are stunning, but for the do-it-yourself types like me, I'd rather keep the smaller painting jobs in-house.

I've read a few articles about Krylon's Fusion brand of spray paint being used for tough-to-paint plastics in automobiles and on objects around the house but have never tried it myself (Figure 1). For this project, I decided to get a few cans of flat and gloss black to give it a what-the-heck try. This paint claimed to be much different from others in that it's not simply a colored coating, but a special chemical that bonds to plastic on a molecular level. Sounds pretty cool to me.

After cleaning all the parts of the mod with a cloth and denatured alcohol, I prepared a small piece of white styrene plastic to test the Fusion paint. After a few light coats, I let the test piece dry as recommended by the instruction on the back of the can. In fact, I let it dry overnight just to give this new-fangled paint the benefit of the doubt. The next morning I approached my test piece again, the sound of a drum roll in the background as I picked it up and proceeded to gouge the painted surface with a fingernail. To my absolute amazement, I was unable to reveal the white plastic beneath, even with vigorous digging with said fingernail. This can't be—maybe I'm still asleep! The product really did live up to the hype, and I can't express enough how long I've waited (okay, 20 years or so) for a plastic paint that is this durable. I am now sold on this paint, and I proceeded to give the entire housing a good-looking gloss black paint finish. For once, those 800 numbers on the product labels came in handy because I had a few questions for the Krylon representative about applying an automotive wax coating or clear coat spray paint. I was told that other clear paints are incompatible, but after 7 days curing time, I could do a light polish with rubbing compound and finish off the paint with a clear automotive glaze. Impatient as I am, I did this about 5 days later with pretty good results. I was also told that Fusion would soon be manufacturing a clear coating that is compatible with Fusion paints. Hallelujah.

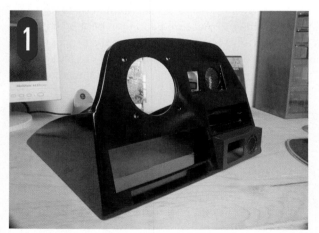

I had been wanting to try Krylon's Fusion brand of spray paint and found a good candidate with this project. Fusion bonds to hard-to-paint plastic surfaces on a molecular level, creating a durable and scratch-resistant finish. Gloss black and burgundy (which matched the red of the backpack nicely) were the two colors I chose.

As you might imagine, a number of steps were involved in painting the backpack (or any mod for that matter). I thoroughly covered painting—such that can be done by non-professionals—in Chapter 4, "Painting Cases." Bear in mind, however, that unless you have access to expensive painting tools, a booth, and so on, you are severely limited in what you can pull off when it comes to painting your own mods. I used spray paint for this mod, and it worked great. However, your needs might go beyond what can be achieved with spray paint. In that case, you most likely need to seek the services of a professional painter. I provide some recommendations for professionals who can apply a kick-ass paint job at a reasonable price. Trust me, even if the quote does leave you a little sticker-shocked, it won't be a tenth as pricey as you can expect if you try to purchase the necessary tools to apply a professional-grade paint job yourself.

Step 6: Installing the Hardware and Final Modding

When it came the time for final assembly of the parts, it felt like I had done it a hundred times before—only because I had, during the construction (Figures 1–7). The only difference this time around was the degree of finishing such as wrapping cables, installing wire management clips, and the general tucking away of loose wires. The final assembly had to be fairly neat and tidy because of the small space, but also because it's good modding practice to do so. With such a tight space, I had to be very careful to keep wires and cables out of the path of fans and to keep in mind the overall clearances for airflow once the housing was placed in the backpack.

I also used split-loom tubing and heat-shrink material to tidy up the wires inside the backpack (refer to Chapter 7, "Laying Cables," for details).

> Note that I haven't gone into a lot of detail here on the actual hardware assembly. I assume that, if you're thinking about taking on a serious mod such as this, you're already pretty accomplished with PC hardware assembly. If you do need some additional assistance with PC building, see *Maximum PC's Guide to Building a Dream PC*. You'll learn everything you need to know about PC building in this excellent book written by Maximum PC's own Will Smith. Another excellent—and deep—PC hardware reference is the venerable *Upgrading and Repairing PCs*, by Scott Mueller.

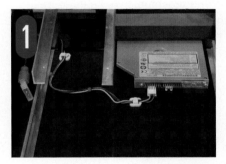

When using slim-style optical drives in full-size systems, you need to use an IDE adapter, shown here. Meant as replacements for laptop drives, these are the best choice when making small found object mods. Self-sticking wire management clips keep things tidy and prevent bunching in tight spaces.

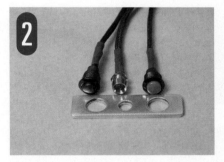

A very simple button bezel was made from aluminum bar stock and mounted on the front of the housing. Shown are the power (in red) and reset buttons and the power indicator light.

Here you can see the fan bracket I made for the X-800 videocard. Warm air is exhausted from underneath the card and out into the open areas of the case.

This Swiftech CPU cooler is a massive but extremely well-designed block for both Intel and AMD processors. With a high CFM (but very loud) fan, you see temperatures almost as low as water-cooled rigs with this cooler.

Step 6: Installing the Hardware and Modding (Continued)

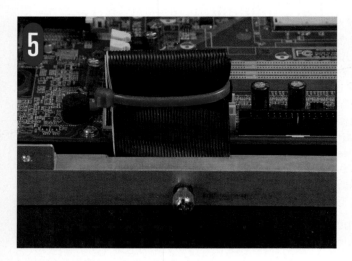

We all make mistakes, and I did by forgetting to make room for the optical drive cable. I solved this by cutting a channel in the framework of the motherboard mounting tray. A zip tie keeps the folded cable in place.

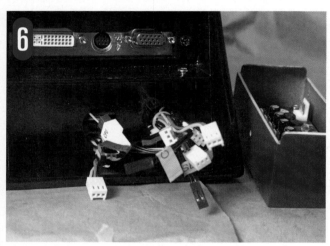

By using a label-making machine, I was able to make sense of this spaghetti by clearly marking each cable. It's a good idea to mark every cable using labels or by writing on pieces of masking tape. Tracing wires in a system as crowded as this is not a fun task.

Every piece of hardware is in place, and the system is ready to fire up. You can see here the two intake fans—80mm and 60mm—mounted at the rear of the housing. It was time now to install the OS and let the system run for a few hours. It's critical to double- and triple-check your physical connections as you build a system like this to prevent hair-pulling rants and hours of extra work.

Step 7: Cutting the Intake Vent

My final bit of hacking on this project was cutting a good-sized vent in the shell of the backpack for ventilation. I had an 80mm fan and a 60mm fan at the rear of the housing that would draw in fresh air, and a single 80mm on the front bezel for exhaust. To protect the finish of the shell and provide a surface to draw on, I laid a few strips of blue masking tape down (Figure 1). With a spade bit and power drill, I made a starter hole so I could begin shaping the opening with my rotary tool and sanding drum (Figure 2). I finished the edges of the opening with sandpaper, starting with 100-grit and working up to 800. With a small artist's brush I painted the edge with some flat black Fusion paint I had sprayed into a tin can to collect (Figure 3).

The only major modification done to the backpack was the cutting of an intake vent toward the back of it. Blue masking tape was used to plot out the opening and to protect the factory finish.

To make a clean opening, a starter hole was first drilled into the shell of the backpack.

The rest of the material was removed using my rotary tool fitted with a coarse grit sanding drum attachment. The opening was then sanded clean and smooth by hand, and the raw plastic edges painted with a small brush.

Step 8: Adding the Mesh Grill

With a pair of metal snips, I cut an over-sized piece of modder's mesh, a superbly made steel screen material that was sent to me for the project by master modder Bill Owen of www.mnpctech.com (Figure 1). I had never used the material before, and I can say that I'll be using it again for other projects that require a good-quality mesh. The mesh was then glued onto the interior of the case using a fast-setting epoxy around the edges (Figure 2).

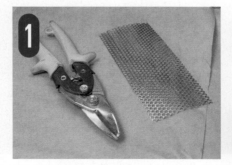

Good mesh and grill material is hard to find. This modder's mesh was perfect for the opening on the backpack.

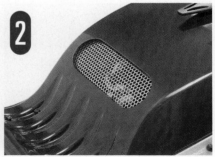

After it was cut to size with a pair of metal snips, it was glued to the inside of the case using 5-minute type epoxy resin.

The Finished Mod in All Its Glory!

When I slipped the housing into the backpack, it was a pretty good feeling having accomplished my first found object mod. The PC needed an operating system, and I did so without a hitch; then I allowed the mod to run for 24 hours to test for stability and monitor system temperatures. After that, a few hours of gaming and stressing the system proved again its LAN worthiness. I must say that the unit is no lightweight, and using components typically found in desktop boxes was surely the cause (not to mention the monster CPU cooler) because the housing and framework were quite light. Style and portability was the name of the game after all, and after it was strapped to my back, the weight wasn't so terrible. I do think it will make a great LAN conversation piece if anything.

Build a mod like this one and you'll have the ultimate portable PC. You'll still have to attach a monitor to it (I couldn't fit one of those in there, too) after you get to where you're going, but how hard is that?

I can hear the words echoed from 50 years ago, as one in a group of shirt-pocket slide-rule geeks stood before a room-sized computer and uttered, "Some day you'll be able to carry a computer on your back." Well, today I did, just for the fun of building it.

Keep an eye on your case, er, backpack, temp with the built-in Aerogate controller.

The power and reset buttons, as well as the power indicator light, are in easy reach.

Maximum PC Fave!

And It Might Even Hit 12,000 Kesselmarks, Too!

We thought we had seen true *Star Wars* fandom when *Maximum PC* senior editor Gordon Ung had the movie score playing during his wedding—*as he and his bride exited down the aisle.* Does Russ Caslis trump the Ungster? That's debatable. But if you could hold in your hands the wee Millennium Falcon model that serves as Russ's PC enclosure, you'd be impressed. In the grand pantheon of found-object PC mods, the Falcon project was surely a wicked pisser to handle.

Caslis owned the model as a child, but as he puts it, "After finding one on eBay, I realized that either the toy had shrunk or I had grown…. Many hours were spent simply looking at the toy, trying to figure out how to fit everything inside and where all the connections would be."

Thank the PC gods for delivering mini-ITX motherboards to the masses because without these smallest of all mobos, shoe-horned mod jobs like this wouldn't be possible. But you know what we'd really like to see now? A functional PC stuffed into a Millennium Falcon model, and then *that* model stuffed into a bottle!—J.P.

Russ was determined to include a window through which the internal workings of his rig's laptop hard drive could be observed.

It's a tight fit, but six laptop fans (not pictured) keep these close quarters cool.

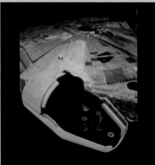

A homemade control panel is home to power, reset, and engine buttons. An LED that transitions through the three primary colors serves as the PC's power light.

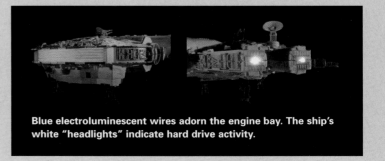

Blue electroluminescent wires adorn the engine bay. The ship's white "headlights" indicate hard drive activity.

Chapter Ten

Building the Ultimate Scratch-Built Mod

PC case? Who needs a stinkin' PC case?
We show you how to build your own case.

Mark Weitz built this eye-popping tribute to Microsoft's Xbox game system from scratch. Mark's creation was featured in the March 2002 issue of *Maximum PC*.

Blood fin tetras, zebra danios, and red wagtail platies all call this PC home. Katie Hoch, an engineering student in Pennsylvania, captured our hearts with her 20,000 Leagues Under the CPU mod that's not only fully functional, but doubles as a fish tank. Katie's mod won our 2003 Coolest PC Case Modding Contest.

Barney Lascola proved that a mod can come from the most unlikely and useful sources—an actual desk! Barney's creation swept us away, winning our March 2004 Rig of the Month contest.

Case modders and aficionados often say that the true measure of a craftsperson's skill lies in the enclosures he builds entirely from scratch—raw materials that have been cut, carved, sanded, glued, and assembled into unique master-pieces of art and engineering. These "scratch-built" cases represent the pinnacle of case-modding craft, in large part because they allow the builder's imagination to determine every aspect of even the smallest design detail.

The scratch-built case is the PC geek equivalent of the custom chopper—custom-built from the chassis all the way to the paint finish, and like no other bike on the planet. So, if you want a case mod that stands out from the cookie-cutting crowd of stock enclosures, this chapter will help you on your way to designing and building a rig that's worthy of your artist's signature.

The Importance of Reverse-Engineering

Let's face it, the basic geometry of stock cases is restricted to squares and rectangles. Manufacturers might try to mask these obvious limitations with round-ed corners, protruding plastic decorations, and fancy front bezel designs, but if you remove all this injection-molded garb, the naked truth is exposed: That fancy prefab case is nothing but a metallic box.

Enter scratch-building, which gives you complete control over box; you can think outside it or completely ignore it by creating a wild and original shape. My most enjoyable case-modding projects have always involved building enclosures from scratch. There have been challenges at every turn, even for an experienced modder and craftsperson like myself. And every irritat-ing engineering problem that ever resolved itself in a cry of "Eureka!" has given me a rush of satisfaction. Elegant solutions are the sweetest rewards.

Nothing has helped more in my scratch-building adventures than my practice with taking things apart. For example, if you were to take an old VCR and remove the outer shell, you'd find an amazing assortment of

Rob Arnold fashioned this scratch-built mod with an exposed hard drive hardware hack, winning our December 2002 Rig of the Month honors.

parts, all living in harmony with one another. Indeed, industrial engineers put immense creative effort into conceiving delicate balances of electronics and mechani-cal elements, and deconstructing their designs can lead to better case-modding strategies. I found that pok-ing around inside a VCR provides great ideas on how to mount hardware in tight spaces by using clips, springs, rails, posts, nuts, and bolts. And examining how an outer shell comes apart can provide useful clues on making seamless joints for a computer case.

So, go ahead. Take something apart (safely!) and learn from it.

Actually planning your scratch-built case is, needless to say, quite important. There's no need to map out every bit of minutia during the early planning stages, but for a good starting point, you should definitely sketch out your basic design on paper. When I make custom cases, I try to establish an overall set of outer dimensions and then build on this basic structure in an organic manner. In effect, I use a freestyle method of engineering that allows my projects to take on lives of their own. Of course, by not planning every last detail, I often find myself with a few problems that require a bit more caffeine and a little head-scratching, but for me, this all adds up to fun.

Ed Downing proved that a computer can be both functional and portable, while still maintaining and air of class. This mod was Maximum PC's November 2002 Rig of the Month. Ed's classy wood-en case includes storage space for a mouse, keyboard, and other peripherals.

Online message boards devoted to case-modding are an excellent source for help when a project hits a snag. I've found solutions to the most confounding problems from fellow craftspeople who generously offered their advice. And when you visit these enthusiast websites, you'll also find scratch-built case mods from people all over the world, perhaps giving you that boost of inspiration for your own project.

So How Do We Teach That Which Defies Teaching?

The very nature of scratch-built case-modding makes it virtually impossible to provide you with a fully actionable, step-by-step guide to making your own. After all, every scratch-built case is a unique expression of its creator's vision, so I really can't show you how to build your own. I can, however, show you how I built one of my own, alerting you to tricks of the trade and giving you a general idea of the scope of a scratch-building project.

Later in this chapter, we get into the nitty-gritty of my Project Jujube mod, but for now let's get into some general issues you'll need to tackle regardless of your personal vision. Here are some points to consider.

Hey, It's Still a PC

Scratch-built or not, your mod must still function as a working computer, so you'd do well to learn as much as possible about how systems are built into stock cases. Indeed, a good stock case can teach you some very important lessons: how structural components are mounted, the best placements for various types of hardware, basic airflow and cooling requirements—the list goes on. Although scratch-building is about breaking the rules of design, you still have to apply good practice when it comes to basic PC functionality.

Gene Phipps, veteran case mod builder and avid LAN gamer, found a way to marry his two favorite pastimes when he saw the ad about CompUSA's Mod Contest in *Maximum PC*. On the plane, right after his January wedding, Gene convinced his wife to let him cut the honeymoon short so he could meet the 20-day contest deadline. She supported his idea to build a mod based on Half Life 2, but with one caveat—if he won the $10,000 grand prize, she got a longer vacation. Eighty percent of Gene's case mod is based on off-the-shelf retail products. Congratulations and bon voyage, Gene!

Function Precedes Form

Your ultimate goal should be to create a one-of-a-kind working computer inside a really interesting-looking case, so the first questions to ask yourself should be what will the PC be used for, and where do I intend to use it? If you're building a workstation or a gaming PC, for example, you know that you'll be swapping parts in and out quite often, so you'll want to design a case that provides easy interior access.

In fact, even if you don't plan on upgrading too often, you still need to make sure that your case can be easily opened for repairs and troubleshooting. After I built my The Matrix: Rebirth 8.0 project, I found myself having to take notes and photographs just so I'd remember the steps needed to gain access to the inside of the case! (The lesson learned with that project was to create a simple instruction manual during the build for reference later.)

Many of the best scratch-built cases I've seen were created to blend in with particular environments. For example, a finely crafted wooden case blends in beautifully when placed in a home decorated with warm furniture accents. By the same token, a sleek, streamlined cases made from acrylic or polished metal integrates nicely into a modern home or office.

Finally, if you plan to take your scratch-built case on the road, consider that it should be fairly durable and made of a strong material that can withstand a lot of movement and changing environments. Acrylic scratches, for example, so it's definitely not the best material on which to base a LAN party rig.

Form follows function. Respect that credo.

Johan "Mashie" Grundstrom's Y2k Bug is a stunning example of a scratch-built case mod. The shell of this entomological masterpiece is made entirely of carbon fiber, an expensive but extremely strong and lightweight material. To learn more about creating custom cases with carbon fiber material, visit Johan's website (www.mashie.org) for a step-by-step tutorial.

Choosing Your Poisons

When it comes to picking a base material of your scratch-built mod, your choices are endless. Acrylic, wood, styrene, and metal are but a few examples of the more common materials you can go with, while exotic materials, such as carbon fiber and polyester casting resin, are appropriate for sculpted, lightweight enclosures

If you plan on painting your case, the materials you choose for your outer shell have to be carefully considered. Plastic, metal, and wood all require a certain amount of careful thought and preparation before a decent paint finish can be applied.

Considering an acrylic or Plexiglas case? These materials require a very clean, clutter-free working environment to minimize scratches, chips, and other damage that can occur during such a build.

Before starting a scratch-building project, you have to consider the tools you'll need for successful completion. The old saying "get the right tool for the job" should be your scratch-building credo. So, when deciding on the materials for your rig, create an inventory of the power

and hand tools you already have in your arsenal. Wood cases call for sharp, well-maintained tools to cleanly and precisely cut the pieces for your case. Plastic- and metal-based projects require specialty hand and power tools that you might have to purchase or borrow. Without them, you won't be able to create a case with accurate cuts and finely crafted details.

Having the right tools and the know-how to use them safely and properly can prevent your projects from stalling or ending up in the scrap heap. The best safety equipment to prevent serious injury is knowledge. So, if you're unfamiliar with the operation of a certain tool, ask for assistance from those with experience.

Before we move on to the project for this chapter, here is a heads-up on the types of tools that might be required to complete your scratch-built project:

Wooden Cases

- Circular saw
- Table saw
- Jigsaw
- Wood-cutting blades for power tools
- Power drill
- Hand chisels
- Router
- Belt sander and finishing sander

Acrylic and Plastics

- Jigsaw
- Table saw
- Hand drill or drill press with bits made for plastics
- Plastic-cutting blades for power tools
- Plastic-polishing compounds

Metal Cases

- Jigsaw
- Metal snips (hand or powered)
- Propane torch for brazing and soldering
- Arc welder
- Grinders

See Chapter 1, "Prep Work: Laying the Perfect Foundation," to learn more about the tools I'm using in this chapter.

Hands-on How-to: Building a Scratch-Built Case

Project Jujube: A Home Theater PC

Materials Used for Our Project

- Intel Pentium 4 2.8c
- Micro Star International (MSI) Micro ATX main board
- ATI All In Wonder 9800 Pro w/remote
- Creative Labs Sound Blaster Audigy2 ZS
- Sony DW18A DVD-R/RW drive
- 1GB Corsair DDR400 Value RAM
- 200GB Western Digital Serial ATA hard drive
- Griffin Technology Power Mate USB multimedia controller and input device
- Matrix Orbital 2x24 VFD (vacuum fluorescent display)
- Shuttle Brand 250-watt power supply
- Windows XP Professional
- UV reactive cable sleeving
- Heat-shrink tubing
- Plexiglas
- Furniture glides
- 60mm and 80mm stealth fans
- Metal speaker mesh
- Spare power and reset wires
- Silver spray paint
- Silver contact paper
- DupliColor simulated anodized paint
- 1/4'' acrylic sheets
- Extruded aluminum door saddle (door sill)
- Aluminum tubing
- Aluminum angle
- Socket-head screws
- Brass and nylon standoffs

Tools Used for Our Project:

- Pencil and paper
- Jigsaw and plastic-cutting blades
- Belt and/or disk sander
- Sandpaper (100-, 300-, 600-, and 1200-grit)
- Power drill
- Wood and metal drill bits
- Center punch
- Hammer
- Small countersink
- T-style hand tap
- Spray lubricant
- Hacksaw
- Foredom rotary tool
- Allen and/or hex wrenches
- 6'' combination square
- Hobby knife
- Assortment of hand files
- Riffler files
- Hole saw
- Scroll saw
- Hot glue gun
- Cable ties

Estimated Time Commitment

- 72+ hours

Step 1: Gathering Materials

With the growing popularity of TiVo and other personal video recorders (PVRs), I wanted to build a home theater PC to replace the aging components in my entertainment center. Upgrading to a digital media center PC replaced my need for the bulky, low-quality VHS tapes that were gathering dust and taking up precious New York City apartment space. My initial step on the project was to jot down a needs assessment—in other words, what the heck do I want this PC to do for me.

First on the list, I wanted to record my favorite shows to the hard disk and be able to effortlessly program them to do so. Several excellent video capture cards are available, such as the ATI All In Wonder and the Hauppauge WinTV PVR, that record and play back video on your VGA monitor or television. These cards are often bundled with software that creates a front end or user interface that displays on your television. With these applications, you can integrate your satellite or cable service to download program guides and schedules from the Internet to record live broadcasts.

My lust for technology didn't stop at mere video recording: I also wanted to burn DVDs and finally get rid of all those VHS tapes. So, on the project hardware list a DVD burner was added. Because my shows would be eventually burned onto DVD, the need for mega storage was eliminated, and I chose a Western Digital 200GB drive to temporarily store the recordings. When the time came to decide on a video card, I chose the ATI All In Wonder Pro 9800, giving me both video capture *and* the ability to play the latest games when the nephews are visiting. SnapStream Media's BeyondTV3 software was chosen for its robust front end and user-friendly interface.

For the purpose of this chapter, I wanted to build a case from parts that were available at the local plastics shop and one of the big home improvement stores. Cruising these stores in what I like to call "mod mode," I come across endless ideas and possibilities for project hardware and materials. The one product that sparked the entire look of project Jujube was the extruded aluminum door saddle (or door sill) that makes up the front faceplate of the case. As soon as I

With all my hardware and materials gathered for the project, my next step was to do a rough layout of the internal parts.

grabbed it off the shelf (and took some dimensions with my trusty key chain tape measure), I began designing the case in my head around this one part. Not too far from the door saddle was the aisle that had all the aluminum tubing and angle I would need to make the frame and mounting rails for the case. After a trip to the hardware department, I had all the socket head screws I would need to fasten it all together.

My next visit was to the plastics shop, where I had 1/4'' acrylic sheets rough cut to my dimensions. Another good source for acrylic sheet is a custom sign shop in your area. Some good advice is to visit these shops and introduce yourself. Starting a friendly dialogue with the owners and salespeople can get you expert advice and help you locate hard-to-find materials, and they might even let you scrounge around in the piles of scrap for free stuff. If you spend some cash there and become a regular, you'll never have to venture far for parts for your next project.

At the end of the planning phase, I had all the hardware and materials I'd need to start roughing out the design and dimensions of Jujube.

Step 2: Laying Out and Mocking Up the Hardware

The construction principle of this project was to create a ridged frame from aluminum angle and "skin" it with acrylic side, top, and bottom pieces. This type of building is pretty basic and doesn't require an entire shop full of tools, so you beginners out there should be able to follow along without getting lost. The computer hardware I chose dictated the final dimensions of the case and was the reason I had the acrylic cut oversized at the plastics shop.

With the bottom and side pieces mocked up (Figure 1), I played around with the placement of the internal hardware. Avoid the impulse to cram the components together because this leads to problems with airflow and when cables have to be attached and wires routed. Most of the components are mounted to the bottom piece of acrylic, and I was careful to remember that the motherboard and other hardware would eventually be up on small posts. I decided on the ATI All In Wonder 9800 Pro and installed it temporarily on the motherboard along with the audio card. (Figure 2) This gave me the dimensions I'd need for the overall height of the case and allowed me to see how the aluminum framing would fit. As you're doing the mock-up, keep in mind the length of your power supply leads and how your cables and wiring will be installed. Leave yourself some room inside the case for fingers and tools to make the assembly easier later. Decide if you'd like to upgrade your system in the future with additional hard drives and PCI cards, reserving a place for them at this point in the mock-up stage. Give some thought to thermals and airflow and where fans will be placed to keep all that hardware running cool and comfy. Typically, air should enter the front, side, or top of your case; flow past the components; and exhaust out the back, much like a stock case. Take as much time as you need with the mock-up; calculate each and every step you'll need to fire up a working computer later.

The acrylic I purchased for the project conveniently came with a paper backing, perfect for marking up all the holes for hardware mounting. If the acrylic you buy doesn't have a backing or has a plastic film, cover it with strips of blue masking tape. You can even cover the acrylic with craft paper with some spray mount adhesive applied. Marking is very critical, so choose the best way to make clear, easy-to-see indications. With a sharp pencil, I traced the shape of each component onto the paper as a guide for drilling the holes (Figure 3). With the final placement of the components chosen, I now had the final length and width of the bottom piece, so on to the acrylic cutting. I used a jigsaw and plastic-cutting blade for the cuts. Plastic-cutting jigsaw blades with at least 14 teeth per inch (TPI) are good for straight, fine cuts in acrylic, Plexiglas, and soft metals such as aluminum and brass. You'll find jigsaw blades for just about every material and thickness you'll encounter, so always have the proper type on hand for the task. Medium speeds are best when cutting plastics to avoid heating up and melting the material and therefore binding the blade. I cut with the jigsaw on the outside of my pencil marks, leaving about 1/16'' to be removed next.

To save on the hand filing, I used a belt/disk sander combo machine (Figure 4) to clean my cuts accurately down to the pencil marks. Using a 100-grit belt on the machine, I held the bottom piece against the fence and as straight and upright as possible while applying pressure downward. I kept a close eye (behind safety glasses, of course) on the pencil mark as I sanded. After the rough cut was sanded, I used a smooth hand file to remove the marks the belt left on the edge. The edge was cleaned up with 100-grit wet/dry sandpaper, then 300-grit paper, and finally a good polishing of 600-grit paper with a bit of water. For a glass-smooth edge on acrylic, you can wet sand all the way up to 1200-grit and then polish it off with a plastic polishing compound like Novus brand.

Now that my bottom piece was cut to size and sanded clean, I prepared to mount the first component. With the motherboard in position on the bottom piece, I marked the holes with my pencil. If your pencil is too big, simply take a utility knife and whittle the shaft of the pencil down until it will fit easily into the screw holes. After the holes were marked, I readied my power drill and drill bits. When drilling in hard plastics, your standard wood and metal drill bits are not the best ones to use. Conventional wood and metal drill bits can cause the material to ride up the drill bit, possibly cracking the plastic. Bits made for plastics have a sharper point and less of a pitch, creating a clean hole and preventing damage. Ask for these at a plastics shop, or you can order them online from specialty hardware stores. Drilling plastic takes a slow speed to prevent melting and a steady hand, so practice on some scrap to get the hang of it.

I'm glad now that I save all the mounting hardware that comes with stock cases, and for this project the brass motherboard mounting posts were the perfect solution. After I drilled the holes for the brass posts, I used the proper-sized tap to thread the acrylic. The posts screwed in nicely and gave me a clean, accurate way to mount the motherboard to the acrylic.

After the hardware was mocked up and final decisions were made on best placement, I used a pencil to trace the shapes of the components right onto the paper backing of my acrylic bottom piece. This was then used as a guide for hardware mounting holes, posts, and screws.

A rough mock-up of the components on the acrylic sheets gives an overall sense of dimensions for the case. The decisions you make at this stage dictate future upgrades and expandability. The paper was left on the acrylic for protection and for layout purposes.

This belt/disk combo machine saves a lot of time cleaning up rough cuts in acrylic.

Installing the VGA and PCI cards is critical to roughing out the interior layout. If you plan to upgrade, think ahead and leave plenty of space for additional hardware.

Remember to save all those brass mounting posts that come with stock cases. These are just the thing for mounting motherboards and hard disk drives in your custom case.

Step 3: Framing with Stock Aluminum

To hold all the acrylic parts together, framing pieces made from aluminum angle stock worked out nicely. This material is not only easy to find at home and hardware stores, but is also very strong and can easily be cut, drilled, tapped, sanded, and polished. What more can you ask for? After the aluminum pieces were cut to size with a hacksaw and cleaned up on the disk sander, a center mark (Figure 1) was drawn along the length of each one. A tick mark was made with a pencil at every point where a socket head screw would be threaded. With a center punch and hammer, I lightly tapped (Figure 2) each mark. Making a dimple with a center punch prevents the drill bit from walking (Figure 3) along the material when a hole is drilled on the press. Again, slow to medium speed on the drill press is all that's needed to make a clean 9/64" hole in the aluminum. After my holes were drilled, I used a small counter sink on my power drill (Figure 4) to lightly clean off any burs on the aluminum.

I decided to thread the aluminum pieces rather than the acrylic, and for this I used a basic T-style tap and die set. Made from hardened steel, taps create inside (or female) threads for screws; a die is used to cut male threads, making the screw itself from metal rod. The 9/64 hole diameter in the aluminum is drilled slightly smaller than the tap, allowing the 8/32 tap to cut the proper threads. Using a tap (Figure 5) is simple and

makes for a clean, professional-looking job. Turn your tap clockwise in the hole 1/3 to 1/2 turn; then after you feel some resistance, back off (or unscrew) the tap slightly. Be sure to keep the tap perpendicular to the hole and the material so you don't create a crooked set of threads. On thicker metals, you might have to back the tap out of the hole completely to clear away any metal chips and debris. Some light machine oil or WD-40 on the tap helps make threading easier and cleaner.

Taps are made from hardened steel, but they are very brittle. On thicker metals, go slowly and try not to bend the tap accidentally, which will surely snap it off. To test the newly threaded holes, you can take an 8/32 bolt and thread it in a few turns.

Once the aluminum angle was drilled and tapped, I used the holes to transfer marks onto my acrylic bottom piece. I drilled the acrylic with an 11/64 bit and slightly larger than the socket head screw. The screws were far longer than I needed (Figure 6), so each was clamped in a small bench vise and cut with a few strokes of a hacksaw lubricated with some WD-40. The hacksaw generally leaves a rough cut on the screw, so this was remedied with my Foredom rotary tool and a metal grinding accessory bit. The proper-sized Allen (or hex) wrench was used to tighten down the screws, but don't tighten too much or you'll crack the acrylic.

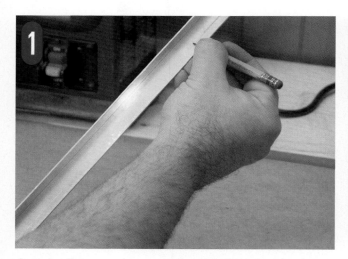

A center line was drawn on the aluminum angle pieces after they were cut to size. Using my fingers as a guide against the edge of the metal, this carpenter's trick of drawing a center line free-hand is pretty accurate—after many years of practice!

A few taps with a center punch prevents the drill bit from walking while making holes.

The speed adjustment belt on my drill press was set at medium—all that's needed for soft metals like aluminum.

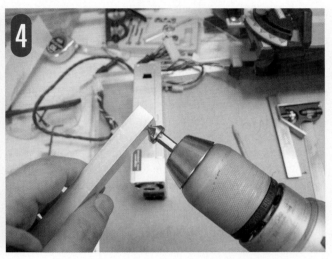

A small countersink on a power drill removes the burs that are left behind by drilling.

Hand taps can be purchased individually or in small sets. After you get the hang of using them, a whole new world of fastening is opened up.

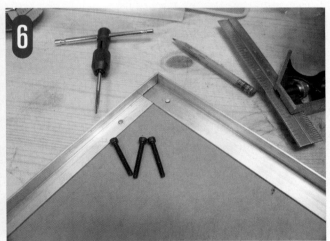

Holes in the acrylic are drilled slightly larger than the diameter of the screw. Because the holes are bigger, there's a small amount of play that allows you to make slight adjustments in alignment before tightening the machine screws.

Step 4: Mounting the Remaining Hardware

Now that the bottom of the case was framed out, I began to mount the remaining components. I cut two pieces from aluminum the same length as the PSU, and these became rails that the unit would sit on. The PSU had several threaded mounting points along the sides, and to transfer these accurately to my aluminum angle, I did a simple rubbing. I made a 90° fold in a piece of paper (Figure 1) and placed it on the PSU. I gently rubbed the side of a pencil point on the paper until the mounting holes beneath began to appear in the strokes. I could now use the paper pattern to transfer the mounting holes (Figure 2) onto the aluminum rails, hit them with a punch, and drill the holes. Small aluminum standoffs (available at home improvement stores in many sizes) were used on each rail (Figure 3) to raise the PSU off the bottom and also to help with the airflow inside the case.

The last piece of hardware to be mounted to the bottom of the case was the hard disk drive. Using the same technique as the PSU, I made a pencil rubbing of the mounting holes located on the bottom of the drive. The holes were then drilled, plastic standoffs placed in between, and finally four 6/32 machine screws were added to hold it down. For this project, all I needed was a single, dependable hard drive for temporary video storage. If I were making a video file server, I would have used multiple drives that could easily be swapped out and replaced.

A pattern for the PSU mounting holes is created by rubbing a piece of paper with a pencil.

The pattern is then placed on the aluminum stock, and the holes are marked with a center punch.

The PSU was raised up on small standoff bushings to help airflow inside the case. Standoffs are available in steel, aluminum, and plastic at hardware stores and home improvement centers.

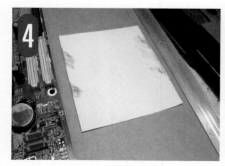

Another pencil-rubbed pattern was made for the hard drive mounting holes. The motherboard was put in place temporarily to double-check the spacing.

Hard disk drives have 6/32 mounting holes on the sides and bottom. The brass standoffs used for mounting motherboards in stock cases is also 6/32 and could have also been used here.

Step 5: Cutting and Mounting the Side Panels

Now that I had the hardware mounted to the bottom of the case, I measured and cut the side panels. The rough cuts were made using a jigsaw and plastic-cutting blade, and the piece was then cleaned up on the belt sander. The 1/4'' acrylic is very ridged, so only three mounting screws were needed to securely fasten the 14''-long piece to the aluminum framing. When drilling holes in acrylic, it's important to go slowly and accurately, especially when drilling close to the edge. A good trick is to back the drill bit out while cutting and remove the chips by blowing on it. This helps prevent the bit from binding and pulling the drill down, and possibly damaging the plastic.

After my second side panel was cut, drilled, and screwed in place, I carefully measured for the front bezel. With the door saddle securely clamped in my bench vise, a hacksaw lubricated with a blast of WD-40 (Figure 2) gave me a good cut. With the door saddle on the disk sander, I cleaned the cut to a near perfect 90° angle. You'll notice

on the end of the side panel (Figure 1) that I angled the corners. This created a shape that complimented the profile of the door sill (Figure 3) that would become the face plate of the case. With the scrap piece from the door saddle, I used a combination square (combination because it gives both 90° and 45° angles) to mark the profile of the bezel onto the side pieces. Notice the flat aluminum stock I mounted to the bottom of the case (Figure 3) that fit the bottom channel of the door saddle perfectly. When using found objects like this door saddle, keep a sharp eye out for interesting ways to integrate them into your own projects. Lastly, the bezel was put in place temporarily (Figure 4) to check for square. A tape measure was used to check the readings on both the top and bottom of the bezel. Because the holes made in the acrylic are slightly larger than the screws, I was able to loosen the bottom panel and make very small adjustments to get a tight fit for the bezel.

The front corners of the side panels were cut and angled to compliment the shape of the bezel. Resist the urge to remove the protective paper from acrylic pieces; you'll need it for marking throughout the project!

The aluminum door saddle was cut using a hacksaw with a blast of WD-40 to lubricate the blade. Notice the scrap piece of cloth in the bench vise that prevented scratches and marks on the aluminum.

A 6'' combination square was used to mark the bezel on the side panel at a 90° angle. Sometimes a found object works out perfectly. The channel in this door saddle became a great way to secure it to the front of the case.

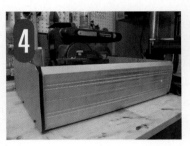

With the front bezel in place, I checked both sides of the case to make sure it was square.

Step 6: Cutting the I/O Shield Panel and Fan Hole

Once the back panel of the case was cut to size, I began plotting out the I/O panel (input/output) for the motherboard. I mounted and screwed the motherboard into the case (it has enough sides to call it a "case" at this point) and, using the I/O shield that came with it as a pattern, carefully measured and transferred the holes (Figure 1) and slots onto the acrylic. Instead of cutting every opening individually, I could have cut a single rectangle and simply used the I/O shield. I've always found these shields rather flimsy, so I decided to go for broke and cut all the openings right into the back panel. I used the scroll saw (Figure 2) to rough cut the shapes of the holes, saving me a lot of time. The flex shaft tool (Figure 3) with several different-sized bits was then used to shape and clean the cutouts. Even with the scroll saw rough cuts, this was a very time-consuming task that was done very carefully.

Because I was using 1/4'' acrylic, the holes for all the ports had to be cut oversized so I could easily plug in the various cables. When I was cutting the holes and slots, I tested their sizes (Figure 4) using a spare USB cable, mouse, keyboard, VGA, and audio cables. Now that my I/O port holes were cut, I installed the VGA and audio cards on the motherboard so I could mark the slots for cutting on the back panel. After a single slot

type cut was made for the cards (Figure 5), I secured the top of them with a single screw, tapped and threaded (Figure 6) right into their plates. It's extremely important that your VGA and PCI cards are seated completely and squarely in their respective slots. An accurate 90° angle of the motherboard and back piece must be made to get a good fit of all the cards. If your angle is out of square, a good trick is to use small washers as shims on the screws that hold the acrylic and aluminum frame together. Before you install the motherboard, use a combo square to double-check your work.

For the rear exhaust, I chose a 60mm Stealth fan with a low decibel rating to help keep down the noise of my home theater PC. My trusty method of pattern making (Figure 7) was once again used to plot out the mounting holes for the fan. A 2 1/8'' hole saw on the drill press was used to cut the fan exhaust port on the back panel. A scrap piece of metal speaker mesh cut with a pair of scissors made for a decent fan grill. The standard screws supplied with the fan were not long enough for mounting onto the acrylic, so I used a hand tap (Figure 8) to thread four new holes. After the back panel was complete, I removed the motherboard and stored it in a safe place, removed the exhaust fan, and went on to the next step.

When plotting out the pattern for the I/O panel, accuracy is very important for a clean, finished look. Take your time, measure twice, and cut once!

A scroll saw was used to rough out the holes and slots of the I/O panel.

A flex shaft rotary tool and various plastic-cutting bits were used to clean and shape the ports.

All the ports and holes were cut oversized to allow plenty of room for the cables and wires to be plugged in. Here I used a spare USB cable to test the fit.

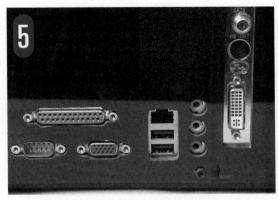

Slots were cut into the acrylic for both the VGA and audio cards. If you plan to upgrade by adding hardware to your custom case, now is the time to make a few extra slots for PCI cards.

A single screw was threaded into the plate of the VGA and audio cards to hold them securely to the back of the case.

Another of my pencil-rubbed patterns was used to plot the holes for the fan. A 2 1/8'' hole saw made a good-sized port for the 60mm exhaust fan.

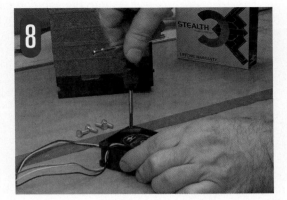

The supplied fan screws were too short for the 1/4'' acrylic so I tapped new holes in the fan and used longer ones.

Step 7: Making a Support Frame for the Top of the Case

For the top of the case, I planned to use a piece of 1/4'' clear acrylic. I needed a way to fasten the top to the rest of the case so I made a frame using aluminum angle. After I attached the sides and the back piece to the case, I took careful inside measurements to determine the size of the frame. A nice feature of the belt/disk sander is the capability to make very good 45° angles using the included guide fence. To calibrate a perfect 45° angle, I removed the blade from my combo square and used the handle to adjust the angle (Figure 1) on the fence. After the fence was locked down, I started the machine, slowly pushed the aluminum stock into the sanding disk (Figure 2), and fed the material until I had a nice 45° angle on the end. The same process was repeated for the three remaining frame pieces. With a hack saw, I cut four small brackets (Figure 3) that would hold the corners of the frame together. These brackets were then tapped for a machine screw, and the framing was drilled for the corresponding holes. I named and numbered each framing piece (Figure 4) and bracket just to make sure all the holes would line up properly when assembled.

I cut eight machine screws to size and began to assemble the frame. As you can see, this frame-making method (Figure 5) made a very clean, accurate 90° corner. While tightening one corner, I cranked the hex wrench too tight and stripped out the threads on the bracket. A few minutes later I had a new bracket and was careful this time not to over tighten the machine screws. With my framing complete, I mounted it on the top of the case using three screws on each side. On the back of the case, I made two notches (Figure 6) in the framing with a jigsaw to allow for the VGA and audio cards. Now that the frame was complete, it was time to mount the DVD burner and install the front bezel hardware.

I used the handle of the combo square to adjust the fence on the disk sander to 45°.

The aluminum stock was held firmly down to the table and against the guide fence; then it was slowly fed into the sanding disk.

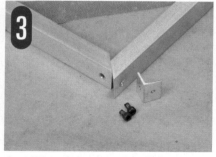
Small brackets were cut from the same stock to create corner supports for the frame.

Each corner bracket was then drilled and threaded with a hand tap. Be sure you don't over tighten the screws or you'll strip the threads.

Using the disk sander made for an accurate 90° corner.

Before the frame was mounted to the case, notches were cut to make room for the VGA and audio cards.

Step 8: Installing the Optical Drive

To save space inside my custom rig, I decided to mount the DVD burner so it slightly overlapped the hard disk drive. This also put the disk tray of the drive right in the center of my front bezel and much easier to cut out. Every situation will be different with custom cases; the trick is to take your time during planning and mock-up stages to make the right decisions. The first step was to remove the plastic bezel from the DVD drive. I inserted a paper clip into the small emergency tray release hole located under the door of most optical drives. A slight push inward with the paper clip and the tray came out slightly, enough for me to grab the tray and pull it out. I could then remove the plastic lip on the end of the tray. The plastic lip had to be removed before the rest of the bezel could come off the drive. Then I pushed in small tabs on the side of the drive, and the bezel came off easily.

That scrap piece of door saddle (Figure 1) came in handy again, helping me properly align the mounting holes for the drive. The DVD burner was attached to the side of the case using standoff bushings and machine screws. At this point, I also made small brackets (Figure 2) that would be used for mounting the front bezel of the case. On the right side of the DVD burner, I made an L-shaped leg from stock aluminum (Figure 3), and this became a mounting bracket. The stock aluminum bar was cut to length and then clamped securely in the table vise. I used my hand to slightly bend the aluminum and then finished it by tapping it lightly with a hammer (Figure 4). When I drilled the mounting holes in the acrylic and drive bracket, I made each one slightly oval shaped, allowing me to make slight adjustments if necessary. Now that I had the drive mounted and in position, I could mark the front bezel and begin cutting.

With the scrap piece from the front bezel taped in place, I was able to take the proper measurements for mounting the DVD burner in the case.

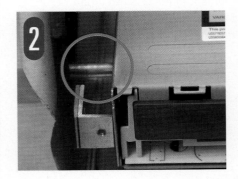

Standoff bushings (circled in red) were used to mount the left side of the DVD burner. You can also see the small bracket that would later be used to mount the front bezel to the case.

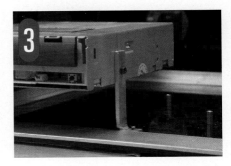

On the right side, an L-shaped bracket was made from a bar of stock aluminum. This was cut to size and the support leg bent by clamping it in a table vise and tapping it with a hammer.

The aluminum was carefully bent back by hand and then tapped into place with a hammer.

Step 9: Cutting the Front Bezel and Mounting Hardware (Part 1)

An interesting feature of the case was the addition of the Griffin PowerMate USB multimedia controller that was mounted on the front bezel. This aluminum device has the solid feel of a control knob found on expensive stereo equipment. For this project, it would become just that—a volume control device for multimedia applications. The PowerMate is meant primarily to sit on the desktop next to your mouse; therefore, the USB interface cable was not in a great position for mounting to the front bezel without being unsightly. My instinct to take things apart kicked in so I prepped for some surgery on the PowerMate.

As it turned out, the spinning control knob was glued in place with a dab of silicon at the factory, and this was easily pulled off by hand. After the knob was removed (Figure 1), I found a nut inside that was holding the entire mechanism in place. With a pair of needle-nosed pliers, I unscrewed the nut and disassembled the rest of the device. My plan was to relocate the USB cable (Figure 2) from the side of the device to the back, so I heated up my soldering iron and grabbed a pair of tweezers. When the iron was heated up, I carefully desoldered the four USB wires and pulled them from the circuit board, taking note of the wiring and making a small diagram. The back of the PowerMate had an acrylic disk, a hole was drilled in this, and the USB cable was inserted. I then soldered the wires back onto the circuit board according to the diagram and used a dab of hot glue (Figure 3) to secure the wires in.

In my hole saw kit, I was lucky to find a bit that was ever-so-slightly smaller than the diameter of the PowerMate controller. With the hole saw mounted in the drill press, I cut the opening for the knob into the front bezel. A half-round file was then used on the hole to make the PowerMate fit perfectly (Figure 5) into the bezel. Later, I would use small dabs of fast-setting epoxy on the back of the bezel to glue the knob in place.

The USB wire on the Griffin PowerMate had to be relocated to the back of the unit for clean mounting to the front of the case. This photo shows the unit after it was disassembled.

The four USB wires shown here were desoldered from the circuit board. I made a small note of the wiring diagram for later use.

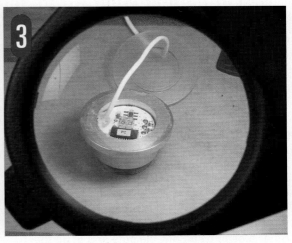

With the pesky cable now coming from the back of the unit, I used a small dab of hot glue to prevent the delicate USB wires from pulling out.

I drilled the opening for the PowerMate knob. Having a good selection of hole saws in various sizes is critical when making custom cases.

The opening was then filed by hand until the knob fit perfectly. Precision and accuracy at this stage of building can set your custom rig apart from the crowd.

Step 10: Cutting the Front Bezel and Mounting Hardware (Part 2)

The opening for the DVD burner was another step that I took slowly and carefully. I wanted to use the plastic lip that came with the drive, so I used the old bezel as a template (Figure 1) to make precise markings. The hole for the open/close button was also marked out for cutting. I made sure to include a small hole (Figure 2) for the emergency release mechanism on the DVD drive. With the opening for the drive cut out (Figure 3), I could now drill the holes on each side of the aluminum bezel and mount it to the brackets I made earlier.

I made the remaining cutouts for the Matrix Orbital display, power/reset buttons, and DVD button. I used small riffler files to clean out the cuts and fit all the hardware in nicely. The black plastic button for the DVD burner (Figure 4) was later super glued onto the back of the bezel. To mount the VFD display, I made a plate from scrap styrene plastic (Figure 5) and threaded a hole on each side. The plastic piece was then glued to the display using epoxy adhesive. To check the fit of the parts, I installed them on the bezel and made any slight adjustments with a small file (Figure 6). The last elements to be mounted on the bezel was the auxiliary USB and audio ports. I had this little unit (Figure 7) left over from a previous project and thought it would make a nice addition. To support the unit, I made a bracket from aluminum (Figure 8) that prevented it from being pushed inside the case.

At this point, the hardest parts of the project were behind me, so it was time to review the work and prepare for finishing, painting, and final installation.

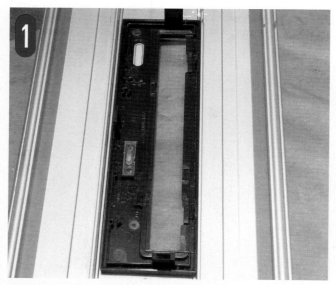

Using the old faceplate from the DVD burner as a template, holes for the disk tray and button were traced onto the back of the bezel.

It's a good idea to make a hole for the emergency release mechanism so you can open the disk tray without powering up the drive.

Once the opening for the drive was cut, I could mount the aluminum bezel to the front of the case using the brackets I made earlier.

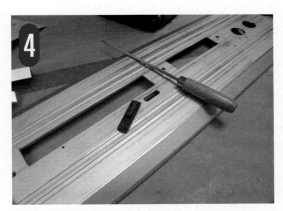

Riffler files are indispensable for cleaning out very small holes. Aluminum can be easily filed by hand to create precise openings.

A plastic mounting plate was made from scrap styrene sheet and glued with epoxy onto the VFD display.

Hardware was dry-fit on the bezel and any slight adjustments were made with a hand file.

The auxiliary USB and audio ports were a leftover item from a stock case.

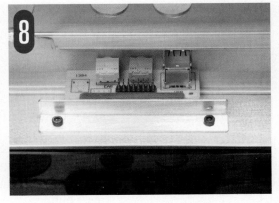

A support bracket was made to securely mount the unit inside the case.

Step 11: Putting It All Together

The finish on the aluminum bezel wasn't great to begin with and took a bit of a beating while making all those holes and cutouts. The solution was to give it a nice finish using DupliColor simulated anodizing paint. I chose a gold paint (Figure 1) for a classy look and thought it would be accented nicely by the glossy black acrylic of the case. Once painted, I set the bezel aside to dry and began wiring up (Figure 2) the power and reset buttons. For a clean look, internal wiring would be covered with ultraviolet (UV) reactive cable sleeving. Spare power and reset wires from an old case were soldered (Figure 3) onto the new switches. The helping hands device (Figure 4) with the alligator clips and articulated arms serve two purposes. Great for holding small parts, the alligator clips also serve as a heatsink and protect the LED lights from overheating while soldering the wires on. Heat-shrink tubing was used on both leads to give a nice clean look to the wires. The buttons are now sleeved (Figures 5 and 6) and ready for installation inside the case.

Next came the task of sleeving the PSU leads and peripheral cables. While it's good practice to sleeve cables and wires, I've found that too much cable wrapping creates even more of a mess inside a small case. Wrapped cables can become inflexible and hard to manage, and they can even come off the small pin connectors on motherboards. Good judgment will tell you when you've wrapped too many cables considering the size of your enclosure. Small wires can be traced along the walls and bottom of the case using self-stick wire management clips, and zip-ties can help group wires together and create a tidy-looking harness.

I began installing the hardware (Figure 8), ticking off a checklist item by item. I double-checked all the connections for power and reset buttons and made sure the RAM and VGA cards were seated properly in their slots. You should be sure to check the connections of critical fans such as the CPU and the Northbridge fan, if any. Exposed or poorly soldered wires can be disastrous, so inspect each one carefully before installing it. Project Jujube was beginning to take shape (Figure 8), and I could finally see what this case was going to look like once completed.

The bezel was painted with a simulated anodized finish from DupliColor.

Tools and materials were at the ready for wiring up the power and reset buttons.

Spare wires from an old case were used on these vandal-proof-type buttons.

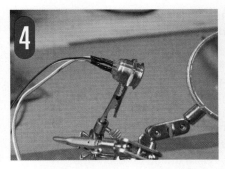

After the wires were soldered on, heat-shrink tubing was used to give a clean, professional look.

The power button was sleeved and ready to install inside the case. Always check the length of the wire leads by dry-fitting the button prior to soldering.

Zip ties helped organize wires into a neat-looking bundle.

Here you can see the black box inverter for the ultraviolet CCFL and the PowerMate glued in place. The green UV cable wrapping reacts with the light and appears to glow.

System hardware was installed and ready to fire up. Double-check that all components are properly seated in their slots and that critical devices such as CPU fans are plugged in.

The case had started to take shape, and at this point, I could really get a sense of the final look of the project.

Step 12: Making a Top and Wrapping Up the Project

The last piece to be fabricated and installed was the cover for the case. I wanted to take a peek inside the case from the top, so I decided to create a window using a sign maker's technique. A 1/4'' sheet of clear acrylic was cut to fit the top of the case, flush on all sides; then all the edges of the acrylic were hand-filed, wet-sanded, and polished. I chose a spot for my see-through window and used the lid from a large cooking pot as a guide for my circle. With the circle drawn, I made the opening for the case fan (Figure 1) using a hole saw and cordless drill.

With the lid in place and held firmly down, I used a sharp hobby knife to gently trace around the lid and cut the protective paper on the acrylic. The paper makes the best masking material when painting designs on acrylic. I removed the paper and left the round window area in place. With canned air and glass cleaner, I carefully cleaned the dust and fingerprints from the clear acrylic in preparation for painting. I gave what would become the underside of the acrylic (with the window mask) three coats of silver spray paint from a can and let it dry. When the paint was dry to the touch (about 2 hours), I peeled off the window masking paper (Figure 2) and was left with a pretty nice-looking clear area.

I bought a roll of silver contact paper, the kind used to line kitchen shelves with. This sticky-backed vinyl material is basically the same kind sign makers use to cut lettering. I cut a piece of contact paper slightly larger than my acrylic and peeled about 1/2'' of the backing from it. Starting from one end, I placed the contact paper on the painted side of the acrylic top. The backing was slowly peeled off the contact paper and, with a soft cloth, I

pressed (Figure 3) the vinyl down until the entire side was covered. Any bubbles that were trapped under the vinyl were pierced with a straight pin to release the air and then rubbed flat with a cloth. The vinyl served two purposes—to protect the painted finish on the acrylic and to make it opaque, or lightproof. It would have taken far too many coats of paint to make the clear acrylic opaque. With a hobby knife, I next trimmed the excess vinyl from the edges of the acrylic top and from the mounting holes that were drilled on each side.

I could see the slight impression of the painted circle through the thin vinyl, and this helped me position the lid (Figure 4) back so I could cut the window. Once in position, I cut the vinyl using the lid as a guide and then peeled (Figure 5) it off. The intake fan was then mounted on the window (Figure 6) and ready to be screwed down to the top of the case. Furniture glides (Figures 7, 8, and 9) with self-adhesive backing were placed on the bottom of the case, protecting the acrylic from scratches and giving the project a finished look.

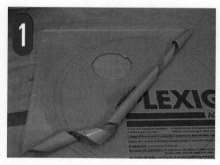

For the case cover, I used a piece of 1/4'' clear Plexiglas. With the paper left on as a painting mask, I cut a circle using the lid from a sauce pan as a guide. Very light pressure with a sharp hobby blade created a clean circle. It was also a good time to drill the bolt holes on the edge of the piece and cut the blow hole for the intake fan.

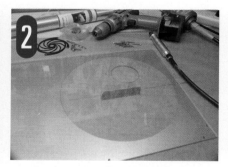

Using a sign maker's technique, I used a few coats of bright silver spray paint to back-paint the Plexiglas. I removed the paper circle mask before the paint was dry to prevent it from peeling or lifting.

It would have taken dozens of coats of paint to make the silver area lightproof, or opaque. To remedy this, I cut an oversized piece of self-sticking vinyl shelf paper and laminated it right over the painted side. Any small air bubbles in the vinyl were pushed out with a soft cloth, and the stubborn ones were pierced with a straight pin.

The sauce pan lid was repositioned carefully back on the cover. I was able to see the faint lip of the paint under the vinyl, and this helped position it just right. With very little pressure on a hobby blade, I cut the vinyl slowly and carefully using the edge of the lid as a guide.

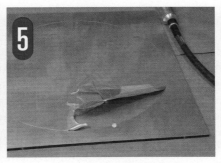

The circle of shelf paper was peeled off starting at the edge. I always purchase #11 hobby blades in bulk not only to save a little cash, but to ensure I have a fresh blade on hand for critical cuts like this one.

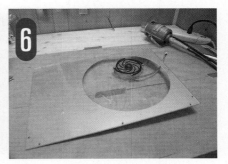

The 80mm intake fan was then mounted on the cover, and a swirl design steel fan grill polished it off. I left just enough slack on the fan power cable so it would be easy to plug in to the motherboard header pins. Not enough slack and it would be difficult or impossible to plug in.

Self-sticking furniture glides and rubber pads can put a nice finishing touch on a custom-built case, and they also help prevent the acrylic bottom from getting scratched.

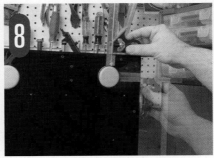

With my small combo square, I positioned the four plastic glides on the bottom of the case. The tape backing used on these glides is extremely aggressive, so try and get it right the first time.

Now was a good time to check all my bolts and make sure they were tightened properly. After the top was fastened on, the entire unit became much stronger and sturdier.

Project Thoughts

Jujube was basically a success and now has a new home in my entertainment center, as the central tool for everyday TV viewing and recording. Looking back on the project, there are several improvements to the design I should have made and will keep in mind for the next HTPC case. Additional cooling with another intake fan is my first thought because the case is mostly plastic and acts like an insulator. Although the temperatures inside the case are acceptable, a few degrees cooler would have made me happier. A bigger VFD display or possibly a small touch screen LCD monitor would have been a nice (albeit expensive) touch. We live and learn.

I really liked making this case for the simple fact that the parts were easy to find and very affordable. It just goes to prove that interesting case mods don't have to be expensive if they are at least *clever* in some way or make use of everyday items we take for granted. In retrospect, I could have, for instance, used chrome-finishing screws instead of the black machine screws. However, the latter was much more readily available at my local hardware store.

Every case project should leave you with a sense of accomplishment and, dare I say, pride. Each step you take in the process is knowledge learned, either on your own or with the help of others. Knowledge is a wonderful gift. Share it with a friend.

The Finished Jujube Mod in All Its Glory!

With this home theater personal computer (HTPC), I've replaced the aging VCR and DVD players in my home entertainment center...and good riddance!

Building a custom case from scratch is time-consuming but doesn't have to break the bank. What can make your case mod unique is clever use of materials and found objects and, of course, a little imagination!

I've also integrated a Griffin PowerMate programmable USB knob into the front bezel. This great little aluminum knob can be programmed to control volume and launch programs and has tons of other uses.

Also on the front bezel is the Matrix Orbital VK202-24-USB vacuum fluorescent display (VFD) running the always excellent LCDC software.

Caution: Contents Extremely Evil

Call it a remarkable display of ingenuity or a brazen flouting of evil, but either way you put it, this box is bad. Inspired by Clive Barker's horror classic *Hellraiser*, Sheffield Abella carefully crafted a 10'' × 10'' Plexiglas replica of the movie's demonic prop—the Puzzle Box—to house his custom PC. In the movie, the Puzzle Box is a receptacle for man's dark side. But in this September 2002 Rig of the Month winner, we were happy to find something a little less creepy.

Sheffield told us that a college course gave him entry-level experience in plastic craft, but wouldn't you know it, he also used some of the same planning strategies described in this book to execute this incredibly complex mod. "I built a full-size mock-up of the box out of Gatorfoam," he says, "and taped photocopies of the components to the sides so I could get a clear picture of where things would go. Doing the Gatorfoam box enabled me to solve design issues that I hadn't anticipated."

Interior lighting includes electro-luminescent tape skirting the box's base and two blue LEDs on each of the fans. "I designed the box so that, if lit from the back, light would bounce and reflect throughout the inside," Sheffield says. For the complete step-by-step details on this amazing hacking job, check out the Projects section of www.sheff.com. You'll find a treasure trove of scratch-built instruction that will help complement the tips in this book.—J.P.

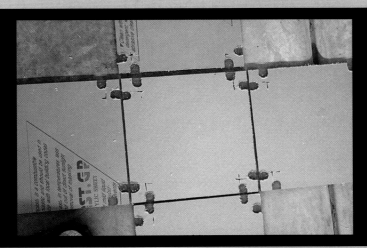

Here we have the raw Plexi pieces, lying flat and still protected from workshop elements.

With a little web research, Sheff was able to find authentic Puzzle Box patterns. "That thing is pretty damn evil once you learn the meaning behind the symbols, so I made some changes to make it nicer."

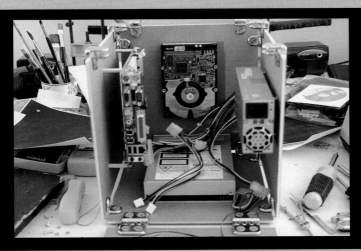

As this mock-up demonstrates, the Puzzle Box is cramped, but it's certainly not the most cramped case mod we've ever seen. The PC is based on a Shuttle FV24 Flex ATX motherboard and a 1GB P-III Coppermine CPU.

Chapter Eleven

Exotic Cooling

Increase your rig's pimp factor with extreme cooling hardware

Cristophe Janbon's extremely popular Blackmesa HL^2 *Half Life2*-inspired case is not only water-cooled, but its hand-painted exterior, custom cut window, and top-mounted fans make it one of the most famous of all custom PC mods.

Jason Catanzaro's St. Anger mod is inspired by the metal band Metallica and sports an Innovatek reservoir and convection radiator. Catanzaro's rig also includes a simulated stained-glass window (not shown here) depicting the band's 2003 CD, *St. Anger*. Assuming Jason's creation doesn't house any bootlegged MP3s, we're guessing this mod does the band proud.

Now, before you have visions of beautiful, scantily clad Pacific island natives waving palm fronds in your direction and feeding you chilled pineapple slices as you swing gently in a rope hammock (is it too late?), for the record we're talking about exotic PC cooling. We're talking about over-the-top, void-your-warranties, hardcore thermal hardware to keep all that sexy new circuitry cool and comfy. While cooling electronic components with liquids is nothing new to the industry, for the PC enthusi-

ast, it was born on the workbenches of overclocking pioneers. With their collective slogan "heat is the enemy," they borrowed concepts, parts, and practices from the refrigeration and automotive cooling worlds and adapted them for use inside the personal computer.

What all their late-night experimentation with PC plumbing has achieved for the rest of us is not only a slick alternative to noisy fan-based cooling, but also a reliable performance-boosting technology that is common practice today among case modders. Heat and power consumption have always gone hand-in-hand. Now more than ever, as CPU and graphics card manufacturers push the envelope of current technology, outfitting our rigs with exotic cooling might just be all we can do in the near future to keep up with them.

We just wouldn't be able to sleep at night if we didn't give you a stern, grab-you-by-your-Abercrombie-T-shirt-and-shake-you warning about the dangers of messing with the exotic cooling schemes discussed in this chapter. While we wholeheartedly support your intrepid nature, we feel it imperative that we also warn you that you can cost yourself some serious cash, lose valuable data, and even set your house on fire if you don't get it right. If you decide to tinker with the exotic cooling schemes discussed here—and we hope you do—then be sure to pay close attention, read the manufacturer's instructions, bug your techie friends for answers, and (most of all) take your time. We don't recommend undertaking mods such as these on mission-critical PCs or on computers that must be up and running after only a short downtime. There. You've been warned and we'll sleep better.

Who says you have to break out the sabre saws, sanders, and paint to create a slick modded case? As we explain in Chapter 8, "Building the Ultimate Off-the-Shelf Mod," you can use a case with a pre-cut window, add an Innovatek water-cooler, and—BAM!—you've got yourself one stylish rig that will draw a crowd. Slap a couple of cold cathodes inside and you have created a respect-worthy mod without breaking the bank or getting in over your head.

Installing reliable liquid cooling components inside your computer is not as difficult as it might seem. Entire websites and community forums, where free expert advice is shared, are dedicated to the alchemistical practice of hardcore cooling. There you'll find tutorials and work logs as well as theories and hypotheses from water-cooling masters and gurus. If you decide to take the plunge, you'll find that water-cooling parts and supplies are sold à la carte or in complete kits on just about every retail modding website you can click on. Products from Danger Den, Hardware Labs, and Asetek are at the pinnacle of liquid cooling performance and craftsmanship and are among some of the brand names you'll definitely come across.

For the PC-building thrill seeker, installing water-cooling components has both its risks and rewards. Improper installation, and in some cases, hardware defects, spell disaster for a good number of your rig's components if they get wet. On the other hand, a well-planned and stable water-cooled PC is certainly grounds for major kudos and bragging rights.

Cristophe Janbon's Blackmesa HL^2 mod is nearly as menacing as the game that inspired it. Janbon, aka Piloux, lives in Belgium and provided a work log—with lots of photos showing how this mod was created—at http://members.home.nl/gis/.

Up Close: The Physics of Water-Cooling

Water-cooling systems send liquid to water blocks attached to your key components (candidates include your CPU, GPU, and hard drive). The cool liquid draws heat away from your searing component and then flows to some type of cooling device (usually a fan-cooled radiator), which dissipates the heat outside of your case. The liquid is circulated through each water block with the help of a pump—the literal heart of the water-cooling system. This ticker, usually a high-end fish tank pump, can pump thousands of gallons a day throughout your rig.

The liquid within a water block can absorb four times the heat of a traditional fan/heatsink combo. Even better, it can transfer heat 30 times more effectively than regular cooling methods and doesn't produce an excessive amount of fan noise. In short, water-cooling is an extremely effective tool for overclockers—it not only cools key components, but also keeps heat away from your case's general interior. Just be aware that if one of your circulation tubes becomes undone, you'll probably royally bork your system.

This Innovatek water-cooling rig will keep your PC cool, and it's virtually silent to boot.

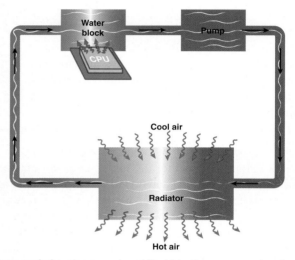

Water-cooled systems send cool liquid to the component and then pump the heated water to a radiator, where it is cooled before the cycle starts again.

Up Close: How Phase Change Cooling Works

A *phase change* occurs when matter shifts between any of its liquid, gaseous, or solid states. For example, water phase changes when it turns to ice in your freezer, when it boils away in a cooking pot, and when steam condenses back into water.

To change from liquid to gas, water (like all matter) needs a significant amount of energy. At room temperature, for example, one gram of water needs just one calorie of energy to increase in temperature by 1° Celsius. But at 100° Celsius (the boiling point of water near sea level), water needs to absorb 540 times that amount of energy to phase change into steam. Conversely, all that energy is released again when the steam vapor condenses back into a liquid.

Here's the plot twist that makes phase change cooling possible: Boiling and condensation can be forced to occur by manipulating pressure, and if you put water in a container holding a vacuum, the water boils at a lower temperature than it would at regular room pressure. Water in this vacuum container still requires 540 calories of energy to convert to steam and absorbs this energy from the most convenient heat source—such as a scorching CPU.

In a phase change system for your PC, a compressor sucks air from one side of the system to the other, creating a low-pressure side and a high-pressure side. In the low-pressure side, boiling is induced at extremely low temperatures in a chamber called the *evaporator*. Once the heated gas moves out of the vacuum, an air-cooled radiator—also known as a *condenser*—causes the gas to turn to liquid again.

This phase change from gas to water—known as *condensation*—releases all the heat drawn from your CPU. The liquid passes through a tight passage called a *restrictor*, which keeps the low-pressure and high-pressure sides separate.

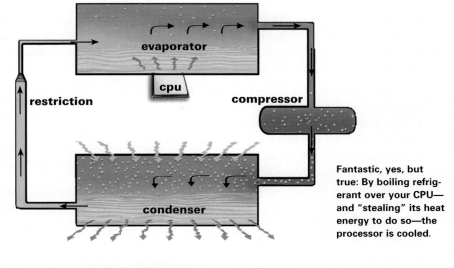

Fantastic, yes, but true: By boiling refrigerant over your CPU—and "stealing" its heat energy to do so—the processor is cooled.

The heating element is mounted in the back of the motherboard, directly under the CPU socket.

Phase change systems require a roomy enclosure, as shown in this Prometeia phase change cooling unit from Chip-con, to house the extra hardware needed to keep your PC frosty cool.

In case it isn't readily apparent, phase change cooling is a little more involved (and much more expensive) than a basic water-cooled system and is a lot more involved than an air-cooled heatsink system. To that effect, we have not covered installing a phase change system. In most cases, it's best to buy a system with a phase change cooling system preinstalled. For the most courageous among you, however, you can find detailed installation instructions and artwork at http://www.extremeoverclocking.com/reviews/cooling/Asetek_VapoChill_LS_1.html.

Water-Cooling: It's Like a Little Splash of Evian for Your PC

Now that liquid cooling has proven itself to be a reliable, alternative method of thermal control, the abundance of products available for it has caused the practice to branch off into several categories:

- **Extreme**—This type of system typically uses a large case; one or more high-flow-rate pumps; 1/2'' (or bigger) tubing; large or multiple radiators; and high-quality water blocks for CPU, VPU, North Bridge, and hard disk drives. Some of the more skilled overclockers handcraft their own parts, such as water blocks, copper tubing, and reservoirs. In addition, building a custom phase change cooling unit is not an uncommon practice for these serious overclocking and benchmarking enthusiasts.

- **Gamers/case modders**—Gamers and case modders tend to favor water-cooling systems that allow them to push their hardware beyond its specs and increase benchmarks, but they generally aren't looking to push the envelope and break records. They want a stable, cool-running rig with an overclocking edge. This setup might include a single high-flow pump, 1/2'' tubing, single 120mm radiator, and CPU and VPU water blocks. A favorable style of case might be an all-aluminum mid-tower for portability.

- **Silence seekers**—For those looking for peace and quiet, water-cooling can be the answer. If you don't plan to push your system with overclocking, a good choice might be a small low-noise 12-volt pump, single-fan 80mm radiator, 3/8'' or 8mm tubing, and CPU/VPU water blocks. To eliminate noise even further, passive (fanless) convection-type external radiators are available. See "Quieting Your PC," later in this chapter, for more on making your PC as quiet as a church mouse.

- **Externals**—For those who have existing cases and are short on internal space, external water-cooling units are available, such as the Corsair HydroCool 200EX, Thermaltake Aquarius 2, and the Koolance Exos. These units house the pump, radiator, fans, and reservoirs into a single box. All that's needed to get it up and running is bringing the tubing and water blocks inside the case and mounting them. These are not the most portable or space-saving models, but they are perfect for you noncommittal types who would like to experiment.

This Koolance external water-cooling rig might just be the answer if you're short on space or just prefer to keep the inside of your PC nice and tidy.

This Corsair HydroEX External Water-cooling System is a fully contained, highly efficient external water-cooling unit, capable of removing up to 200 watts of dissipated power from your computer. This cooling block is compatible with both Pentium 4 and Athlon XP and MP processors.

Water-Cooling Hardware

The Pump

If you're into aquaria, some of this equipment is definitely familiar to you. The pump is the heart of the water-cooling system, moving thousands of gallons a day through the network of hoses and water blocks. From left: The Eheim 1250 is a 110/120VAC pump manufactured for outdoor ponds and water gardens. With the capacity to move 317 gallons per hour (GPH), this pump is one of the most well liked. The Hydor L25 is another popular 120VAC model. However, it's almost half the size of the Eheim and rated at 185 GPH (325 GPH with the similar-sized L35 model). The Alphacool AP700 is a 12VDC centrifugal pump powered from the system PSU and moves about 190 GPH. Another measure of a pump's performance is known as the *delivery head*, or the maximum height it can push liquid through a hose vertically before it stops. When purchasing your water-cooling components piece-by-piece, the size and type of pump need careful consideration, given the limited space you might have inside an existing enclosure to mount it.

When using 110/220VAC pumps in your water-cooling setup, it's obvious you won't be powering that baby up with your system PSU. If you have the memory of an elephant, you could simply remember to plug the pump in before firing up your system. However, this can be risky. By installing a PCI relay card such as the Criticool Powerplant, you won't toast your rig when, after a long night of beer and football, you forget to plug in your pump. Installation is simple: After cutting off the plug end and wiring your pump's AC cord to the relay card's terminals, you install it as you would any other PCI device. Plug the supplied cord into the relay card bracket and then into your surge suppressor. When you turn on your system, the relay card senses the current from the PCI slot and fires up the pump. No fuss, no muss.

Radiators

The basic copper cooling radiator is a design that hasn't changed much since it was invented and put to use. The design is simple, capable of both distributing heat and removing it from a closed loop water system depending on its application. In cooling systems, the water is passed through the radiator's plenum chamber where slender louvered fins work to shed and draw off the heat. A fan attached to the radiator is necessary to force cool air through the fins and efficiently shed the heat as the liquid passes through. Radiators, or *rads* as we call them, come in many sizes and configurations. The smaller ones accommodate a single or double 80mm fan, while the larger models sport single or double 120mm fans. The type and size of your radiator largely depend on how many components are being water-cooled in your system loop. Cooling a CPU might require only a single 80mm radiator; however, as you add more components to be cooled to the loop, the size of your radiator should increase respectively.

Water Blocks

Water blocks are similar to fan-cooled heatsinks in that they are blocks of metal that mount directly to, say, a CPU die and draw the heat away from it. The magic of the water block is it sheds heat much faster, quieter, and many times more efficiently by forcing cool water in and out of it very quickly. Inside a well-engineered water block is a maze of channels that directs the inlet flow of water across the entire surface of the block and then to the outlet in a constant cycle. There are water blocks for every major CPU, such as the Intel Pentiums, Xeons, 775 processors, AMD XP/MP, and Athlon 64. To cool the graphics processor, blocks are available that fit ATI Radeons and X-800 series as well as blocks for the NVIDIA GeForce and 6800 series of videocards. For keeping the motherboard's North Bridge chipset cool, you can use water blocks designed specifically for them. In addition to the water blocks for processors, some excellent blocks are also available for hard disk drives.

Reservoirs

Reservoirs are both the holding tanks and fill stations for the water-cooling system. Although not absolutely necessary, in a typical setup their removable water-tight caps make filling the system with coolant and bleeding off trapped air inside the loop easier. The exquisitely crafted clear acrylic reservoirs from Danger Den come in several sizes that fit perfectly inside single and multiple 5 1/4" drive bays and even floppy bays. The Alphacool res, (in red) is milled from solid aluminum and then anodized and includes two 8mm compression fittings.

While it might go without explaining if you're a bona fide PC hardware maven, we find many hardware enthusiasts out there who don't have a clear understanding of the differences between North Bridge and South Bridge chips. Collectively, these chips are known as the *chipset*.

North Bridge—The component of the core logic chipset that primarily functions as a memory controller, allowing the CPU to interface with main memory and the AGP videocard (provided the motherboard supports AGP). In some systems, such as those based on the AMD Athlon 64 processors, the memory controller is built in to the CPU.

South Bridge—The component of the core logic chipset that provides the interface between the North Bridge and the slower interfaces in the PC, such as PCI slots, USB, IDE, and other I/O interfaces. In other words, everything other than the main memory and AGP falls under the charge of the South Bridge chip.

Tubing

Tubing is, of course, the vascular system of any water-cooling setup. Typically found in 1/2" inside diameter (ID) and 8mm and 3/8" ID, tubing connects to all the components in your water-cooling loop. The tubing is connected to the components by the use of barbs and hose clamps, or in some water-cooling kits, compression fittings. Brand names like Tygon and PrimoFlex are the top choices of PVC tubing for case modders because of their outstanding quality and reliability. Some brands are also available in UV reactive colors that fluoresce when exposed to ultraviolet lighting.

This Lucite-topped Danger Den water block uses massive 1/2" ID tubing and fittings for a very high flow rate. The plastic hose clamps are ratcheted and adjustable for both 3/8" and 1/2" tubing.

Coolant

The water in water-cooling is usually the distilled type mixed with some measure of metal-protecting additive, such as automotive coolant. To prevent corrosion, algae growth, and oxidation, and to increase heat transfer inside the loop, specialty fluids are the best choice. There are also a number of UV reactive coolants that give an otherworldly look to clear tubing systems.

Basic Water-Cooling Setup

Here I demonstrate how you might install a basic water-cooling system. The Alphacool Cape Red kit I am using came complete with three water blocks, a 120mm radiator, a Pabst fan, a 12-volt pump, 8mm tubing, and compression fittings. While this German made kit isn't geared toward overclocking hardware, it has exceptionally well-crafted and good-looking parts that

are perfect for the water-cooling novice. To install a similar kit, you need the following tools:

- Jigsaw
- Power drill and drill bits
- Flat and Phillips screwdrivers
  - Pliers or open-ended wrench
  - Metric Allen (hex) wrenches
  - Scissors
  - Tape measure
  - Masking tape

Step 1: Planning and Hardware Placement

Considering the shape, architecture, and size of cases vary greatly, there might be few or many choices for mounting the cooling components. If you have an existing system, you must remove the hardware down to the bare walls before hacking up the case. While planning hardware placement, you have to consider the route of your tubing and how that might or might not interfere with your PC components.

Radiators are best placed where outside air is forced onto the louvered fins (there is an endless debate with regard to whether fans should blow onto or pull air through the radiator) and cool the radiator. Suggestions might be the top or rear of the case or, if room permits, the inside front of it. In any custom water-cooling setup, be prepared to cut up your case to some degree to mount the parts. Think through this part of your project extremely carefully—120mm blow holes are very hard to cover up if mistakes are made. A nice potted plant maybe....

Step 2: Mounting the Radiator

I decided to mount the 120mm radiator to the inside top of the case, and this required cutting the appropriate sized hole. To protect the factory finish on the Silverstone case from the shoe of my jigsaw, I put a few strips of masking tape down. I then used a 120mm fan grill to mark the intake hole and fan screw holes.

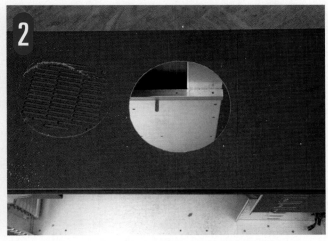

After the hole was cut, the edge of the hole was de-burred with a smooth half-round file and 150-grit sand-paper.

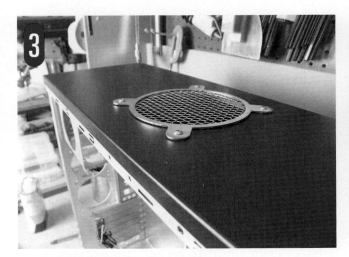

I took a cheesy-looking steel fan grill and made it much nicer by replacing the center portion with some hexagonal modder's mesh.

The radiator was then bolted into place. Again, be sure you plan this step out carefully ahead of time. Remember the carpenter's adage: measure twice, cut once.

Step 3: Installing the Water Pump

Check the installation instructions that come with your pump to make sure you have all the mounting hardware. If you purchased your pump from a highly reputable retailer, such as Danger Den, you can also get step-by-step installation instruction from the retailer's website.

To install the pump where I wanted, I found I had to add a small extension piece of stock aluminum bar to the drive cage to create a mounting plate.

To help prevent vibration and noise from the pump using the case like a big amplifier, I slipped some rubber grommets over the bolts before mounting the pump to the case.

Step 4: Prepping the Motherboard for the CPU Water Block

The reservoir was a tricky part to place, and after a bit of head-scratching, I decided to put it on the back burner and move on to preparing the motherboard for the CPU water block. For both Intel and AMD motherboards, the stock heatsink mounting brackets have to be removed to accommodate the custom hardware for the water blocks. For the Asus motherboard shown here, it was a simple matter of removing the four Phillips head screws.

Once the bracket was removed (and stored safely away, in case the mobo has to be returned for defects—ahem) I installed the four threaded mounting posts for the CPU water block with the included hex nuts and nylon washers. The motherboard was then put aside and I began assembling the water blocks.

Step 5: Installing the GPU and CPU Water Blocks

1 The Alphacool Cape Red kit comes with threaded compression fittings that needed to be screwed into the blocks and tightened down before mounting them. These 8mm fittings have a rubber O-ring that seats and seals against the body of the water block, and on the opposite end, a compression fitting for sealing the tubing.

2 Although this type of hose barb/compression fitting is supplied with a rubber O-ring for making a water-tight seal, it's still good practice to wind some common Teflon plumber's tape around the threads. Apply one and a half wraps clockwise on the threaded area only, avoiding the rubber O-ring and the top of the fitting. When installing noncompression-type metal and plastic barbs, always use Teflon tape.

3 The trick is to tighten it by hand as far as it will go and then use a pair of pliers or an open-ended wrench to seat it. These O-ring-type fittings should never be over tightened; when you feel the O-ring beginning to compress, all you need is a slight tightening with a tool to create a waterproof seal.

4 I then removed the stock heatsink and fan from this ATI Radeon 9800 Pro graphics card and mounted the two threaded posts supplied with the water block. I installed the block on the card in a dry run (without thermal grease) to make sure the mounting procedure was correct and that the bottom of the block seated correctly against the VPU die. I repeated the process for installing the CPU block and proceeded to mount the motherboard and graphics card temporarily in the case.

Step 6: Installing the Reservoir

A cup of good coffee helped to find a suitable spot for the reservoir and, as it turned out, I mounted it horizontally (the reservoir is threaded for a bolt on the bottom) right onto the motherboard plate. I now had all my components installed and ready for a little tubing action.

By taking one end of the tubing and holding it near a water block, I could estimate an approximate length to cut it with a pair of sharp scissors. If anything, cut the tubing a little longer than you think you might need, but be sure to trim it down as described in the next step. You want the cut tubing to be nice and square on the end and not on an angle that would prevent it from seating properly on the barb. The fitting has a knurled compression nut that should be leak-proof when hand-tightened; for the paranoid, a half turn with a wrench is all you need.

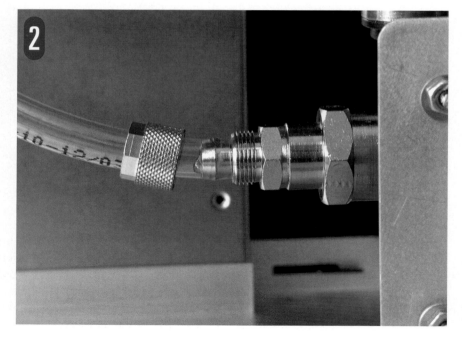

Step 7: Making Tubing Connections

My first tube was attached to the outlet fitting of the pump; then it was brought up to the radiator. From the radiator, the second hose went directly to the inlet side of the CPU block. The third hose went from the outlet on the CPU block to the inlet of the VPU block. From the outlet of the VPU block, a fourth hose went to the inlet side of the reservoir. The fifth and last hose went from the outlet side of the reservoir to the intake of the pump. Got that? See the diagram on the next page for help.

Here is the entire setup outside of a PC case. Of course, you'd never want to actually set one up this way, but this is for illustrative purposes.

To prevent kinks in the tubing, you have to leave the proper amount of slack for each connection made. Kinks essentially act as a valve, slowing down or even shutting off the flow of coolant in your loop—and leading to nicely toasted hardware. That's why I suggest cutting your tubing a little longer than necessary and then trimming it to fit when you're sure about the final placement of all the components.

Up Close—Water-Cooling Setup

The following diagram shows the correct connections for a water-cooled system. Be sure to consult the instructions that come with your water-cooling system:

1. Outlet pump fitting to radiator
2. Radiator to CPU block inlet
3. Outlet of CPU block to GPU block inlet
4. Outlet of GPU block to reservoir inlet
5. Outlet of reservoir to pump intake

Note that you also could connect your system according to the following (not shown in this graphic):

1. Outlet pump fitting to CPU block inlet
2. Outlet of CPU block to GPU block inlet
3. Outlet of GPU to radiator
4. Radiator to reservoir intake
5. Outlet of radiator to pump intake

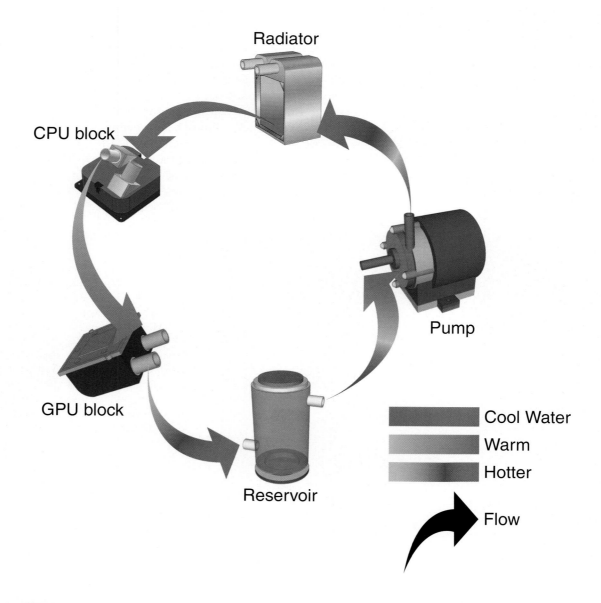

Radiator

CPU block

GPU block

Pump

Reservoir

Cool Water
Warm
Hotter

Flow

Step 8: Filling the System

Now that I had all my hoses locked in place, it was time to get things wet. Because I mounted my reservoir horizontally, obviously I had to lay the case on its side to fill the system. I removed the water blocks carefully from the motherboard and graphics card before I began. I then laid out some blue paper towels around all the components inside the case so any leaks in the loop would be easier to see after it was up and running.

The kit came with a nice little 20-pin adapter for hot-wiring your PSU and firing up the 12-volt pump during filling. With the filler cap removed and the pump plugged into the PSU, I filled the reservoir up until the fluid began to flow toward the pump; you don't want to run the pump dry, even for a few seconds, because you can burn it out.

I flipped the switch on the PSU and continued pouring the fluid into the reservoir. It only took a few moments before the loop was filled and the reservoir could hold no more; at that point, I switched off the PSU. There was air trapped in the loop for sure, so I capped the reservoir, picked up the case, and rotated it until I could get the trapped air back into the reservoir. I then opened the reservoir and topped it off with fluid. I had to repeat this several times to get most, if not all, of the air out. The biggest culprit of trapped air is always the radiator.

It's good practice to let the water-cooling setup run for 12–24 hours before installing hardware, such as the motherboard and graphics card, to make sure the loop is absolutely leak-free and stable.

After the components have passed the 24-hour test, it's safe to install (very carefully!) all the major components (motherboard, CPU, videocard, and the like) of your new water-cooled rig. You have the choice to either drain the system or mount the blocks to the components with it filled. In my experience, with a simple setup, draining the coolant is unnecessary if all your tubing connections are solid and the system is stable. If you have a particularly complicated hardware install, it might be best to drain it. When your components are in place, you might want to, once again, test the water setup for a few hours before installing the rest of your system hardware.

CPU Coolers—Fever Reducers for Your Binary Reactor!

While the majority of this chapter discusses exotic cooling schemes, we'd be remiss not to tell you about standard CPU coolers. Though not considered exotic or extreme by most case modder standards, we believe adding a high-quality, stylin' CPU cooler to your PC gives it some bling.

Modern CPUs pack millions of transistors into a tiny amount of space. As a result, they're not just highly advanced silicon brains, but they're also intense furnaces that generate massive amounts of heat. And heat reduces performance, introduces instability, and can seriously abbreviate the life of your components.

If you don't plan to overclock your CPU (running it at a higher clock frequency than its official, posted rating), you'll most likely be satisfied with the heatsink and fan combo that came with your CPU. But if you intend on raising some overclocked hell with your processor, or if you bought a bare CPU in some shady back-alley deal, you'll need to devise your own cooling strategy.

The more surface area your heatsink has, the more it is able to transfer your CPU's heat to the air inside your case. Hence, the blooming flower design of Zalman's CNPS6500B-CU.

If you decide an aftermarket CPU cooler is in the cards, Thermaltake's Volcano cooler is a good choice. Its classic polished styling makes us think of performance car parts.

You might have heard of the dangers of futzing with the cooler that came with your Intel or AMD CPU—and you probably said, "Damn the torpedoes!" Right? Well, as much as we hate to bring the party down, we have to tell you that those warnings aren't without merit. In fact, AMD and Intel spend millions of dollars on the research and engineering of their products. The coolers that ship with a boxed processor are field tested and guaranteed to run for the warranty period (and usually longer). Think about it: It behooves Intel and AMD to extensively test their coolers, ensuring they don't fail during the warranty period. If the cooler does fail, your CPU is likely turned into a charcoal briquette and they have to replace it for free.

Also, Intel and AMD test their coolers to work within the rated specifications for the particular CPU. If you overclock the CPU and the cooler isn't capable of cooling it effectively, you're S.O.L. if the CPU dies a fiery death. The same holds true if you install an aftermarket cooler on a CPU under manufacturer warranty (regardless of whether you overclock the CPU). So keep all this in mind if you're adding an aftermarket cooler to a boxed processor with a warranty. If you purchase a bare-bones CPU or your CPU is no longer under warranty, you can overclock to your little heart's content, assuming all the risks if things don't go as planned.

This poor little CPU died a painful death when the CPU cooler failed. Please join us in a moment of silence....

Fun with Classic Air Cooling

The job of any CPU cooling setup is to move heat from your CPU and dissipate that heat into the air. Heatsinks squat directly on your CPU and transfer heat from the die (or, in Intel's case, a heat spreader plate) to its fins or spires, which pass the heat into the air, which should then be swept out of the case by your case fans (as long as airflow isn't obstructed by tangled cables and whatnot).

Four major factors affect cooler performance: the kind of metal the heatsink is cast from, the design of the radiating fins, the fan (if present as part of a heatsink/fan combo), and the contact surface between the heatsink and the CPU.

As far as the material goes, copper is the finest material a heatsink can realistically be made from. It's the third-best conductor of heat after silver and diamond, which are somewhat more expensive. So, look for a cooler with a copper heatsink or, at the very least, a heatsink with a copper contact plate.

Heat is dissipated from the heatsink through contact with air, so the more surface area on your heatsink, the better. That's why you should look for heatsinks with numerous thin fins or spires rather than a few thicker ones.

A heatsink alone won't cut it for overclocked CPUs. A heatsink/fan combination wicks the heat off the heatsink radials much faster. Keep in mind, however, that the bigger the fan, the more noise it's likely to make.

Finally, it's important that the surface where the cooler contacts the CPU be as smooth as possible. Although the base of a heatsink might look smooth to your eye, it's actually replete with microscopic gaps and crevices that inhibit maximum heat transfer. This is where thermal paste enters the picture. Thermal paste, such as our preferred Arctic Silver 5, fills in these tiny gaps to improve the conductivity of your heatsink. But don't go crazy with this stuff; more is *not* better here. When applying thermal paste, apply just enough to create a *very* thin film over the CPU. Remember, you're just trying to fill in microscopic gaps, not smother your CPU or clean up goop that spills out over your mobo's circuitry!

Intel's stock Pentium 4 cooler is a hefty beast. The boxed processor comes with this cooler, mounting brackets, thermal paste, and instructions.

Athlon CPUs come with a similarly beefy cooler unit; use extreme care when mounting the cooler on Athlons with an exposed chip die so you don't crack the die and hose the chip.

Adding an Aftermarket Cooler to Your Pentium 4

Any retail CPU package includes a stock heatsink that has been approved for use by the CPU's manufacturer, but the upgrader in you might desire more cooling, less noise, or both. A high-speed fan provides better cooling for your P4 but can sound like an airplane taxiing down the runway. Meanwhile, a fan with multiple speed settings allows you to strike a balance between cooling and noise. Most fans have a noise-level specification printed on the box—anything around 32 decibels or lower should be tolerable.

Fan speed aside, you should look for two characteristics in a CPU cooler: First, look for either an all-copper heatsink or an aluminum heatsink with a copper base. All-aluminum heatsinks don't transfer enough heat to meet the demands of today's fastest processors, but copper does a terrific job. Second, the larger the diameter of your CPU fan, the more air it moves at a given rotational speed.

The heatsink/fan isn't the only part of the CPU cooling equation—the thermal compound you apply between the processor and heatsink is just as important. We prefer Arctic Silver 5 (www.arcticsilver.com). Carefully clean off any residual thermal compound from both your CPU and heatsink using rubbing alcohol before applying a new layer of Arctic Silver.

To install a new P4 heatsink/fan, you need to follow the instructions in the box because installation procedures can vary. (Most Pentium 4 coolers somehow lock onto the plastic frame surrounding the CPU socket.) After your new cooler is mounted, don't forget to plug the fan into the power header on your motherboard!

We recommend monitoring your CPU temperatures for a little while after installing a new heatsink/fan, especially if you're overclocking. You can do this in the BIOS (usually on the Health screen) or from within Windows using a free utility like Motherboard Monitor. In general, a Pentium 4 processor should not exceed 115° Fahrenheit under a heavy workload.

Pentium 4 heatsink/fan contraptions reside within a plastic frame with four posts. Each post clips into a bracket surrounding the CPU socket on the motherboard.

The Pentium 4 is Intel's darling; note that the chip die is covered by a metal heat spreader.

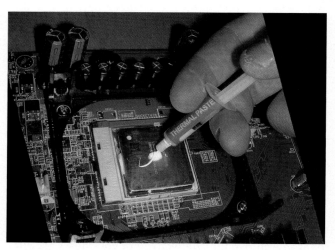

A dab'll do ya—don't get crazy with this stuff. Add a small dollop and call it a day.

Adding an Aftermarket Fan to Your Athlon CPU

Picking a heatsink/fan for your CPU inevitably involves a tradeoff between noise and cooling performance. You can either have massive cooling with a lot of noise or less cooling and quieter operation. If noise pollution is a concern, look for a fan that generates 32 decibels of noise or less (most manufacturers provide a decibel rating on a fan's retail box).

The two features you should look for in any Athlon cooler are a big fan, which offers better cooling than a small one without spinning as fast. However, some Athlon motherboards have capacitors positioned very close to the CPU socket, preventing the installation of large coolers. Second, choose a heatsink that features a copper base or an all-copper design because these are better at wicking away heat than all-aluminum heatsinks.

Our recommendations? The Zalman CNPS7000A-Cu (www.zalman.co.kr) is an excellent heatsink/fan that's compatible with both the Athlon and the Athlon 64 and can be set to either silent or normal mode. Meanwhile, the Thermaltake A4002D (www.thermaltake.com) is an inexpensive cooler that uses new Tip-Magnetic driving fan technology to funnel air directly to the heat source for better performance with less noise.

Before installing the cooler, be sure to clean off any leftover thermal compound from both your CPU and heatsink using rubbing alcohol (assuming you are adding an aftermarket cooler to an already installed CPU).

Installing an Athlon heatsink/fan for the first time can be tricky. Apply a small amount of thermal compound to the heatsink and then place the heatsink directly on top of the die. Clip one side of the heatsink to the CPU socket; then grab a flat-head screwdriver and push the other clip down and slightly outward, hooking it onto the CPU socket. Be very careful not to push too hard because you might inadvertently crush your processor's delicate core! Finally, don't forget to plug the fan into your motherboard's fan power connector.

When your new cooler is installed, keep tabs on your CPU temperatures. You can do this through the Health screen of the BIOS on most mobos or through Windows using a program such as Motherboard Monitor (mbm.livewiredev.com). In general, an Athlon shouldn't exceed 130° Fahrenheit during heavy usage.

Meet Intel's official nemesis, the Athlon XP. Note that, unlike the Pentium 5, the Athlon has an exposed chip die that can be easily damaged during the installation of a cooler.

This Zalman heatsink/fan moves a lot of air and is one of the best cooling solutions on the market.

North Bridge Chipset Coolers

Some motherboards have fans on their North Bridge chips and some have heatsinks. Then there's the kind of motherboard that has neither, and looks the worse for it. Place this shiny blue porcupine of a heatsink on your bare North Bridge chip to cool it off a few degrees, and increase your mobo's style tenfold. The heatsink is passive, meaning it should provide enough cooling without a dedicated fan. Be warned: Once the thermal paste goes on, the aluminum heatsink ain't coming off. The heatsink is packaged with thermal grease and thermal adhesives.

Be sure to look around for a variety of North Bridge (and South Bridge) chip coolers in both active and passive models. Most chipset coolers cost about $30 or less.

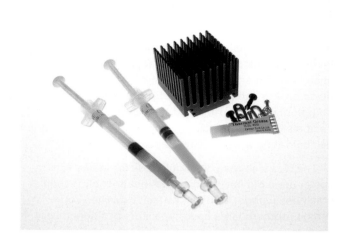

Hard Drive Coolers

Aside from a defrag every now and then, do you really need to concern yourself with hard drive health? You do if you want to protect that 5,000-song MP3 collection. And now that hard drives are capable of moving up to 160GB of data and spinning at a staggering 15,000rpm, it's about time you started seriously thinking about cooling. Hard drives are built from mechanical, moving parts, and just like car engines, they break down if allowed to run too hot. And if you're fortunate enough (let alone rich enough) to run SCSI drives, you already know that those suckers can get hot enough to sear a steak.

In this roundup, we ran the file system benchmark in SiSoft Sandra for one-half hour and then used a Raytek thermometer gun to take temperature readings from two locations. We first measured the temperature coming off the top of the drive and then grabbed a reading from one of the chips located on the bottom of the drive. Without a cooler, this lean, mean, grilling machine hit 120° on the top and 139° on the bottom. With our baseline temps established, we were ready to test the cream of the hard drive cooling crop.

PC Power and Cooling Bay Cool

The Bay Cool is your basic, working man's hard drive cooler. The solid construction and simplistic design make it ideal for entry-level computer hobbyists

who want to "set it and forget it." After you install your hard drive in the Bay Cool's mounting bracket, you just slide the assembly into an open 5 1/4" drive bay. Then you simply plug it into your power headers, and you're swinging to the low purr of two 40mm fans. The whirling duo whisks 6.5 cubic-foot/minute (CFM) of air over the hard drive. A small air filter on the front of the assembly keeps harmful dust from clogging up the fans but still allows cool air to make its way into the interior of the case.

The two minis worked pretty well considering their size. While the SCSI drive was churning away on its meal of data bits, the Bay Cool dropped the top of the drive from 120° to 95°. And even though it appeared that the fans blew most of their air over the top of the drive, the chip underneath was cooled from 139° to 113°. We were amazed that two dinky fans could make that much of a difference. The Bay Cool might not possess any of the extra features other hard drive coolers offer, but its simple design and great performance make it a worthwhile investment for anyone who's serious about hard drive cooling.

GlobalWin I-Storm II

The I-Storm II is a unique hard drive cooler in more ways than one. The first thing we noticed was that it looked a little too porky to fit all the way inside a 5 1/2'' bay. Turns out we were right. The ugly cooler actually extended about 2 inches beyond the front of what had previously been a stylish case. Are we scaring you? Well, if you don't mind being ridiculed for having one of the most ridiculous-looking hard drive coolers ever made, read on.

Affectionately nicknamed Elephant Nose by our editors, the I-Storm II actually yielded decent performance. Even more amazing, it cooled our SCSI drive without all the noise of its competitors. The cooler's distinctive fan uses a single ball-bearing, rotary-style assembly to push a rated 35 CFM of air, all at low rotation. This engineering adds up to less noise. In fact, the only noise you'll hear is from the built-in alarm, which sounds if the I-Storm senses a problem.

So it looks stupid and runs silent. But what about job one—cooling the damn hard drive? The I-Storm got the temperature of the top of the drive down to 96°. The bottom, meanwhile, hit 121°. Aside from its goofy design, the I-Storm is a nice buy. It offers good cooling without all the eardrum punishment. Just be prepared to ruin the beauty of your case.

Antec Hard Drive Cooling System

At first glance, we could tell this thing meant business. It's the only drive cooler in the roundup to feature a heatsink, and it comes with a digital readout. The digital display is connected to a pair of thermal sensors. The first sensor monitors ambient case temperature, and the second monitors the hard drive and controls the drive cooler's fans. If your drive reaches a critical temperature, the fans kick into high gear. After the drive cools, the fans slow down again. Ingenious!

The Cooling System's stylish front panel pops off to reveal fans similar to the ones used in the PC Power

and Cooling Bay Cool. The Bay Cool's fans are positioned farther apart than the Antec's fans, and one would think this would promote better cooling across the entire hard drive—but this wasn't necessarily the case. With the Antec, the bottom of the drive was cooled to 119° after one-half hour of duress. That's a 20° drop. We couldn't get a direct reading off the top surface of the drive because of the heatsink. But it's worth noting that the temperature of the heatsink was a "chilly" 95°, which is probably a few degrees cooler than the drive itself. The Antec has style, features, and cooling. With its slick design and thermal sensor display, it's the total package.

Slot Coolers

Many PC enthusiasts doubt the effectiveness of slot-based coolers for add-in cards. Some claim that these devices don't move enough air because their fans are too small. Others say the coolers' basic design is flawed; they just move hot air over even hotter components. Well, enough bellyaching. It's time to enter the Lab and debunk these weak-hinged arguments. In this segment, you'll met three types of coolers, each working in a different way to achieve the same objective—to get your components to "simah down now!"

The Vantec is an exhaust fan. Its goal is to flush hot air out of your case and away from hot components. The Buss-Cool from PC Power and Cooling sits in the PCI slot closest to your videocard and blows cool air directly onto one side of it (the rest of your case fans then take care of the heat exhaust). Finally, the Card Cooler from TheCardCooler.com mounts at a 90° angle over your videocard and blows air over both the top and bottom.

Unless you're downloading MP3s 24/7 and your modem is overheating, most people use these products to cool videocards. Because of its massive heat production, we decided to use an ATI Radeon 8500 for testing. To generate near-meltdown temperatures, we ran 3DMark2001—specifically, the Nature demo—at 1280×1024, 4x AA, and 32-bit textures, looping without pause for one-half hour. This is sort of like the video-card version of the Navy Seals' hell week. To record baseline temperatures, we aimed a Raytek thermometer gun on the card's core (the bottom of the card), heatsink (the top of the card), and RAM. Under extreme duress, these three components hit 141°, 119°, and 142°, respectively.

Vantec Exhaust PCSC-100

The Vantec Exhaust's simple design and solid construction make it a good value for anyone looking to simply move air away from components. But although it lagged behind the other two coolers as far as performance, it was nearly silent in comparison—in large part due to its single brushless fan. During our stress test, it dropped the core down to just 137° and the heatsink to 115°. In both cases, that's only a 4° difference from no cooling at all. The Vantec did have more success cooling the RAM—it dropped 12°.

We weren't expecting much from the Vantec and that's exactly what we got; the fan just doesn't have enough cooling prowess to keep video-card overclockers feeling safe and secure. To offer the most effective cooling, a fan must blow air directly onto a videocard, instead of just pulling air away from it. That said, even though exhaust-type coolers aren't very popular with overclockers, OEM system builders are beginning to see their advantages. Take, for example, the PCFX Xbrat system, which *Maximum PC* reviewed in August 2002. It was one of the smallest systems we've ever reviewed, and all its components were packed in tight together. Due to the small size of the case, there wasn't much room for a large exhaust fan, so PCFX installed one of these exhaust coolers, placing it in the heart of where the PCI cards reside. This is an ideal application for a cooler like the Vantec Exhaust—inside a small case, where any extra cooling is helpful.

PC Power and Cooling Buss-Cool

Since 1985, the folks over at PC Power and Cooling have been coming up with unusual and innovative components. The Buss-Cool is no different. Its two superthin fans are spec'd to rush 26 CFM of air onto the card sitting adjacent to it. Out of all the components we tested, this one was the easiest to install. Forget about messy fan wires; the two fans simply draw power directly from the PCI bus. Worried about the electrical stress on your motherboard? Don't be. The device demands a mere 3.2 watts of power; less than most high-end videocards.

When we fired up 3DMark2001, we noticed the fans were quieter than we expected, but still noticeably noisier than the Vantec Exhaust cooler. The Buss-Cool's performance, however, makes up for the added noise. Although the heatsink didn't get much cooler (it dropped 5° to 114°), the core dropped 8°, hitting a low of 131°. Considering the size of the fans, we were also surprised to see that the Buss-Cool chilled the RAM to 117°—that's a 25° difference!

The Buss-Cool offers solid performance without creating too much noise, and its installation couldn't be simpler. Plus, considering that it draws power directly from a PCI slot, it doesn't add any wiring jumble to your case interior. The Buss-Cool might not be the highest-performing slot cooler available, but with all its great features, it's definitely worth considering.

Card Cooler Featuring Sunon Fans

With two huge fans whooshing about 70 CFM of air above and below the videocard, we expected big things from the Card Cooler. And it did not disappoint us.

The device's massive airflow comes from two 80mm Sunon fans, each spinning at 2800rpm. The Card Cooler also benefits from its unique mounting approach. Both the Vantec and the Buss-Cool move air on only one side of the card, but when properly mounted perpendicular to a videocard, the Sunons cools both sides of the card. The benchmarks pretty much speak for themselves. The core temperature plummeted from 141° to 111°. Yikes! Both the heatsink and RAM dropped to 97°—that's a 44° drop in RAM temperature!

With perform-
ance like this, who
wouldn't want the
Card Cooler? How
about gamers who
are trying to enjoy
a late-night frag-
ging session with-

out waking their girlfriends, or their parents, or their girlfriends' parents? Adding the Card Cooler is essen-tially like putting in two additional case fans. Because these fans are installed on two metal brackets that use PCI mounting screws, the Card Cooler is also a bitch to install. And anytime you want to swap out or move an expansion card, you have to fiddle around with the Card Cooler, which usually means placing the case on its side.

Still, if you can handle the significant noise this thing puts out, it's definitely worth the purchase price.

Quieting Your PC

Once upon a time, your average PC builder worried about excessive heat about as much as people in Antarctica do. PCs of yore didn't run all that hot, so only minimal cooling was required. But in today's world of 3GHz CPUs, 15,000rpm hard drives, and high-perform-ance videocards, proper cooling has become essential for any system. The trouble is, most people worry so much about keeping temperature levels down that they sacrifice their tranquility with tons of loud fans.

If you want to quiet a noisy PC, there are some things you can do to knock off a few decibels and make your PC sound a little less like a nuclear reactor.

Keep in mind that quieting your PC *does* increase your case temperature. If you're planning on over-clocking your PC, you might look to more exotic techniques such as water-cooling, described in detail earlier in this chapter.

For this project, you'll need

- Papst 80mm 8412-NGL fan (www.plycon.com)
- Noise Control Magic Fleece (www.plycon.com)
- PC Power and Cooling Silencer 410 ATX (www.pcpowerandcooling.com)
- Foam padding or standard air-conditioner filter
- Felt pen
- Sharp scissors
- Ruler or measuring tape
- Phillips screwdriver
- Duct tape

The biggest contributors to noise in any modern system are the fans. Adding a superquiet hard drive or power supply doesn't quiet your PC at all if you don't also do something about those bloody fans. The prob-lem is, as a general rule, quiet fans don't move as much air as loud fans do, so they're less effective at cooling your hot components. The trick is to find the balance between noise and heat. For our PC, we tested the 80mm Pabst fans that are sleeve-bearing and run at a quiet 12dB but move just a paltry 19.5 CFM of air. At the other end of the spectrum is the 80mm over-clocker Delta fan that puts out an amazing 80 CFM of air, but at a deafening 52.5dB. Remember that the decibel scale is logarithmic, not linear. A 6dB sound is twice as loud as a 3dB sound, but a 9dB sound is twice as loud as a 6dB sound. Funky, ain't it?

- **Buy a better fan**—First, take stock of your case's cooling system. Determine which fans you want to replace with quieter ones. Measure them diago-nally to determine the fan size before ordering replacements (most case fans are 80mm, while most CPU heatsink fans are 60mm). Next, locate the retention mechanism (either screws or plastic clips) and remove them. Then disconnect the fan power cable from the source—either the mother-board or a four-pin Molex—and remove it from the case. Install the new fan by securing it with the retention mechanism; then plug it into either the motherboard or four-pin Molex. Make sure the fan is blowing in the correct direction—most fans have small arrows on one side that show both the direction of airflow and the rotation of the blades.

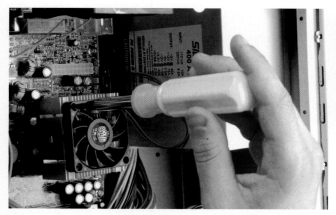
Take care not to start up your PC while the CPU fan is unattached. You'll be able to roast a tamale on the heatsink if you do.

This is a typical clip mount system for an 80mm fan. They're not standardized, so be sure you know what you're doing before you try to swap fans.

- **Filters look hooptie, but they work**—Filters are a cheap way to reduce fan noise while keeping the inside of your case dust-free. First, find the appropriate material; we used the foam padding that came with our motherboard box, but you can buy cheap air filters at almost any hardware store that do the same thing. Next, cut a square section of your filter material to go over your fan's air hole. Then simply apply tape (duct tape works best). You can mount the filter on either the inside or outside of the case, but if it's outside, make sure it's underneath the case panels to prevent your case from looking hooptie. You might need to use more than one layer if the material is thin, but verify that there's adequate airflow by placing your hand in front of the filter while the fan is blowing.

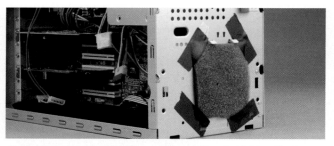
It might look undignified, but making a filter is highly effective and won't break the bank.

- **Disable those extraneous fans**—If you feel like your case is stacked with a few too many fans, you can always remove or disable a couple. To do this, simply unplug the fan's power connector from the motherboard, or the power supply if you're using a four-pin plug. To remove the fan, either unscrew it or unclip it from its mount and simply pull it out. It should be said that, unless your case is absolutely jammed with fans, it's probably best to replace the fans with quieter ones rather than removing them altogether. But if you're on a budget and your CPU temps are south of 100° F, it doesn't hurt to excise a few of these little noisemakers.

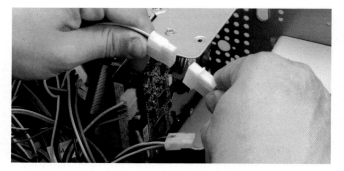
Don't go crazy and disconnect every single fan unless you want to start booking beach vacations inside your case.

Sound Dampening

Noise-dampening materials work by absorbing sound, keeping noise inside your case where it belongs. European manufacturer Noise Control meets this need with Magic Fleece—a polyester microfiber specifically intended for quieting a noisy PC. Magic Fleece can greatly reduce your PC's noise levels, but at the price of higher case temperatures.

Before you begin, make sure the airflow in your case is adequate. See Chapter 5, "Fans, Fans, and More Fans," for more information on airflow. The catch is that installation of the Fleece is pretty much permanent. We recommend taping the material to your case before you install it permanently, so you can make airflow adjustments if your PC overheats.

1. First, decide to which sides of your case you want to apply the Magic Fleece. We recommend placing Magic Fleece on both sides and the top. Then measure the dimensions of the piece you are applying. When covering side panels, be sure to take pains not to cover pieces that affix the panel to your case. You should also make sure you have enough room between the side panel and the motherboard tray. Magic Fleece is 12mm thick and doesn't fit in many cases without some adjustments.

2. When you have the measurements of the sheets you need, use a felt pen to mark your cut-out on the plastic covering the adhesive side of the Fleece. Then use scissors—sharp ones because this stuff is hard to cut—to cut your desired segments.

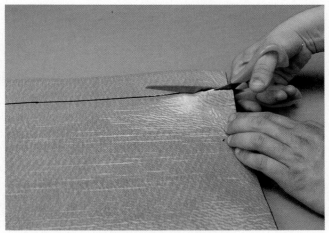

3. Next, lay the surface of the case panels flat and mark with a felt pen where the corners of the sheet will be placed. Then remove the plastic adhesive cover and apply the sheet—corners first—to the panel. Be very careful because this stuff is an absolute nightmare to reapply, so take care to do it right the first time.

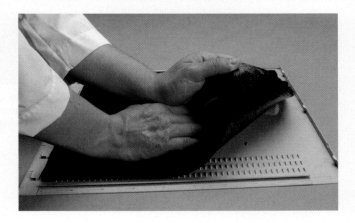

Power Supply Replacement

A power supply replacement is a nifty way to take your PC's noise level down a notch, but it's not for the faint of heart. Replacing a power supply is a major system upgrade, on par with a motherboard replacement. The PC Power and Cooling's Silencer line of power supplies are reliable, are really quiet, and can be had with up to 410W total output.

First, open your PC's side panel and put the case open side up on a table. Locate all the power connections to your current supply and remove them; this includes optical drives, hard drives, floppy drives, fans, and the big 20-pin connector on the motherboard (plus possibly four-pin 12v connectors for P4 systems). You might want to write down the number of connections

you're disconnecting so you don't miss any when you plug them back in. Next, locate the four screws on the back of the PC that are holding the power supply in place, and remove them. Then simply pull the supply out of the case, being sure not to snag anything.

To install the new supply, put it in the case where the old one was (unplug the old one first!). Then make sure the four screw holes line up; if they do, screw them in. Next, reconnect all the power leads you just unplugged. Take your time and be sure to reconnect everything; otherwise, your stuff won't function. After you do that, power on your PC and make sure all the drives are recognized and all the fans are spinning.

If you're using the power supply that came with your case, you might be able to upgrade to something quieter. A 400-watt supply is shown here, although PC Power and Cooling now offers a 410-watt version.

Maximum PC Fave!

Yeah, But Where's the Hemi?

At first glance, you would think the ExtremeMHz PC is most noteworthy for its hand-fabricated acrylic case. Yeah, the case *is* impressive. But, in fact, this project was named Rig of the Month in April 2003 for its amazing water-cooling system. See the big, black floating mass that consumes more than half of the back-panel real estate? That's the freakin' radiator! Originally manufactured for motorsports application (that is, competition race cars), this baby is capable of cooling a 600-horsepower vehicle. According to the rig's creators, the radiator provides "maximum cooling in low airflow environments." Perfect. It was painted black, but rest assured, this beast is all copper.

The ExtremeMHz was created by the IT department of Del Valle Food Products, based in Miami, Florida. Other noteworthy cooling parts include a modified water pump featuring clear PVC fittings, glass-encapsulated thermistors to capture water temps, two CompuNurse recorders that keep tabs on CPU temps, and various front-panel display and control bays that allow a direct interface between the machine and its human operators.

All in all, this might be one of the most ambitious water-cooling projects *Maximum PC* has ever seen—if only dust bunnies didn't collect in the oh-so-public case interior. (Words of wisdom, case-modders: These acrylic rigs *must* be kept tidy.)—J.P.

Here you can see the massive copper water-blocks attached to the CPU and chipset. Think this rig's Athlon MPs aren't overclocked? Think again.

That radiator doesn't cool itself, Jimbo. So, when in doubt, blow a gentle wind with two 120mm fans. Yeah, for a radiator this large, even two 120mm fans can be considered "low airflow."

Chapter Twelve

CPU Overclocking

The Overclocker's Handbook

Increase your CPU speed—*for free.* Here's how in vivid detail....

So far, we've focused the bulk of this book on concocting and building your ultimate PC mod. The first 11 chapters have dealt with defining your vision; collecting the right parts; and getting busy with your power tools to cut, assemble, paint, light, and cool your custom rig. By now, your mod should have lurched to life. Now that you're finished raising your PC from the ground, why not spend a little extra time eeking out every last drop of performance from your creation?

In this chapter, we show you how to overclock your CPU, adding a few extra horses to your already ragin' mod. The tricks you learn here will help you match your mod's actual performance to its already tight look.

Chapter 13, "Tweaking Your BIOS Settings," shows you how to tweak your BIOS, memory, and video cards to squeeze yet a little extra performance from your mod.

This Might Look Familiar . . .

Avid readers of *Maximum PC* might recognize much of the material presented in this chapter—and they'd be dead on correct. We first ran this material in the July 2003 issue. Since then, we've spruced it up to include here with this book. The information presented here—pulled from one of our most popular articles ever published—deals with slightly archaic CPUs but is entirely accurate and bears repeating. Although a vast majority of the material presented in this book was written specifically for this publication and has never before been seen, the editors at *Maximum PC* felt that we nailed CPU overclocking instruction the first time around, so why mess with a good thing, right?

All Men Are Created Equal . . . Processors Are Not

All PC processors are *not* created equal. Sure, your Pentium 4 and your buddy's Pentium 4 might both be clocked at 2GHz, but this is only because Intel rated the processors for 2GHz before the two CPUs left the factory. But when it comes right down to it, every processor is a unique entity. One marked to run at 2GHz might actually run just fine at 2.2GHz, while another marked for 2.2GHz might not have any headroom at all.

These speed tolerance variances are inevitable—each CPU is unique, and on the microscopic circuit level, some are more accepting of higher frequencies than others. That's why each CPU is individually tested for its speed potential after it pops out of the toaster, so to speak. If a proc can run days on end at, say, 2.2GHz without giving up the ghost, then it's labeled accordingly and tossed into the 2.2GHz bin. If not, it's given a more modest rating. This way, CPU manufacturers can reasonably guarantee 100% reliable performance—and thus reduce warranty claims.

CPUs manufactured during the launch of a new processing technology tend to have less frequency headroom than CPUs manufactured at the end of a processing technology's lifetime. That's because after the initial CPU launch, chip designs are tweaked and refined and manufacturers such as AMD and Intel find craftier and craftier ways to produce CPUs capable of running at faster speeds. So, for example, a 1.6GHz P4A manufactured at the launch of Intel's Northwood process technology might have much less frequency headroom than a 1.6GHz P4A manufactured at the end of the Northwood's run. And get this: It's typical for CPU companies to manufacture a whole slew of extremely capable processors and then label them with lower speed grades to fulfill orders for lower-priced CPUs! That's right—the processor that's been sitting inside your system for two years might actually have been created to run at faster speeds.

And you can make it run at faster speeds if you practice the dark art of overclocking. In the following pages we teach you the basics, walk you through four case studies, and show you how to exploit the quirks of chip production to realize the full potential of your CPU.

The Basics

So, what is overclocking? Simply put, it's the practice of running a computer chip at a higher frequency than it's been originally set to run. CPU overclocking can be accomplished in two ways: by increasing the speed of a system's frontside bus (abbreviated to FSB, the bus that connects the CPU with the chipset) and by changing the CPU's multiplier setting. Because a CPU's frequency is determined by multiplying FSB speed by the multiplier setting (for example, a 133MHz FSB paired with a 10x multiplier equals 1333MHz), you can increase the frequency of your CPU by upping either value.

The overclocking process varies from motherboard to motherboard, but in most cases, settings for the frontside bus speed can be changed by making an adjustment in your system BIOS. The multiplier ratio setting is often located here as well, but with some mobos, you can only change the multiplier ratio via a physical switch on the motherboard itself. Sometimes you also need to increase your CPU's core voltage because a faster chip has a larger appetite for power. The voltage setting usually hides in your BIOS as well. Consult your motherboard user's manual for specifics on where your FSB, voltage, and multiplier settings might be hiding.

More on BIOS Tweaks

We dig deeper into jacking with your BIOS to increase performance in Chapter 13. If there's additional performance to be had, we show you how to get your little fingers on it.

Overclocking involves many risks, the least of which is invalidating the warranties on your processor and related system components. System instability is also a possibility, and in extreme cases, you could irreparably damage your computer—though this is usually caused by an inadequate cooling setup. So, as you consider overclocking as a feasible means of increasing CPU performance, you must also consider adding extra cooling to your rig. At the very least, this might mean adding a high-performance fan/heatsink to your CPU. This will get you through a "modest" overclock. If, however, you're considering a drastic overclock or are dealing with a CPU that just doesn't take well to *any* overclocking, you might need to consider exotic cooling—namely watercooling—to prevent system instability and damage.

We discussed the dark art of cooling in Chapter 11, "Exotic Cooling." While some of the cooling options discussed there might be used for aesthetic reasons, others could spell the difference between successfully boosting processor performance and turning your CPU into a charcoal briquette. If you haven't read Chapter 11, do so before futzing with your CPU's speed. As much as we'd like to be there to console you if your CPU goes belly up, the best we can do is give you accurate info, copious warnings, and Godspeed. Beyond that, you're on your own.

For purposes of this chapter, we will simply encourage you to use the following products for your ventures into the world of overclocking:

- **Conventional heatsink/fan combos for P4s**—Intel's newer bundled P4 coolers are very efficient, featuring a powerful fan, radial fins, and a copper central post. Chances are you'll find this combo to be adequate for modest overclocking adventures. For a more serious solution, try Swiftech's MCX478V, combined with a quality 92mm fan. As to fan choice, the Tornado TD9238H is the best performing but loudest (56.4dBA) 92mm available: 119CFM at 4800rpm. If noise is a concern, the Thermoflow TF-9225 is good choice. It features a thermal probe for active rpm throttling between 1850rpm and 3100rpm, with peak ratings of 58.5CFM at 40dBA.

- **Exotic cooling for P4s**—If you plan to throttle up your CPU into the red, we recommend investing in either liquid cooling of Koolance's Exos system (www.koolance.com) or a phase-change system care of the Chip-Con Prometeia www.prometeia.com). Both the Exos and Prometeia are mainstream designs with superb efficiency. An additional possibility is thermoelectric peltier cooling, such as the Swiftech MCW5002-PT hybrid peltier/liquid cooler. See http://www.swiftnets.com/products/mcw5002-PT.asp.

  A cooling enhancer for liquid systems is available in the form of the Swiftech MCW-CHILL 452, an inline peltier cooler. See http://www.swiftnets.com/products/MCWCHILL-452.asp.

- **Conventional heatsink/fan combos for Athlon XPs**—If you have a late-model AMD that came with a copper-based cooler, you'll find that it works well for sober overclocking. Otherwise, try the Cooler Master Aero7 (www.coolermaster.com.hk), which features a quiet and powerful centrifugal blower. The Swiftech

MCX6400-V is the AMD64 premier air-cooled heatsink currently on the market when combined with a quality 92mm fan.

- **Exotic cooling for Athlon XPs**—If you're going to really turn up the heat on your Athlon XP, we recommend the same water and phase-change systems previously noted for the P4.

Please note that frontside bus overclocking is riskier than simply changing the CPU multiplier ratio because on most mobos, every increase in FSB frequency also causes an increase in PCI bus frequency. And if the PCI bus speed deviates too far from its 33MHz spec, some PCI devices can experience problems. If at all possible, use a motherboard that allows you to keep the PCI bus at or near 33MHz, even when system bus speeds are increased. Check motherboard manuals and spec sheets for details.

Do You Feel Lucky, Punk? Well, Do Ya?

CPU overclocking can sometimes result in destroyed processors, motherboards, and other system components. Don't even consider overclocking unless you feel comfortable with the risks. Overclockers who approach the dark arts with patience, caution, and reason will rarely (if ever) hurt their hardware. But you never know when science will go awry....

Is Your CPU a Prime Candidate?

The quickest way to find out how much extra sauce you can squeeze from your CPU is by researching how far others have pushed similar CPUs. That's what makes online forums so helpful (at the end of this chapter, we point you to our favorites). If you have an Athlon XP 3000+, just ask other owners how much success they've had with the same type of chip.

As a general rule, "mature" CPU technologies tend to be more overclockable. For example, while the original Thoroughbred Athlon processors were fabbed on a 0.13-micron process, they were often less overclockable than the 0.18-micron Palomino Athlons—a seemingly strange anomaly because "thinner" process technologies definitely run cooler than "thicker" process technologies, and coolness aids overclocking. But sometimes even a particularly efficient, cool-running process technology can't mitigate the overclocking constraints of a core design that resists speed increases, and the design will have to be finagled. In the case of the Thoroughbred, AMD said the chip had low frequency headroom because of "congestion" in the circuits. By adding an extra layer to the chip for routing signals, AMD says it was able to accelerate the clock speeds of the Athlon XP.

Most people would agree that Intel's Northwood P4s have been overclocker darlings. The Northwood chip's heat spreader—a slug of metal that helps pull heat

from the tiny core—is just one of the features that make that P4 overclocking friendly.

Nonetheless, the Athlon XP has always been quite popular among overclockers because it can be "unlocked." All P4s and many Athlon XPs sold to the general public are multiplier-locked, leaving the frontside bus as your only overclocking path. Intel CPUs can't be unlocked, but most Athlons can be unlocked with a bit of finesse, making them quite popular with speed freaks.

The Athlon 64 and Opteron processors are FID locked. Only the Athlon FX is unlocked at this time.

Thunderbirds can be unlocked with just a pencil. Palominos require an unlocking kit, such as Highspeed PC's XP Unlocking Kit (www.highspeedpc.com). Thoroughbred B and Barton CPUs, however, require a bit more tinkering to unlock the lower multiplier settings you need for overclocking. Some tricks require shorting pins. Yikes!

Of course, some lucky (or well-connected) individuals have managed to obtain unlocked P4 engineering samples. To see if you're the owner of a rare unlocked P4, head to your BIOS and try changing the multiplier ratio. If it works, thank the processor god for making you one of the lucky ones.

The right motherboard is just as important as the right CPU for overclocking. Boards that allow adjustments to FSB speed, multiplier ratio, and CPU core voltage are your friends. This means most Intel-branded motherboards are not your friends. Even the Intel Bonanza boards, which let you do some mild overclocking tweaks, aren't ideal for overclocking. We suggest you turn to motherboards from Abit (www.abit.com.tw) and Asus (www.asus.com) for features such as voltage controls and PCI/AGP dividers. (These dividers let you lock down PCI and AGP bus speeds while simultaneously increasing system bus speeds—a boon for maintaining overall system stability. After all, the idea is to overclock your CPU, and not the other devices that plug into your mobo.)

Good overclocking mobos also offer temperature monitoring and an emergency shutdown feature to help prevent CPU meltdown. Athlon XP users should seek out a motherboard that supports the thermal diode integrated onto the core of an AMD processor. It's also a good idea to use software that allows you to monitor your hardware sensors while in Windows. Check out Hardware Sensors Monitor (www.hmonitor.com), which allows you to throttle down Intel CPUs.

The very best motherboards include plenty of documentation on overclocking features and allow memory and FSB speeds to be set independently of one another. Because many mobos don't fall into this category, speed freaks opt for memory that is spec'd higher than the speed of their FSBs (for example, they put DDR333 memory on a 266MHz bus). That way, even if the FSB is overclocked, the memory will still run within spec.

Preparations and Precautions

A few simple precautions can minimize the risks of overclocking. For one, you should ensure that your cooling setup—especially the CPU fan—is ready for increased heat. Although Northwood P4s can often be overclocked considerably with just stock Intel cooling, the same cannot be said for Athlons and older, 0.18-micron Pentium 4s. We've said it before, and we'll probably say it again before this article is over—for significant overclocking, we strongly recommend investing in a more powerful heatsink/fan unit and even liquid cooling or phase-change cooling systems for radical speed freaks.

It's also important to use a high-quality thermal compound, which helps to wick heat from the CPU to the heatsink. Our favorite is Arctic Silver 5 (www.arcticsilver.com). Also, if you're planning on overclocking your FSB (and thus your memory) by a large margin, it might be worthwhile to buy memory heatsinks.

Make sure you have time to do the overclocking process thoroughly and with patience. And if there were ever a golden rule of overclocking, it's this: Always overclock in small increments. Don't try to jump straight from, say, 1.5GHz–1.8GHz. Play it safe, and you're more likely to achieve success.

Let's Get Ready to Ratchet

Now that you know the concepts behind overclocking, it's time to get some real-world experience. First, we provide a numbered step-by-step list of the basic overclocking operating procedure, and then we show you four overclocking case studies to give you a better idea of obstacles and how they can be surmounted.

1. Verify the make and model of your CPU by right-clicking My Computer and selecting Properties. Next, check the online resources at the end of this chapter to get a good idea of how far others have pushed that particular CPU. Before you begin, also make sure your mobo manual is handy.

2. Consider whether your present cooling solution is up to the task, or if you want to invest in a hardier method. After all, the point of overclocking is to get the most out of your processor, so you'll want the most aggressive cooling setup you can afford.

3. After you've installed your CPU and cooling solution, you need to get into your PC's BIOS. Most systems indicate how to access the BIOS during bootup. Watch the screen for clues like "Press Del to enter BIOS," the most common method.

   BIOS screens follow basic computer interface navigation rules. Just make sure you don't save changes unless you truly want to change these very critical, system-level controls. That's your only warning.

4. If you're running an unlocked Athlon XP, you can try increasing the multiplier to affect your overclocking (remember, just ratchet up speeds one tick at a time). Dig around in your BIOS until you find the setting that lets you alter the multiplier. If your Athlon XP is an 1800+ that was made when AMD was popping out 2200+ CPUs, there's a chance you might be able to increase the multiplier without having to resort to a bus overclock.

If you're denied multiplier tweaking, or if you have an Intel CPU (which are always multiplier-locked at the factory), dig around for your FSB controls. You'll usually find that the FSB has been set to 100MHz, 133MHz, or 166MHz (these bus speeds do not reflect the double-pumped and quad-pumped strategies that AMD and Intel use, respectively). Take baby steps when adjusting the FSB. For example, if your default is 133MHz, try 135MHz, check for system stability via all the suggestions that follow these steps, and then try a little bit more speed if 135MHz performs okay.

If you push your FSB too far, the mobo may even deny you access to the BIOS screen upon reboot. If this occurs, you need to refer to your motherboard's instructions to clear the CMOS memory and return the BIOS to its ultra-safe default settings. With many new motherboards, rebooting automatically resets the board to low CPU speeds. Older models might reset when you hold down Delete during the boot. Again, refer to your manual.

5. You need to check for stability after every incremental increase in speed. To do this, allow your PC to boot into Windows. If it freezes during booting or within a few minutes thereafter, you've got two options: (1) Return to the BIOS and drop the multiplier or FSB speed, or (2) increase the voltage.

Increase the voltage one increment at a time, and don't exceed an overall increase of 10% unless you have a spare processor or two lying around (voltage tweaking is arguably the most dangerous part of overclocking). And if you do increase voltage, it's absolutely necessary to increase your cooling.

6. When you're satisfied with the initial stability of your overclocked system, you need to put it under some stress. Our initial stability tests begin with simultaneously running Folding@Home and SETI@Home for an hour or two. If the system runs normally without lockups or apparent glitches, we then run a looping Quake III demo—all night long. Another option is CPU Burn-in, a free utility available at users.bigpond.net.au/cpuburn. This useful app performs a series of intense floating-point calculations and error-checks to detect subtle chinks in the armor of an overclocking job.

The next thing to do is run some benchmarks to gauge the performance gain you've netted. Which benchmarks you use is a matter of personal preference, but *Maximum PC* usually runs SYSmark, 3DMark, and a game based on a punishing 3D engine.

That's it—the overclocking process in a nutshell. But, alas, overclocking is a tricky craft that sometimes requires a little improvisation. Things don't always go the way you hope, and the unexpected arises at, well, unexpected moments. So, before you drop this book and begin spelunking in your BIOS, check out our case studies on the following pages. These are real-life overclocking experiences from the *Maximum PC* Lab. A study of these examples will give you a good idea of what to expect on your own. If you can read our examples without breaking into a nervous sweat, award yourself an Overclocker's Certificate and get ready to burn.

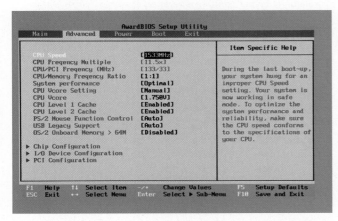

If your Athlon XP is unlocked, you can simply go into the BIOS and crank up the multiplier a notch at a time for a speed increase.

How to Break into Your BIOS

Don't let clock-blockers ruin your fun!

Dell, HP, and other large OEMs write custom BIOSs that don't include any FSB controls, so overclocking is effectively denied. There are, however, a few options for the truly determined. Just remember that overclocking an OEM system will void the warranty—and not just for your CPU, but for the whole config.

Your first option is a software utility called CPUcool. This program lets you adjust your FSB speed directly from within Windows. We used it ourselves to ratchet up an HP system armed with a Pentium 4B mobo. Unfortunately, we weren't able to overclock beyond 50MHz without system crashes. We also had no luck getting the utility to work on any of the Dell machines floating around our office. You can also try CPUFSB and SoftFSB. These utilities also tweak FSB speeds but don't seem to cooperate very well with modern CPUs.

If you're uncomfortable using a software program that might bork your entire system, you can take the drastic step of replacing your mobo with something more overclockable. Open your case and make sure it contains a standard ATX power supply, as well as mounting points lined up in the standard ATX form factor. Also make sure your rig has a front-panel connector (for your power switch, reset switch, and front panel LEDs) that will connect to another motherboard. We've had okay success in upgrading older HP and Compaq machines, but Dell machines usually require a new power supply and serious modifications to their front-panel connectors.

Be sure to check out Chapter 13 for more in-depth info on optimizing your BIOS.

Vamping Your Videocard Velocity

One Small Step for the Clock, One Giant Step for Performance

Videocard overclocking is simple but shouldn't be taken lightly. It's much easier to fry a videocard than a CPU because most videocards don't automatically clock down when they overheat. If you push your card too far or too fast, you can destroy it or drastically shorten its lifespan. Consider yourself warned.

The only tool you need is EnTech's PowerStrip (www.entechtaiwan.com). When it's installed and running, right-click the taskbar icon; then go to Performance Profiles and then Configure. In that screen, you can decrease and increase your videocard's memory and core speeds. After making a modest speed adjustment, test the settings before pushing your card further. We recommend that you start by bumping up your core GPU speed in 5MHz increments and then running a punishing game or benchmark before bumping it further.

When you see artifacts and other visual glitches during testing, you should crank your GPU clock back a notch and then start tweaking the memory clock speeds in the same way described previously. Texture corruption is usually indicative of memory that's been clocked too high. Screen-wide artifacts, meanwhile,

suggest that the core is clocked too high. After you've tweaked your card to taste, you still need to spend a few hours doing some additional hardcore testing—preferably by playing your favorite game.

The Official Word from Intel and AMD: Corporate-speak for Silicon Hot-rodders

AMD: "AMD places a very high value on its reputation as a supplier of PC processors. Our reputation for quality and reliability rests in part on operation of our products within the specified range of performance parameters for each product. AMD is especially concerned that consumers receive products that have not been altered or modified without AMD's authorization…. We appreciate your understanding, cooperation, and your recognition that AMD does not support the unauthorized alteration of AMD products."

Intel: "Intel does not advocate overclocking. Running beyond the speed, temperature, and voltage specifications of your CPU may void your warranty and could damage your hardware. Intel is especially concerned about overclocking where the CPU or system may be remarked and sold to an unknowing consumer at a higher speed than it is rated…. Users who suspect that they have purchased an overclocked CPU can download our Frequency ID utility at http://support.intel.com/."

Overclocking Case Studies

Case Study 1—P4 Northwood A: 2.0GHz to 2.52GHz on Abit IT7-MAX2

Entry-level P4s are excellent OC candidates. Featuring the Northwood A core fabbed on a 0.13-micron process, most of these processors have a good amount of frequency headroom. At stock speeds, they run a 100MHz bus, quad-pumped to 400MHz.

We mounted our 2.0GHz CPU on an Abit IT7-MAX2 motherboard using Intel's bundled heatsink and cooler. The mobo's illustrious roll call of BIOS features includes everything an overclocker could want. With the PCI bus set to a fixed rate of 33MHz, we stepped up the FSB speed from 100MHz—5MHz at a time—until the system failed to boot at 130MHz. We then reduced the FSB 1MHz at a time until we were able to attain rock-solid operation with a 126MHz bus. This yielded a processor speed of 2.52GHz—a mighty 26% increase over the CPU's rated speed. We also increased the BIOS's CPU core voltage settings from 1.5V to 1.55V for an added stability margin.

By adopting a 3:4 FSB-to-memory clock ratio, we were able to operate the DDR memory at 336MHz, which was pretty close to the 333MHz rating the Abit motherboard was designed for. We used two sticks of 512MB Corsair DDR400 CL2 memory, but running at 336MHz shouldn't be a problem with the majority of high-quality DDR333 CL2 memory modules. Other testing organizations running Northwood A P4s have taken their buses from 100MHz to 133MHz, so we believe that our actual CPU specimen, one of the first Northwoods ever fabbed, limited our overclocking attempts. An ambitious overclocker with a late-run chip and a more elaborate cooling solution might achieve even better results.

The BIOS in the Abit IT7-MAX gives you an assortment of OC options, but we're partial to the bus speed setting. We took our FSB from 2.0GHz to 2.52GHz.

The BIOS in the Abit IT7-MAX gives you an assortment of OC options, but we're partial to the bus speed setting. We took our FSB from 2.0GHz to 2.52GHz.

Case Study 2—P4 Northwood B: 2.8GHz to 3.21GHz on Gigabyte Titan CA-SINXP1394

Featuring a 133MHz FSB quad-pumped to 533MHz, the Northwood B is a clean-up version of the original Northwood A. The chip is available today with factory speed ratings from 2.26GHz to 3.06GHz, which puts our 2.8GHz specimen near the top of the CPU type's frequency spectrum. Conventional wisdom says the 2.8 shouldn't have much headroom, but we were able to push our example relatively far with stock cooling.

Seating the P4 in a Gigabyte Titan CA-SINXP1394 motherboard along with Intel's efficient bundled cooler, we increased the FSB in 5MHz increments until our system crashed upon booting at 158MHz. We then dialed back the FSB until rock-solid stability was achieved at 154MHz. In the final configuration, our 400MHz CL Corsair memory module was operating in dual-channel mode at 384MHz CL2 (192MHz memory clock)—the highest available setting that doesn't exceed the module's 400MHz rating.

During our OC attempts, we didn't attempt to manually increase the core voltage beyond the "normal" BIOS setting, but we noticed that the BIOS's own PC health status screen showed a core voltage of 1.602V—0.1V higher than the factory specification of 1.5V. It seems that the folks at Gigabyte, perhaps to foster stability in overclocked systems, had programmed their mobo to default to a higher-than-normal core voltage. While we don't feel that the 0.1 over-volt was harmful or objectionable, we would prefer that the user make such decisions.

All in all, our efforts netted a 14.6% increase in clock speed. We think that's impressive, considering we were upclocking one of the fastest-rated Northwood Bs. All things being equal, a 2.8 Northwood B should have much less headroom than, say, a CPU with an assigned speed of 2.6GHz.

The Gigabyte SINXP1394 features a six-phase power module (next to the CPU fan) to make overclocking more stable.

Case Study 3—Athlon XP Palomino 2000+: 1.667GHz to 1.813GHz on Asus A7V333

We expected a lot from this combination—late-production Palomino silicon on a hearty Asus A7V333 motherboard, with the same cooler AMD uses on its 3000+ Barton and 400MHz CL2 Corsair memory. Unfortunately, as with many overclocking ventures, things didn't turn out the way we hoped. As usual, we started edging up the FSB speed in 5MHz increments but slammed our heads into an unexpectedly low ceiling. The system crashed at 148MHz, prompting us to decrease the FSB until reaching stability at 145MHz. It came as a huge surprise that our Athlon XP 2000+ absolutely refused to accept a faster FSB speed. After all, for our Lean Machine 2002 project, we pushed a 2000+ to run its FSB at 166MHz on the exact same motherboard.

At first, we suspected that we'd hit the core clock limit. However, after unlocking the chip using High Speed PC's Athlon XP unlocking kit and setting the CPU clock multiplier down to 8x (from 12.5x), we still couldn't reliably run the processor above a modest 145MHz FSB setting. Not even a core voltage boost to 1.85V remedied the situation. Because

Athlon XPs rated at 2000+ and slower support a core multiplier between 5x and 12.5x (even when all the L1 bridges are connected), we were stuck at 1.813MHz (12.5 × 145MHz). Oh well. So goes the bad luck of the CPU draw.

We've hit far higher speeds using this Asus A7V333 before, but with the 2000+ we dug up, we couldn't get past 1.8GHz.

Case Study 4—Athlon XP Barton 3000+: 2.167GHz to 2.327GHz on MSI K7N2G

Back in their heyday, AMD's fastest-rated Athlons were quite OC-friendly. But today, as AMD struggles to squeeze more clock frequency from a relatively short-pipeline architecture, some recent top-rated Athlon XPs have proven to be poor overclockers. So, when we got our hands on an Athlon XP 3000+ featuring the Barton core and a 166MHz FSB (double-pumped to 333MHz), we were anxious to see if it would buck the trend and make the Socket A platform the overclocker's preferred diet once again. The Barton core uses the now-dated 0.13-micron process (moving to 90nm would certainly provide more frequency headroom) and is almost identical to the older Thoroughbred B save for a double-size L2 cache. We didn't expect tremendous overclocking potential, but we had to give it a try.

We installed the Athlon XP 3000+ on an MSI K7N2G mobo (featuring the new nForce2 chipset) and threw in two sticks of 512MB Corsair DDR400 CL2 memory. Edging the FSB gingerly forward, we were able to go from 2.167GHz to 2.4GHz (that's a bus speed of 185MHz). However, trouble soon reared its head. The system worked fine as long as we didn't run any serious graphics benchmarks, which ended in abrupt crashes.

Eventually, we were able to achieve unwavering stability with an FSB of 179MHz and a corresponding CPU speed of 2.327GHz. Running a 1:1 FSB-to-memory ratio, we were

operating the DDR memory at 358MHz in dual-channel mode—well below the 400MHz speed the modules were rated for. At this setting, everything ran beautifully and CPU temperatures stayed at a comfortable 52° Celsius using AMD's bundled cooler and heatsink.

If you're willing to undertake the tricky process of unlocking an Athlon's CPU multiplier, you might get better results. Just don't expect any stratospheric headroom built in to the Barton core.

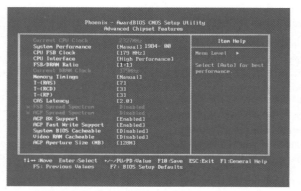

By using the straight bus overclock, we goosed our Athlon XP 3000+ to 2.32GHz.

The Proof Is in the Benchmarks

CPUs	Clock Speed[1]	SiSoft ALU[2]	SiSoft FPU[3]	Quake III Arena[4]
Northwood A	2.000	5385	2632	187
Northwood A	2.520	6624	3318	217
Barton 3000+	2.167	8046	3267	285
Barton 3000+	2.327	8676	3512	305
Northwood B	2.800	7226	3714	348
Northwood B	3.210	8305	4240	375
Palomino 2000+	1.667	6211	2504	214
Palomino 2000+	1.813	6756	2708	237

1. *Gigahertz*   3. *MFLOPS*

2. *MIPS*   4. *Frame rate*

The Five Most Overclockable CPUs

Pentium 4 Northwood 2.4GHz

The 2.4GHz P4 (running a stock FSB of 533MHz) is a favorite and can often be OC'd beyond 3200MHz, even with traditional forced-air heatsink coolers. The average overclock often reaches upwards of 3000MHz with minimal tweaking, often needing only a quick FSB BIOS bump. An Intel i875 Canterwood chipset motherboard is a definite recommendation, as this CPU has great performance potential when paired with dual-channel DDR memory.

Athlon XP Barton 2500+ Mobile

The Barton core Athlons, especially the elusive power-efficient mobile models, have become particular favorites from a price perspective because they yield above-average overclocking results due to their advanced 0.13-micron core technology. Average returns are usually in the 2200MHz–2300MHz range (up from 1.83GHz). Top-end cooling combined with an NVIDIA nForce2 or VIA KT600–based motherboard should yield results up to 2500MHz, but don't expect to go much further with even the most radical of cooling configurations.

The Book of Overclocking

The remainder of this chapter was written by Scott Wainner, president/CEO of online retailer reviews and price comparison site ResellerRatings.com and coauthor (with Robert Richmond) of *The Book of Overclocking* from No Starch Press (ISBN 1-886411-76-X) a book that we've dog-eared here in the *Maximum PC* Lab. This material appeared in the July 2003 issue of *Maximum PC*.

Please note that while there are newer processors that could be added to this list, we still believe the processors we identified in the July 2003 issue remain the most overclockable processors available.

Athlon XP Thoroughbred 2100+

The 2100+ (1.73GHz) was once the most popular Athlon model for overclocking. While not as speedy as the latest Barton core models, this chip is generally good for clocking past 2000MHz with a minimal core voltage increase. Extreme cooling and high voltages can offer the best overclocking reward, often in excess of 2200MHz with a quality nForce2 chipset motherboard.

Athlon XP Thoroughbred 1700+

Although it's becoming difficult to find, the low-cost Athlon XP 1700+ (1.47GHz) provides a great offset when purchasing a more expensive NVIDIA nForce2 chipset mobo. Average overclocks often reach well beyond 2000MHz, often at default core voltages with the low-power DLT3C core models. Extensive cooling and a slight core voltage increase can offer the bump needed to push this inexpensive chip beyond 2200MHz.

Pentium 4 Northwood 1.8GHz

The 1.8GHz Northwood P4 (running a stock FSB of 400MHz) is a great overclocking option for true hard-core enthusiasts. Its low fixed multiplier, combined with a quality Intel i845 chipset motherboard, can allow for tremendous overclocking potential. Overclocks in excess of 2600MHz are not uncommon, and getting beyond 2800MHz is even possible with radical peltier or water cooling.

And 4 Others That Might Just Break Your Heart
(In order from least generous to most generous in terms of overclocking potential)

VIA C3 (Any Model)

VIA processors are currently attracting a lot of attention for their low power demands and minimal cooling requirements. Oddly, however, even with a thermally efficient core, the C3 offers only minimal overclocking potential at best. Expect maximum overclocking returns in the 50MHz–100MHz range. Whee.

AMD Athlon Thunderbird 1400MHz

The Athlon Thunderbird was put out to pasture after hitting 1400MHz. With an early-generation 0.18-micron core, this processor has massive power demands and dissipates tons of heat. Overclocking upwards of 1600MHz–1700MHz might be possible, but only with quality cooling and potentially dangerous voltages.

Pentium III EB 1000MHz

The Pentium III Coppermine core was hitting its maximum frequencies when the 1GHz chip was released. In fact, its limitations were clearly evident when Intel released—and eventually withdrew—the P-III 1.13GHz from the marketplace. Lucky overclocks are generally in the 1150MHz–1250MHz range with traditional heatsink cooling.

Athlon XP Barton 3200+

The Athlon 3200+ (2.20GHz) is one of the best-performing processors, but its overclocking potential leaves much to be desired because of the limited frequency scaling of the Barton core. The expensive 3200+ often slams the proverbial wall around 2400MHz, even with the best cooling and maximum voltages.

Top 10 Tips for the Hardcore Overclocker
Tricky, dangerous, over-the-top, foolhardy, brazen, gonzo, imprudent...

1. **The Crayola Trick**—When trying to connect a CPU's L1 bridges with conductive fluid to unlock the multiplier, do those pesky holes in the surface of the Athlon XP annoy you beyond belief? Sure, you could break out the epoxy or superglue, and spend countless hours trying to fill the holes, but there's an easier way, and it's often the simplest ideas that are overlooked. A cheap coloring crayon can fill the surface pits with just a few passes and a little pressure.

2. **Smoking the Core**—Processor burn-in is perhaps the most controversial topic you'll hear discussed in overclocking circles. Start by running the processor at its default frequency with an increased core voltage for several days. Assuming the chip runs fine in this condition, drop the voltage back to default and then push the chip to its maximum stable frequency. Now adjust the voltage as necessary to reach the desired overclocking range. Do you

actually "break in" the electronic circuits? Probably not. The benefits of the procedure probably have much more to do with getting the CPU's thermal paste to settle and even out. Regardless, burn-in seems to help in pushing a chip to its maximum limits.

3. **String 'em Up**—Have a motherboard that offers no way to change the CPU voltage? Coated magnet wire might be the key to overclocking bliss. Strip the ends and wrap the small wire around specific pins on the bottom of the processor to unlock many features, such as voltages and multipliers. A quick glance at the Intel or AMD technical documents of your CPU model will serve as a guide to the maze of socket pins. Be sure to pay close attention to your heatsink when installing the processor in your motherboard because the magnet wire can cause the CPU to seat differently, requiring either heatsink clip retensioning or wiggling the heatsink a bit to realign its base with the chip.

4. **Computer and a Beer?**—You've probably already seen slick hobbyist systems mounted inside coolers and micro-fridges. But while nice to look at,

they can cause water condensation on electronics parts, which is never good. Refrigeration can work, but all water vapor must be removed before the system can be operated long-term. Damp Rid is a commercial product used to remove humidity from basements. Just fill up the fridge with this powdery substance, crank up the cooling, and wait a couple of days before firing up the system. Those without patience need not apply.

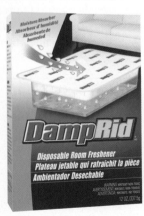

Billed as an "air freshener," DampRid (www.damprid.com) is really a box of calcium chloride salts that harden as they absorb moisture.

5. **Conform to the Rules**—Conform to the rules of condensation, that is. Conformance sealant is a must for any system being cooled below the air's dew point. The sealer is available in an aerosol and can be applied in the same manner as spray paint. Cover the entire motherboard as well as any other electronics surfaces that are near the contact point of the active cooling solutions, such as a

Konform is an acrylic resin that can protect your PC's delicate innards from the effects of moisture. Basically, it laminates your electronics.

chilled liquid waterblock or thermoelectric peltier circuit, to keep water from ruining your day. The stuff is almost impossible to find, but you can go to HMC Electronics (www.mcelectronics.com) and look up "Chemtronics CTAR12 Acrylic Konform AR."

6. **Get the Lead Out**—Magnet wire can also be used along with 60/40 lead solder to manipulate CPU pins. Instead of wrapping the wire around the processor pins, solder it to the matching pins on the back side of the motherboard CPU socket. A micro-DIP switch can be installed inline to allow for easy customization of many different processor models.

7. **The Bling Bling Effect**—Why not pimp out your system with a little silver? Silver-based thermal pastes represent today's top choice for heatsink interface material. Popular brands like Artic Silver 5 can lower core processor temperatures by 5%–10% compared with traditional silicon thermal pastes. Follow the directions to the letter, being careful not to over apply. Keep in mind that it will take about 72 hours to realize the full benefits of thermal paste. But the increased thermal efficiency can often raise a processor's maximum attainable frequency, sometimes upwards of 50MHz.

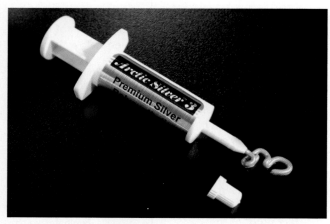

The makers of Arctic Silver ($8, www.arcticsilver.com) advise that thermal compounds can take from 72 to 200 hours after the initial application to achieve their maximum thermal conduction.

rotary tool with polishing cream can finish off the process to provide a mirror like finish for the heatsink base, ensuring maximum thermal transfer for improved cooling efficiency.

9. **Mr. Snow Miser**—Liquid nitrogen has become a favorite of the hardcore overclocking elite—but it's not kid's stuff. LN2 is available through a variety of scientific suppliers for a relatively cheap price. This supercooling liquid can be placed in a reservoir mounted atop the processor to max out a chip's top speed for short periods. Sadly, liquid nitrogen is not a long-term solution, but rather a hardcore trick for demonstrating one's overclocking prowess. Beware: This cooling method can easily snap off a few fingers of anyone not understanding how to handle this dangerous material!

8. **The Final Lap**—Most heatsinks lack a smooth finish on the base side of the cooler, but this can be addressed by *lapping*, a process that entails using ultra-fine sandpaper to remove imperfections in the contact surface. Attach the sandpaper to a glass surface and move the heatsink in alternating figure-eight rotations to evenly sand the bottom finish. Start with 800-grit sandpaper and work toward 1600-grit polishing paper. A high-speed

10. **Deadly Intentions**—Ever thought about drowning your PC? Immersion cooling is used by supercomputers from Silicon Graphics, and now this technology can be deployed in desktops and servers. Fluorinert is the fluid of choice, but it can be expensive at $500 a gallon. 100% pure mineral oil works nicely, but any contaminants like fragrances or colorings will short out your system. A multimeter is recommended to test the fluid for capacitance, and never attempt to submerge any power supplies or drives into any electronics cooling fluid.

Choosing Your Motherboard
A fast car needs a good track

Before you even think about buying a specific motherboard—particularly for overclocking—download the board's manual off the Internet and read it word by word. Make sure the board offers access to frontside bus speed controls. This is the most basic, entry-level feature offered in an "overclocking board." You'll also want the ability to increase core voltage to the CPU. Some boards (such as the Abit IT7-MAX2 used in case study 1) also allow you to independently increase voltage to your AGP card and RAM—a fantastic level of control for hardcore practitioners.

Because overclocking your FSB increases the speed of your PCI and AGP devices, you might suffer instability problems caused by add-in cards that can't handle the faster frequencies. This is why it's always smart to pick a board that lets you adjust AGP and PCI dividers. A healthy list of dividers will let you keep your PCI and AGP slots within spec (or at least closer to spec) even when increasing the FSB in zany increments.

OC success (or the lack thereof) can also be traced back to a mobo's design layout and power dynamics.

Some boards are simply much more prepared to handle the electrical stress. Unfortunately, a board's "overclockability quotient" is difficult to quantify, and you won't find anything about "stability under intense duress" mentioned in the mobo manuals. So, talk to your friends and check online message boards for info on a specific model's OC potential.

In our experience, Abit continues to be the premier brand for overclockers. The company generally exploits every overclocking trick when designing its boards. Asus, MSI, Gigabyte, DFI, Chaintech, and I will also have nice features for OC tomfoolery.

Online Resources
The most overclocking-friendly websites around

The most comprehensive site for overclockers and overclockers-to-be is, not surprisingly, www.overclockers.com. The information here runs the gamut, but the real jewel is the CPU database, a massive, user-maintained compendium of CPUs and their overclocking potential (the database is also available at www.cpudatabase.com). Start here for an idea on how far to push your proc.

At www.octools.com you'll find plenty of traditional fare, such as reviews of motherboards and water-cooling systems, as well as hardware news. But dig a little deeper in the site to find treatises on budget overclocking, condensation prevention, and lapping techniques. And don't pass up Mission: Submersible, a photo essay on total-submersion cooling.

Online forums can also yield a wealth of information, especially if you need quick answers when faced with an overclocking roadblock. Check out the Overclock Intelligence Agency forums at www.ocia.net/forums/ and the forums at Overclockers Online at http://forum.overclockersonline.com/.

Tweaking Your BIOS Settings

Better performance, reliability, and boot speed—this chapter shows
you how to get the most from your PC's BIOS

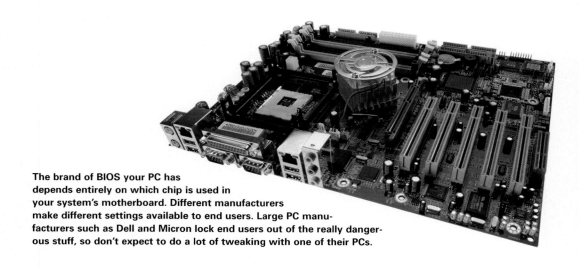

The brand of BIOS your PC has
depends entirely on which chip is used in
your system's motherboard. Different manufacturers
make different settings available to end users. Large PC manufacturers such as Dell and Micron lock end users out of the really dangerous stuff, so don't expect to do a lot of tweaking with one of their PCs.

The BIOS controls your PC's hardware at the very lowest levels. It determines the speed of your CPU, memory, and even some components. Because of this, tweaking your BIOS can net you huge gains in performance and reliability. Changing one minor setting can net you a 10% performance boost, while another could cost you as much as 40%. How do you know which settings will give your system a lift or bring it to its knees? Motherboard manuals usually leave something to be desired when it comes to explaining the workings of the BIOS. Not to fear—you're reading the most comprehensive BIOS optimization guide we've ever produced. We'll show you how to tweak your BIOS three different ways:

- To maximize performance
- To minimize boot times
- To make your PC more reliable

We'd be remiss if we didn't warn you that setting your BIOS incorrectly could keep your PC from booting. Before you make any changes to your BIOS, make a note of all of the original settings. And make sure that you follow the instructions explicitly, as any deviation may do damage. If you're not comfortable with the possibility of breaking your system, you shouldn't be tweaking your BIOS.

Before you begin, reread this text and the figure caption on the chapter's opening page. Done? Let's get started then!

Editor's Note

Avid readers of *Maximum PC* might recognize this chapter as one that appeared in our newsstand special, *The Ultimate PC How-to Guide 2004*. Mark Edward Soper, a longtime computer trainer and writer, wrote this chapter. We feel that the original article is the definitive treatise on BIOS tweaks for PCs, so we would be remiss if we didn't include it in this book. We took Mark's original text and updated it with the most current information so you can tweak *your* dream PC. Enjoy.

Tweak Your BIOS for Maximum Performance

Tweak 1: Correct Your Memory Card and CPU Speeds

```
AMIBIOS NEW SETUP UTILITY - VERSION 3.31a

 Frequency/Voltage Control              [ Setup Help ]

Spread Spectrum          ±0.25 %     Please keyin/select ur
CPU FSB Clock          [ 133 MHz ]   desire FSB. FSB range
CPU Ratio                Auto        100 ↔ 280 MHz.
CPU Vcore (V)            Auto        Select: [Up]/[Dn].
DDR Voltage (V)          Auto        KeyIn: Number+[Enter]
  Termination Vol (V)    Auto
AGP Voltage (V)          Auto
```

Overclocking can give your system a big performance boost, but before you can try upping your system's clock speeds, you should make sure the processor's frequency and clock-multiplier are set correctly. Your CPU's speed is determined by taking your system's frontside bus speed (FSB) and multiplying it by the clock multiplier. Both of these values are set in your system's BIOS. Overclockers are generally limited to adjusting the frequency, because most modern processors will operate at just one clock multiplier.

Many BIOSes correctly detect the processor frequency and clock multiplier for you. However, a lot of systems switch to a default fail-safe setting of 100MHz if the system locks up or powers-down during initial startup. The processor or FSB frequency is multiplied by a factor of two (most AMD CPUs) or a factor of four (most Intel CPUs) to obtain the processor's rated frontside-bus speed. Thus, a 100MHz setting in the BIOS is equivalent to a 200MHz FSB on an AMD system, or a 400MHz setting on an Intel system.

If your processor is designed to use a faster FSB speed (as most newer CPUs are), this fail-safe setting results in a significant performance drop. You should find this setting in the Frequency/Voltage Control menu or the Advanced menu. To determine the correct frequency to use, check the data sheet for your processor model at the vendor's website.

Tweak 2: User-Defined Memory Timing

Step 1: Adjusting CAS Latency

```
                AMIBIOS NEW SETUP UTILITY - VERSION 3.31a
┌─────────────────────────────────────┬───────────────────────┐
│   DRAM Timing Control                │  [ Setup Help ]       │
├─────────────────────────────────────┼───────────────────────┤
│ Current Host Clock           133 MHz │                       │
│ Configure SDRAM Timing by    SPD     │                       │
│   SDRAM Frequency            Auto    │                       │
│   SDRAM CAS# Latency         Auto    │                       │
│   Row Precharge Time         Auto    │                       │
│   RAS Pulse Width            Auto    │                       │
│   RAS to CAS Delay           Auto    │                       │
│   Bank Interleave            Auto    │                       │
│ DDR DQS Input Delay          Auto    │                       │
│ SDRAM Burst Length           4 QW    │                       │
│ SDRAM 1T Command             Disabled│                       │
│ Fast Command                 Normal  │                       │
│ Fast R-2-R Turnaround        Disabled│                       │
└─────────────────────────────────────┴───────────────────────┘
```

Manually tweaking your memory settings can yield big performance gains. The memory timing menu is usually located in the Advanced Chipset screen, or a submenu of this screen. Before you can adjust memory timing, you must change the Configure SDRAM Timing setting from the default of SPD to User. The default SPD setting uses the settings built into a chip on the memory modules to determine the proper memory timings. If you need to determine what the standard timing values are for the memory modules you use, and the BIOS doesn't show the actual values, check the memory vendor's website for the modules' data sheet.

There are two major ways to rate the speed of memory: frequency (measured in MHz) and latency (how quickly the module can send data after receiving a request). SDR memory usually features CAS (column-address-strobe) Latency values of 2 and 3 (lower is faster); DDR SDRAM is available with CAS Latency values of 2.5 and 2. Some systems display the CAS Latency value during startup.

To improve performance, try using a lower latency value. For example, if your memory has a CAS Latency value of 2.5, use 2 instead. If the system won't run properly, go back to the default CAS latency and try other adjustments.

Step 2: Adjusting Memory Timing and Access Factors

```
                AMIBIOS NEW SETUP UTILITY - VERSION 3.31a
┌─────────────────────────────────────┬───────────────────────┐
│   DRAM Timing Control                │  [ Setup Help ]       │
├─────────────────────────────────────┼───────────────────────┤
│ Current Host Clock           133 MHz │                       │
│ Configure SDRAM Timing by    User    │                       │
│   SDRAM Frequency            Auto    │                       │
│   SDRAM CAS# Latency         2       │                       │
│   Row Precharge Time         2T      │                       │
│   RAS Pulse Width            5T      │                       │
│   RAS to CAS Delay           2T      │                       │
│   Bank Interleave            4-Way   │                       │
│ DDR DQS Input Delay          Auto    │                       │
│ SDRAM Burst Length           8 QW    │                       │
│ SDRAM 1T Command             Disabled│                       │
│ Fast Command                 Ultra   │                       │
│ Fast R-2-R Turnaround        Enabled │                       │
└─────────────────────────────────────┴───────────────────────┘
```

Depending on the BIOS your system uses, you can also adjust other memory timing factors, such as row precharge time, Row Address Strobe (RAS) pulse width, and RAS-to-CAS delay. Row precharge time (also referred to as tRP) refers to the amount of time needed in clock cycles to activate the memory bank. RAS pulse width (tRAS) refers to the amount of time in clock cycles to leave the row of memory open for data transfers. RAS-to-CAS delay (tRCD) refers to the amount of time needed to switch to a different row of memory to access data not found in the current row. For maximum speed, these should be set as fast as possible (smaller values are faster).

The following options have variable effects on performance:

Enable SDRAM 1T to synchronize RAM with the CPU's FSB if both run at the same speed. SDRAM Burst Length can sometimes improve performance when set to 8QW (que words). Fast Command controls how quickly the CPU interacts with memory (Normal, Fast, Ultra). Many systems default to Fast, but Ultra can be used in some cases to improve performance. Fast R-2-R Turnaround, when enabled, improves the speed of recovery from a burst operation.

Tweak 3: Adjust AGP Settings

```
          AMIBIOS NEW SETUP UTILITY - VERSION 3.31a
   AGP Timing Control                        [ Setup Help ]

AGP Mode                        4x
AGP Fast Write                  Enabled
AGP Aperture Size               64MB
AGP Master 1 W/S Write          Disabled
AGP Master 1 W/S Read           Disabled
AGP Read Synchronization        Disabled
```

The AGP menu might be located on its own or be incorporated into the Advanced Chipset menu. The first setting to check is the AGP mode. It should be set for the maximum speed supported by your motherboard and AGP card (usually 4× or 8× with today's hardware).

As you might expect, other AGP settings fall into the trial-and-error category. AGP FastWrite bypasses main memory when performing writes to AGP memory, which can boost write performance by as much as 10% when enabled. However, some games have problems with this setting. AGP Master 1 W/S Read and Write settings can be enabled to use one wait state (a memory cycle that performs no operation) instead of the default of two wait states for memory transfers to and from the AGP card. However, if your system uses a default of zero wait states, enabling these options can slow down your system instead of speeding it up. AGP Read Synchronization can cause stability problems if enabled, so it should be disabled. AGP Aperture Size controls the size of the GART (graphics address relocation table) and the amount of memory address space used for AGP memory addresses. A value of 64MB–128MB is recommended.

Tweak 4: Improve PCI Bus Performance

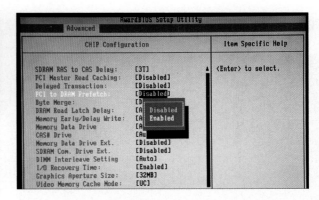

Enable the PCI Delay Transaction option (also referred to as PCI 2.1 Compliance or Delay Transaction) to improve performance if you have ISA cards. Enable the PCI To DRAM Prefetch option to improve the performance of IEEE 1394 and PCI-based soundcards. Enabling PCI Master Read Caching uses the processor's L2 cache to cache reads from the PCI bus. Disabling this option can sometimes help performance by keeping the processor's L2 cache available for other processes. However, enabling this option in some Athlon-based systems helps lower the temperature of the processor. These options are usually located in the Advanced Chipset Features menu.

The PCI Latency Timer option might be located in the PnP/PCI Configuration menu. It configures how long each PCI device gets to control the PCI bus before allowing another device to take over. The maximum range of settings is 0–255, but some BIOSes provide only certain values in this range. Reducing the value from the default of 32 can improve the response time of each PCI device (0 provides the fastest response time and 255 the slowest) to fix problems with some cards. However, PCI bandwidth suffers as a result. Increase this value to increase bandwidth across the PCI bus if your PCI devices work at an acceptable rate.

Tweak 5: Power Up Peripherals

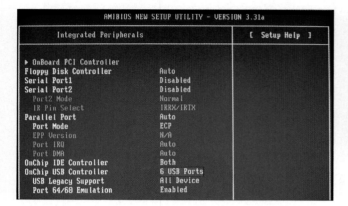

If you still use parallel ports for printers and other devices, you should configure the parallel port to run in EPP or ECP mode. (EPP is recommended for single printers, and ECP mode is recommended for daisy-chaining printers and other devices.) These settings provide the fastest input-output support available, and are typically located in the Integrated Peripherals menu. Make sure you use an IEEE 1284-compliant parallel cable to get the full benefit of this setting.

If you have switched to USB, keep in mind that using a hub to connect several USB 1.1 peripherals on a single USB 1.1 port (still the dominant type of USB port on most systems) can cause device slowdowns. Slowdowns are particularly likely if you connect low-speed USB 1.1 devices such as keyboards and mouse devices to the same port as faster devices, such as printers or disk drives. If you have more than two USB ports, make sure you enable all of them. Then use separate ports for full-speed and low-speed devices. The USB setting is also typically found in the Integrated Peripherals menu.

Tweak Your BIOS for Maximum Reliability

Tweak 1: Protect Your PC from Viruses

Although boot sector viruses are no longer the most common type of virus threat, every time you reuse a floppy disk, you put your system at risk of a virus infection. This feature is a step beyond write-protecting the boot sector, because it can distinguish between legitimate changes to the boot sector caused by operating system upgrades and boot managers and virus infections. You can find this option on the Standard CMOS Features, Advanced CMOS Features, or Boot menus of typical systems.

Tweak 2: Watch for Hard Drive Failure

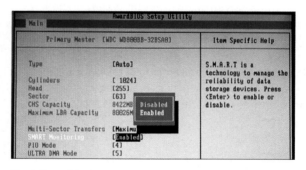

Enabling this feature supports the Self-Monitoring and Reporting Technology (S.M.A.R.T.) feature of recent ATA/IDE hard disks. S.M.A.R.T.-enabled drives can warn you of serious impending problems before the drive goes kaput, giving you time to back up your data and test the drive with vendor-supplied utilities. If you don't run S.M.A.R.T.-compatible software such as Norton System Works, you will only see a warning of a problem with a compatible drive at system startup. You can find this option on the Advanced CMOS/BIOS Features menu of some systems, or as an individual configuration option for each ATA/IDE drive.

Tweak 3: Monitor Vital System Temps

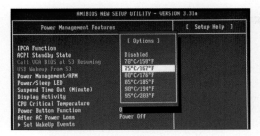

This option is found on the Power Management menu of some recent systems. When you enable it, you will be warned when your CPU exceeds the temperature you specify. Typical temperature options include 70° Celsius (158° Fahrenheit) up to 95° Celsius (203° Fahrenheit) in 5° Celsius increments. Don't substitute this for adequate processor cooling, but use it along with other stability options to warn you of problems.

Tweak 4: Watch for Faulty Fans

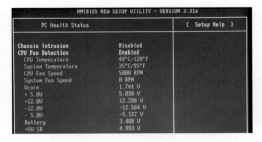

If a CPU or chassis fan fails, your system will crash in short order because of overheating, and you might also fry your processor as a most unwelcome bonus. Some systems monitor the CPU and chassis fans automatically if they are connected to the motherboard. However, in other cases you must enable this feature on the PC Health screen. If your motherboard or system includes software that can receive fan status messages from the BIOS, this setting provides cheap insurance against fan and system failure.

Tweak 5: Don't Fear Losing Power

If you are running a system that always needs to be on (such as an Internet Connection Sharing gateway or a server), enabling this option in the Power Management Features menu will automatically restart your system in the event of a power loss. If you'd prefer to restore the system to whatever state it was in when the lights went out, select Last State instead.

Tweak 6: Free Unused Ports

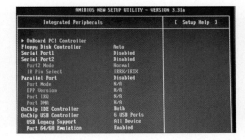

Serial and parallel ports are ISA devices that can't share IRQs with newer PCI devices, such as USB ports. Although systems with ACPI power management can assign multiple PCI devices to the same IRQ, doing so can reduce system reliability and cause conflicts between devices. If you don't use serial and parallel ports anymore, disable them in the Integrated Peripherals or I/O Device Configuration menu to help free up the settings they use for use by newer devices. Serial ports use IRQ 4 (COM 1) and IRQ 3 (COM 2) by default, and the parallel port uses IRQ 7 by default.

Tweak 7: Reserve Resources for Legacy Hardware

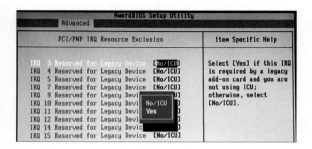

Some systems assume that IRQs from 3 up to 15 are fair game for PCI/PnP devices. However, if you still have non-PnP ISA devices, you'd better reserve the IRQs they use. Disabling legacy ports helps make more IRQs available, but some systems won't use IRQs below 9 for PCI/PnP devices unless you specifically adjust the PnP/PCI menu to enable these IRQs.

Tweak 8: Minimize Component Interference

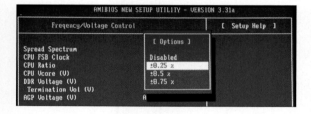

The Spread Spectrum feature in some recent systems' Frequency/Voltage Control menu is designed to help systems pass CE (European) EMI interference tests. However, leaving this feature enabled, especially with large values for the voltage fluctuation, can cause loss of Internet connections and stability problems in overclocking. You can sometimes adjust the voltage difference used as an alternative to disabling the feature completely.

Tweak 9: Use Only USB Legacy Settings If You Must

Originally, USB Legacy mode was intended to support USB keyboards when used at a system command prompt or the BIOS setup program. More recent systems can also support mouse devices and USB floppy drives. In some cases, enabling USB legacy support for devices you don't use can cause other devices to stop functioning when you try to come out of a hibernation or standby mode. The USB Legacy mode might be located on the Integrated Peripherals, Advanced, or other menus.

Tweak 10: Use the Standby State That Makes Sense to You

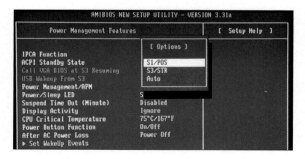

The Advanced Configuration and Power Interface (ACPI) standard supports several different standby modes. The most common are S1/POS and S3/STR. The S3 (Suspend to RAM) option saves more power, but doesn't work with devices that don't support the ACPI specification. If you are using older peripherals or aren't sure if the devices you have connected to the computer work in the S3 mode, enable the S1 mode. This option is typically found on the Power Management Features menu.

Tweak 11: Don't Cache the BIOS

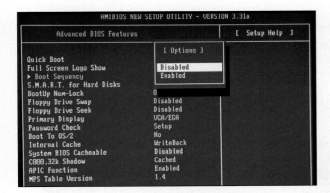

The contents of the system BIOS are copied to L2 cache when this option is enabled (it is usually found in the Advanced BIOS Features menu). However, various problems can result when this option is enabled, including system crashes if programs try to write to the BIOS area and USB conflicts on some systems with Via chipsets. Disable this option to avoid headaches, and you'll suffer little if any real-world impact on system performance.

Tweak 12: Check Your Cache

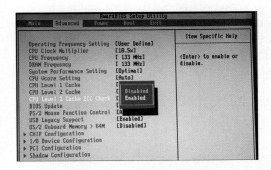

Most systems don't support ECC memory, but if your BIOS (and your processor's L2 cache) support this option, you can get much of the benefit of ECC memory with off-the-shelf non-parity memory. It also helps improve reliability when you overclock your system. This option is typically located on the Advanced or Chipset BIOS menu. To determine whether your processor's L2 cache supports ECC, get the data sheet for your processor from your processor vendor's website.

Tweak Your BIOS for Maximum Boot Speed
Tweak 1: Switch Hard Disks from Auto to User-Defined

Step 1: Finding Your Drives in the BIOS

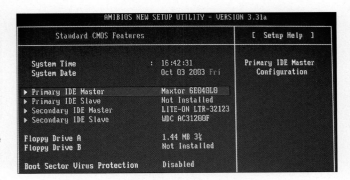

By default, most modern systems are configured to detect the specifics of your hard drive every time you boot your PC. Switching the setting for installed drives to User-Defined bypasses the drive-detection process and speeds boot times. The first BIOS setup screen on many systems is the Standard CMOS Feature screen. It'll display a list of drives currently installed in your PC. If you don't see a list of your drives, look for a setting called IDE Drive Auto-Detect on the main BIOS screen. It works the same way.

Before proceeding, keep in mind that there's one good reason for keeping the Auto-Detect option enabled: If you use a hardware boot selection device such as the Romtec Trios (www.romtec.com), the Auto-Detect feature lets you select which drive(s) to use at startup.

Step 2: Recording Drive Settings

```
         AMIBIOS NEW SETUP UTILITY - VERSION 3.31a
┌──────────────────────────────────────┬──────────────────────────┐
│  Primary IDE Master:Maxtor 6E040L0    │     [ Setup Help ]       │
├──────────────────────────────────────┼──────────────────────────┤
│  Type                      Auto       │ 1-50: Predefined types   │
│  Cylinders                 19680      │ USER: Set Parameters     │
│  Heads                     16         │       by User            │
│  Write Precompensation                │ AUTO: Set parameters     │
│  Sectors                   255        │       automatically      │
│      Maximum Capacity      41111 Mb   │ CD-ROM: Use for ATAPI    │
│  LBA Mode                  On         │        CD-ROM drives     │
│  Block Mode                On         │ Or                       │
│  Fast Programmed I/O Modes 4          │ Double click [AUTO] to   │
│  32 Bit Transfer Mode      On         │ set all HDD parameters   │
│                                       │ automatically            │
└──────────────────────────────────────┴──────────────────────────┘
```

On most modern systems, the Automatic setting displays the drive's configuration. This configuration is read by the system BIOS from the hard disk's firmware using a feature called the Identify Drive command. This feature enables your BIOS to accurately install a hard disk, even if you don't know the correct settings for the drive.

Write down the info corresponding to the Cylinders, Heads, Write Precompensation, and Sectors (per track). Also write down settings for the LBA Mode, Block Mode, Fast-Programmed I/O (PIO), and Ultra DMA Mode settings. Alternatively, you can check the drive vendor's website for this information.

Record this information accurately because you'll manually duplicate these settings in the next step. If you make an error recording the information, you will set the system incorrectly and your computer won't boot.

Step 3: Configuring the Drive As User-Defined

```
         AMIBIOS NEW SETUP UTILITY - VERSION 3.31a
┌──────────────────────────────────────┬──────────────────────────┐
│  Primary IDE Master                   │     [ Setup Help ]       │
├──────────────────────────────────────┼──────────────────────────┤
│  Type                      User       │ Select <Auto> for a      │
│  Cylinders                 19680      │ hard disk > 512 MB       │
│  Heads                     16         │ under DOS and Windows,   │
│  Write Precompensation     0          │ Select <Disabled> under  │
│  Sectors                   255        │ Nerware and UNIX.        │
│      Maximum Capacity      41111 Mb   │                          │
│  LBA Mode                  On         │                          │
│  Block Mode                On         │                          │
│  Fast Programmed I/O Modes 4          │                          │
│  32 Bit Transfer Mode      On         │                          │
└──────────────────────────────────────┴──────────────────────────┘
```

After you record the drive's settings, move the cursor to the Type field (currently set as Auto) and change it to User or User-Defined. The values for Cylinders, Heads, Sectors For Track, and so on are now blank.

Enter the values you recorded in step 2. Use the arrow keys to move from field to field. It's essential

that the drive is configured manually the same way it was detected by the system. If you screw up one or more of the settings, the computer won't boot from the drive or be able to recognize its contents.

Repeat steps 2 and 3 for each ATA/IDE drive installed (select CD or CD/DVD for CD-ROM or other optical drives). If you don't need to make any additional changes, save your changes and exit the system BIOS setup. Your computer will restart.

Tweak 2: Streamline the Boot Sequence

Step 1: Determining the Correct Boot Sequence

```
         AMIBIOS NEW SETUP UTILITY - VERSION 3.31a
┌──────────────────────────────────────┬──────────────────────────┐
│  Boot Sequence                        │     [ Setup Help ]       │
├──────────────────────────────────────┼──────────────────────────┤
│  1st Boot Device   Floppy:1.44 MB 3½  │                          │
│  2nd Boot Device   CD/DVD:LITE-ON LTR-32123S │                   │
│  3rd Boot Device   IDE-0:Maxtor 6E040L0 │                        │
│  Try Other Boot Devices       No      │                          │
└──────────────────────────────────────┴──────────────────────────┘
```

Even when you configure your drives as User-Defined, the typical system that boots off a hard drive still spends a lot of time looking for boot devices that you're probably not using, such as CD-ROM and floppy drives, Serial ATA, and others.

In most systems, the boot menu is part of the Advanced BIOS Features or Advanced BIOS Setup menu, or a submenu of that menu. Note that the floppy drive is listed first, followed by the CD-ROM drive, and then the hard disk. On systems configured this way, the floppy and CD-ROM are checked for boot files before the hard disk, wasting valuable time at each reboot.

Step 2: Making the Primary ATA/IDE Drive the First (or Only) Boot Device

```
         AMIBIOS NEW SETUP UTILITY - VERSION 3.31a
┌──────────────────────────────────────┬──────────────────────────┐
│  Boot Sequency                        │     [ Setup Help ]       │
├──────────────────────────────────────┼──────────────────────────┤
│  1st Boot Device   IDE-0:Maxtor 6E040L0 │                        │
│  2nd Boot Device   Disabled           │                          │
│  3rd Boot Device   Disabled           │                          │
│  Try Other Boot Devices       No      │                          │
└──────────────────────────────────────┴──────────────────────────┘
```

Select the first boot device and change it to the first ATA/IDE drive (this might be referred to as IDE-0). Because this drive will always be used to boot the system, you can disable the other boot devices. If you need to boot from a CD or a floppy disk in the future (such as for an operating system upgrade or repair), you can restart the BIOS setup program and reconfigure the boot sequence menu accordingly.

Tweak 3: Disable Memory Check and Floppy Drive Seek

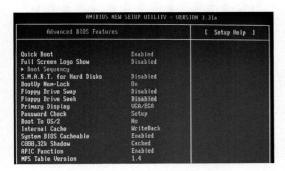

Many systems waste time at startup by performing a memory check and a floppy drive seek. The memory check seldom finds memory problems (even if they exist). If you don't boot from the floppy drive, there's no reason to check the drive at boot time for a boot disk. To disable the memory check, open the Advanced BIOS Features or Boot menu and enable the Quick Boot or Quick Power On Self Test options. Disable the Floppy Drive Seek option in the Advanced BIOS Features or Boot menu.

Tweak 4: Disable Serial ATA (SATA) Host Adapter

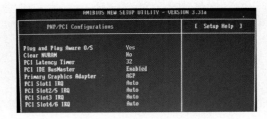

If the SATA host adapter built into many modern systems is enabled but no drives are present, the BIOS wastes time trying to detect drives before giving up and continuing the boot process. The SATA Host Adapter setting is usually located in the Integrated Peripherals menu, or a submenu of this menu. In this BIOS, it is located in the OnBoard PCI Controller menu within the Integrated Peripherals menu. Disable it to more speedily boot!

Tweak 5: Disable Onboard ATA BIOS

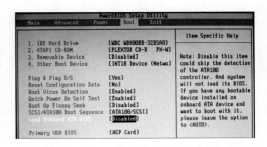

If your system has three or four ATA host adapter connectors instead of the normal pair, it's designed to support additional ATA drives in either normal mode or as an ATA RAID array. We love ATA RAID arrays here at *Maximum PC*, but if you don't have any drives connected to the hard drive controllers, leaving them enabled just wastes precious time at boot. The ATA BIOS option should be located in the Boot menu or in the Onboard Peripherals menu.

Tweak 6: Enable PCI IDE BusMaster

Bus mastering ATA/IDE host adapters provide a huge speed boost when enabled, but if they're disabled, your drives will be stuck using slower PIO access methods. Look for this option on the PnP/PCI menu or Integrated Peripherals menu. Don't forget to install the appropriate bus mastering drivers for your motherboard chipset in Windows to finish the job.

Chapter Fourteen

Case-Modding Resources

Arm yourself with the right tools and right hardware

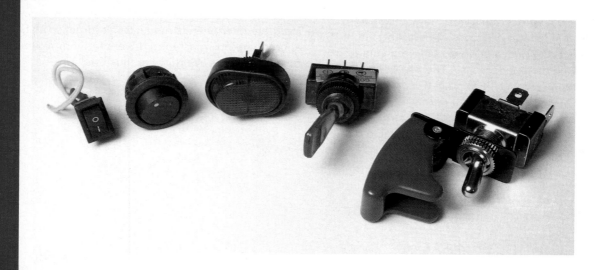

Tools

When you take your job or your hobby seriously, it's time to get some serious tools. A well-made tool becomes an extension of your ideas and inspirations, your goals and dreams. For me, some have become old, trusted friends I can always rely on to get the job done—and done right. Treat tools with respect, keep them well maintained, and always use them with the utmost personal safety in mind.

Foredom Power Tools & Accessories
www.foredom.com

The very best in flexible shaft rotary tools. Thousands of accessories to choose from for cutting, carving, and grinding just about every material. Available at home centers and online retailers such as Amazon.

Dremel
www.dremel.com

The definitive modding tool of choice for beginners and pros alike. Basic kits are available at home centers and online retailers at reasonable prices. A must-have rotary hand tool for any modder's workshop.

Micro Mark
www.micromark.com

Micro Mark has been selling hard-to-find tools for the hobbyist since 1928, and theirs is my all-time favorite catalog to receive in the mail. From miniature milling machines and lathes, to the most unique hand tools for the model maker and electronic enthusiast, they have it all.

General Tools
www.generaltools.com

General Tools is another favorite; it's a company that manufactures both construction grade hand and measuring tools as well as those for the hobbyist. Made to last, I have General brand tools that are over 25 years old and still as good as new.

Binks
www.binks.com

Binks has been making spray paint and finishing equipment for about 100 years now, so it goes without saying that they know their stuff. There are less-expensive look-alikes for finishing and spray guns out there, but they aren't a Binks.

With dozens of head attachments, the legendary Dremel is a small, lightweight, and versatile rotary tool for cutting, carving, sanding, polishing, and drilling—and much, much more. The Dremel company motto is "Tools for the Imagination," and it's a motto that's well-deserved.

Bosch Tools
www.bosch.com

When you get serious about hacking up your next case, check out the wide range of 120v and cordless tools made by Bosch. Sanders, polishers, grinders, and saws—they have a tool for every modding task.

I have to admit that I was intimidated by airbrushes before I decided to purchase one. But after only a few hours of tinkering, I discovered how easy they are to use and operate. Of course, mastering the art of airbrushing can take a lifetime, but these tools do provide the very finest paint finishes for simple applications. Airbrushes can spray acrylic, enamel, and lacquer paints for precise line art as well as entire cases.

Case Materials

Finding the right materials for a custom case mod can be tricky. If you don't live in a big city, you might have a tough time finding the parts and supplies you need to get the project done. The big home centers are a good place to start, but the selection in your area might be limited. Don't underestimate your local, privately owned hardware store either; many of them would be happy to locate and order specialty items and materials.

Industrial Plastics
http://www.yourplasticsupermarket.com

Industrial Plastics in New York City is my favorite store to visit and shop for plastic supplies such as Plexiglas and Lexan. This warehouse-size store also does custom laser cutting, etching, and plastic-blowing to your specs with fax-in orders or over the phone.

Acrylic sheets make the best material for case windows—and they can also be used to form the body of an entire case! Extremely durable acrylic is available in many translucent and opaque colors, from 1/8" to 1/2" thick. Also known as Plexiglas, acrylic is easily cut, drilled, and tapped with hand and power tools. Acrylic can be easily scratched, but these scratches can usually be removed with rubbing compounds.

Lowes
www.lowes.com

A Lowes home center opened in Brooklyn during the writing of this book, and I was happy to find that they are a kinder, gentler monster-size home improvement store—sort of like Home Depot on Prozac. Besides the friendly, helpful staff, I was impressed with the neatly maintained selection of metal stock, such as aluminum and steel. If you need basic materials, you might find them here.

80/20, Inc.
http://www.8020.net/

80/20 is a great source for aluminum framing and extruded shapes for custom case mod projects. They also offer custom fabrication and design assistance for more complex projects.

The Compleat Sculptor
www.sculpt.com

"You supply the talent, we'll supply the rest" is the tag line of the best sculpting supply store in New York City. Here you'll find mold making materials, casting supplies, resins, and tools for advanced modding projects. You can order online, by fax, or by phone.

Modding Parts

Danger Den
www.dangerden.com

The name Danger Den is synonymous with excellence in extreme water-cooling products. Overclockers and performance enthusiasts the world over rejoice at their masterfully crafted water blocks, pumps, and accessories. The extremely knowledgeable staff of engineers can answer any of your water cooling questions.

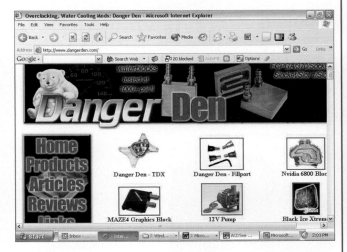

Frozen CPU
www.frozencpu.com

Frozen CPU carries a great selection of quality cooling, lighting, cases, and modding supplies, as well as hard-to-find imported products. Excellent customer service and price have established Frozen CPU as one of my favorites.

Logic Supply
http://www.logicsupply.com/

Logic Supply has the best selection of small form factor computer parts and supplies around. For the Mini-ITX enthusiast, they have many hard-to-find items as well as cases, laptop components, and power supplies.

Newegg
www.newegg.com

Newegg has some of the best prices around for basic computer hardware and peripherals. If you are putting together a new system, visit and compare their prices.

Xoxide
www.xoxide.com

Xoxide is another terrific source for case modding supplies. Popular also are their modding forums where you can discuss your latest project and ask for help. Great deals can be had with their rewards program and weekly X-Hour sales, in which items can be purchased at deep discounts.

Directron
www.directron.com

Everything from modding supplies to complete systems are found at this well-known online retailer. Good selection of cases, fans, and lighting supplies.

Pep Boys
www.pepboys.com

Modding supplies can be found just about anywhere, and auto supply stores are no exception. Many 12v auto accessories, such as lights, work with the power supplied by your PC. Pep Boys has locations in 36 states with a good selection of supplies and interesting parts that can't be found at online modding supply retailers.

Cases

Choosing the right case for your next (or first) modding project or custom rig can take a good deal of research.

Here are a few manufacturers to help you on your way to making the best decision.

Silverstone
www.silverstonetek.com

Antec
www.antec.com

The Aria's ability to handle more hardware than the typical small form factor makes it a great candidate for housing a homebrew personal video recorder. I'm just sayin'....

Cooler Master
www.coolermaster.com

The Cooler Master WaveMaster enclosure is the ultimate blank canvas for serious modders. In fact, *Maximum PC* thinks so highly of this case that we used a heavily modded version of it in our Dream Machine 2003 project.

Lian Li
http://tw.lian-li.com/english/

Thermaltake
http://www.thermaltake.com/

Kingwin
www.kingwin.com

ClearPC
www.clearpc.ca

Chenbro
www.chenbro.com

The Chenbro Gaming Bomb has everything a budget builder needs. If you're doing your mod on a budget or are just getting your feet wet with modding, this could be a good starter case. Trick it out with custom lighting and fans and you'll have a case that'll still make the young girls cry.

Painting Supplies

Whether you want a mirror finish inside and out on that custom rig or just want to airbrush a logo, you should research the right product. Many colors and finishes can be found at your local auto body repair shop, who can also provide custom mixes and specialty chrome finishes.

Krylon
www.krylon.com

These paints are not just for little red wagons any more, with an amazing selection of colors and finishes to choose from. If you plan to paint plastic parts, they also have a line of Fusion brand paints specially formulated for hard-to-paint pieces.

Dupli-Color
www.duplicolor.com

Known for their OEM automotive colors, Dupli-Color also has some of the most interesting finishes out there. Their Metalcast anodized finishes give the appearance of anodized metal parts and surfaces. The Mecanique case mod shown in Chapter 15, "Showing It All Off," is a good example of its potential.

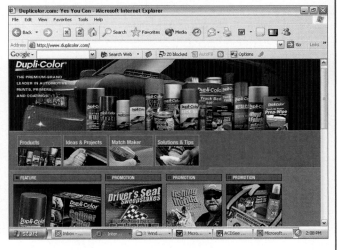

SprayChrome, Inc.
http://www.spraychrome.com

Today's spray-on chrome finishing technology is simply unbelievable, and SprayChrome, Inc., can put a durable, mirror-like chrome finish on just about any object. Visit their online showroom for incredible examples of their work.

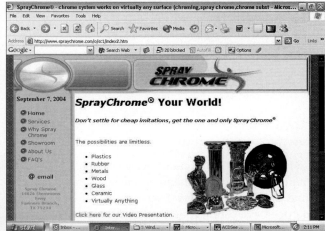

The Alsa Corporation
www.alsacorp.com

Alsa Corporation manufactures chrome and specialty paints and additives, as well as laminates and films. If you want to try your hand at some advanced finishes, you can purchase their paints by the pint, quart, or gallon. They have a great online showroom and application guides as well.

Fans

Vantec

www.vantecusa.com

Vantec is a well-known and trusted name on the modding and overclocking scene for quality fans, cooling devices, front bay devices, and power supplies.

Vantec fans come in a number of colors and sizes—just right for keeping your rig cool and stylish.

Frozen CPU

www.frozencpu.com

Frozen CPU carries a great selection of quality cooling, lighting, cases, and modding supplies as well as hard-to-find imported products. Excellent customer service and price have established Frozen CPU as one of my favorites.

Xoxide

www.xoxide.com

Xoxide is another terrific source for case fans, as well as other fans. Popular also are their modding forums, in which you can discuss your latest project and ask for help. Great deals can be had with their rewards program and weekly X-Hour sales, where items can be purchased at deep discounts.

Directron

www.directron.com

Everything from modding supplies to complete systems are found at this well-known online retailer. Good selection of cases, fans, and lighting supplies.

Lighting and Electronics

Matrix Orbital
www.matrixorbital.com

Matrix Orbital is my first choice for serial interface display modules and VFDs (vacuum fluorescent displays). Their experienced engineers and great customer support and service have made them a popular name with case modders worldwide.

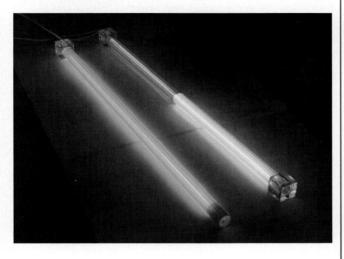

Blue Point Engineering
www.bpesolutions.com

I first discovered BPE when I was researching servos and electronic parts for my Matrix: Rebirth 8.0 case mod project. Specializing in electronic supplies and custom engineering for animatronics, robotics, and haunted attractions, they're also owned by one of the friendliest and knowledgeable professionals in the business.

Jameco Electronics
www.jameco.com

Jameco is an online electronics superstore packed with do-it-yourself electronic and lighting parts and kits for all kinds of projects.

Xoxide
www.xoxide.com

Xoxide is another terrific source for lighting and electronics supplies. Popular also are their modding forums where you can discuss your latest project and ask for help. Great deals can be had with their rewards program and weekly X-Hour sales, in which items can be purchased at deep discounts.

Directron
www.directron.com

Everything from modding supplies to complete systems are found at this well-known online retailer. Good selection of cases, fans, and lighting supplies.

Cables

Cables To Go
www.cablestogo.com

Cables To Go has a big selection of every possible cable for the system builder and case modder.

Directron
www.directron.com

Everything from modding supplies to complete systems are found at this well-known online retailer. Good selection of cases, fans, and lighting supplies.

Xoxide
www.xoxide.com

Xoxide is another terrific source for cables. Popular also are their modding forums where you can discuss your latest project and ask for help. Great deals can be had with their rewards program and weekly X-Hour sales, in which items can be purchased at deep discounts.

Enthusiast Websites

[H]ard OCP
www.hardocp.com

[H]ard OCP is a website and online community that needs no introduction. For years now, it has been the very epicenter of gaming, modding, and technology news and reviews. Join in the forums and you'll find some of the most helpful people you are likely to meet in the modding community.

Gruntville
www.gruntville.com

Gruntville is probably the friendliest tech- and modding-oriented website you'll ever find. Their no-nonsense reviews of the latest hardware and peripherals are matched only by the talented people who make up their online forum community.

The Best Case Scenario
www.thebestcasescenario.com

Okay, you can file this one under "my editor made me do it," but you might want to drop by The Best Case Scenario, a site created and maintained by yours truly. Here, you'll find in-progress photos of my current mods, as well as completed mods, work logs, and more. You'll also find additional photos of some of the mods shown in this book.

Chapter Fifteen

Showing It All Off

Getting the "props" you deserve

It has been said that a picture is worth a thousand words—if that picture happens to be of a killer case mod, it just might be worth a thousand dollars.

There's a lot of potential in the case mod you labored for weeks or months to complete, and having a good visual record of your hard work is essential. The best venue for initially displaying your completed (or work-in-progress) case mod is on the enthusiast websites at the heart of the community. Within hours, thousands of people might be viewing your latest creation, and with fellow case modders as your toughest critics, you want your work to make the best first impression it can. As a perk for existing members and as an incentive to bring in new ones, many websites hold case modding contests several times a year. Entering these contests with a good set of photographs of your rig can mean the difference between winning the latest spankin' new processor or a lighted fan.

Although having good photographs is only part of a winning case mod, it's an important one. There are sure to be special features or details on your rig that can be real attention-grabbers when suitably photographed. You might also find yourself getting requests from magazines and publishers to print your work, and it's likely the editors will want the best photos you can muster. The best advice I can give, other than the tips and tricks in this chapter, is to learn by example. If you're not already a subscriber to PC enthusiast magazines like *Maximum PC*, you should run out and get yourself a copy—I'll wait. Are you back yet? Good. Inside the hallowed pages of *Maximum PC*, you'll find excellent photographs of cases and computer-related peripherals you can study and learn from.

Readers familiar with my real-life mod projects might recognize the mod shown here as my Mecanique mod.

Mecanique is a Danger Den water-cooled case mod with an anodized red paint finish and industrial looks. With a scratch-built cooling tower, the radiator was brought outside the case for enhanced thermals. The round window was water cut from a slab of 1/4'' aluminum by the fine engineers at customwatercuts.com.

The Antec P160 was an excellent candidate for this project, with a rugged build and smart, mod friendly design. The only downside of the Antec P160 was the locking mechanism on the side panel; in my opinion, it's just plain unnecessary. As it turned out, the shape of the locks worked into my design and I decided to leave them.

See more photos of Mecanique at http://www.thebestcasescenario.com/case_gallery.php.

Computer cases are not the easiest objects to photograph, and I've struggled myself to capture decent images. By carefully studying the work of the pros, you get the best possible lessons on how to compose photographs that result in dramatic, striking images. Although it's not the goal of this chapter to be an in-depth lesson in photography (which it isn't), it shows you a few tricks of the trade that can help you capture the essence of your creative case modding projects.

The Equipment—What You'll Need

Get this: You really don't need expensive cameras or fancy photo studio equipment to take a good picture. Whether you're using a pro or consumer-level digital camera or a disposable one from the supermarket, the principles of good photography apply to both. It's not the scope of this chapter to teach digital or even classic photography, so the best advice I can give is to know your tools and practice, man, practice.

The first thing you need is a basic lighting setup; at the very least, it should be a single, strong, reliable source of light. However, two lights work best (Figure 1). Used lighting equipment can be found at reasonable prices at garage sales, at auctions, and from online retailers. Your local home center probably carries 500-watt halogen work lights complete with stands that are an excellent (and cheaper) alternative to studio equipment. I have two halogen work lights in my shop that were bought for under $30 each.

For those beauty shots of your finished case mod, a suitable backdrop should be used. Backdrops can be found in many forms, from a cotton bed sheet to an over-sized roll of paper, and the larger, the better. Velour is another great fabric to use, because it produces a soft, shadow-free background. If your backdrop material is wrinkled, give it the once-over with a clothes iron before using it. The color of the background you choose depends largely on the subject to be photographed. The custom paint job on your rig might benefit from a light-colored background, while a clear Plexiglas case would be better photographed in front of a darker one, or even black. Whatever background material you find that's right for your case, the next step is to set it up on a table, preferably one that can be put against a wall. Make sure you have plenty of space in front of the table to set up the lights and so you can get a good distance from the subject.

The backdrop should be attached to the wall on two corners, a few feet above the subject, and outside the frame of your intended shot. Drape the fabric over the surface of the table to create a nice sloping curve at the back where it comes off the wall. When you place your case mod on the table, smooth out any bunching or gathering of the fabric with your hands. In all likelihood, you want your PC powered up, so you might have to poke a hole to allow the power cord to run through the backdrop and into a wall outlet or surge

This basic setup illustrates the classic lighting technique used in portrait photography. By having your lights located in front of and slightly above the subject at a 45° angle, it creates an evenly distributed light with few shadows. This semi-pro lighting kit from Lowel came with two tungsten light units, aluminum stands, and umbrellas for about $250. Lighting kits like this are built tough to last for many years, and they're a good investment for when you get serious.

suppressor. If you're handy with image editing software and don't want to cut your background material, you can easily edit out the power cord later after your photo is off the camera or scanned in from a hard copy.

If you are using two lights, set them up about 4 feet from the table and raise them slightly higher and then angled down toward the subject. If you are using a single light source and reflector, you can position the light a bit closer to the subject (Figures 2 and 3). Take your time to find the right position for the equipment, using your best judgment to get it looking right to the eye. To create a controlled environment in your impromptu studio, you might want to turn off any overhead lights and close the shades if stray light is interfering—in some cases this might be a good thing, but it all depends on your situation and setup. Make sure the area in front of your table is free from power cords and cables to prevent trip-ups.

You should be prepared to take a lot of photographs (Figures 4 and 5). Whether this means buying several rolls of film or download-ing the images from a memory card every so often, it's all the same. You might have to go through dozens of photographs to get the perfect few, so take as many as you possibly can while you have your studio space set up. Move around and change posi-tions often, looking through but beyond the viewfinder at your sub-ject for interesting angles high and low. If you have a tripod, use it to set up complicated shots and also for keeping the camera steady for long exposure shots of interior case lighting. A step stool, chair, or ladder can be used for bird's-eye views. Just use caution; keep a sharp eye out for stray light and unwanted shadows.

Be prepared to spend a few hours just getting the shots in the can, and if you are using a digital camera, you can take a break and download your images. Digital cameras definitely have an advan-tage over film for reviewing your images. With the images off the camera and onto the computer, you can find just the right angles that look best for the subject and even

By using a reflector, even a single light source can be used. Reflectors are also great for outdoor use, by directing sunlight onto the subject from several feet away.

Bouncing the light from a piece of foam board onto the subject helps avoid the harsh glare and shadows you get by lighting it directly. Here you see the board mounted to a tripod by using a small shop clamp.

This photo does little to capture the interest-ing shapes, colors, and details of the case mod. As you can see, the angle of the photo-graph makes it appear distorted and "squished"—a common mistake with cases.

This image was taken from a slightly lower position and around to the side of the case, creating a much more "majestic" and flat-tering photo. Be prepared to take a lot of pictures before you find just the right ones.

see lighting mistakes and other trouble spots. Get to know the func-tions and features of your camera as best you can. They are all there to help you take better pictures. I

still have to refer to the handbook (that's as big as a phonebook) of my digital camera, so it's a good idea to have it handy while you shoot.

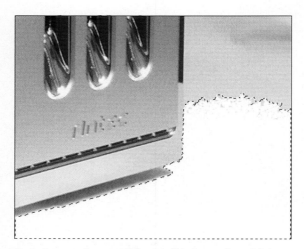

If you have an image editing application such as Adobe Photoshop, you can make enhancements to your photos by spending a little time tweaking them.

Images can be cropped, and backgrounds and unwanted cables can be removed. I find image editing tools to be absolutely necessary for color correction and even adjusting composition. To various degrees, every magazine photograph you ever see has been digitally manipulated in some manner to improve its appearance.

If you have a rig with chrome details or a mirror-like painted finish, reflections are your worst enemy. Chrome details can capture unwanted light, nearby objects, and (in the very worst case) a less-than-clothed photographer (not shown here).

The previous photo shows the reflections of my window blinds as distorted vertical blue lines. Here, you can see I fixed this problem by placing white cardboard on either side of the case and just off camera.

Case modders love to show off the lighting inside their rigs. If your digital camera has manual settings, a long shutter exposure can capture the light in all its neon glory. To prevent blurred images with long exposures, a tripod is greatly recommended. You can get a full-size one for general use or even a small, compact one you can set up on a table for taking close-ups.

If your camera has macro settings or lenses for extreme close-ups, by all means use them! With the macro settings on, use your camera for stunning photographs of the inner workings of your custom PC.

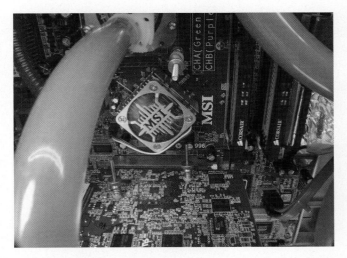

You add an entire new dimension to your work by simply poking the camera inside. Many digital cameras can focus to within inches of the lens.

For this photo, using an image editing program, I completely removed the original background and replaced it with a pure white one. Other enhancements made were color corrections, brightness and contrast adjustments, and sharpening of certain details. The tools available in image editing programs are numerous and can take years to master, but I use the simple ones and those I've become familiar with. With practice, you might find yourself becoming an image editing guru!

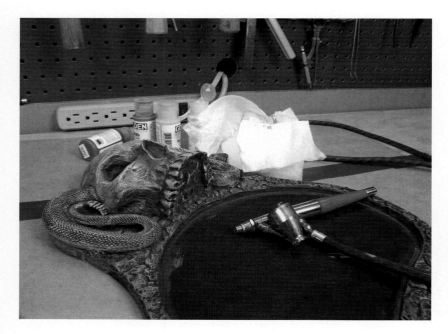

One of the pleasures of case modding is viewing and reading the work logs of other craftspeople. By sharing your work-in-progress with the community, you can give people a behind-the-scenes look into the insight and inspiration of you, the artist. Taking clear, detailed photos of your work leaves a lasting impression even before the work is completed.

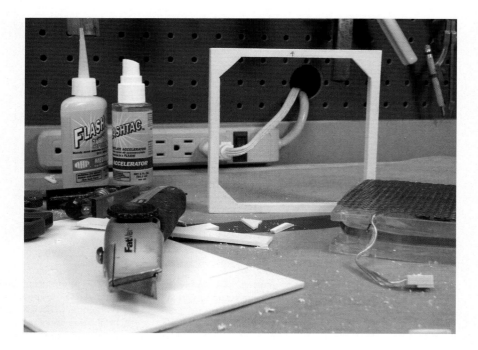

To add some interest to your images, include the tools and materials you work with. I find that some people are actually more interested in how something was made than in the object itself.

For your latest project, you might want to show off all the yummy hardware going into it. Here, you see a simple cyc wall (pronounced *sike*) made from white craft paper. A cyc wall, or *cyclorama*, is simply a curved, seamless backdrop that creates the illusion of infinity behind the subject.

The hardware will make a bigger impression with your audience if the picture isn't a scattered bird's-eye view taken against a carpeted floor. Here, you see an extreme close-up photo of some Danger Den water-cooling gear looking magazine-ready.

Index

B

P

Q – R